Let the Credits Roll

Let the Credits Roll

Interviews with Film Crew

by BARBARA BAKER

Aston House Press

Published by special arrangement with McFarland & Company, Inc., Publishers,
Jefferson, North Carolina.

This edition published in Great Britain in 2005 by
Aston House Press
8 Lower Mall
London W6 9DJ

A catalogue record for this book is available from the British Library

ISBN 0-9547501-1-X

New edition designed by Sherene Poon of earnes, Hong Kong
Printed and bound by Dah Tung Printing Mfg., Co., Hong Kong

For Robin

All photographs, except where otherwise stated are by Barbara Baker

Acknowledgements

I owe huge thanks to my husband Robin, who encouraged me from the start, read each interview as it was completed, scanned and printed all the photos, and gave valued advice and support throughout. I would also like to thank Jacqueline Young, whose editorial skills I sought when she kindly read the manuscript before publication. Many other people have given useful advice or helped to arrange interviews, in particular: Cleone Clarke, Anastasia Edwards, Tim Fywell, Larry Kaplan, Henry Korda, Rebecca Lloyd, Rick McCallum, Madeleine Slavick, Meredith Tucker and the members of BECTU History Project. I am indebted to Alan Parker for generously allowing me to use cartoons from his book *Making Movies* (British Film Institute, 1998). Finally I would like to thank everyone that I interviewed. There are some people who for various reasons but through no fault of their own, did not actually end up in the book; to them I apologize. But everyone whom I interviewed gave their time and effort to make this book possible as well as a pleasure. Thank you.

Contents

Acknowledgments vii

Introduction 1

Editor Teddy Darvas 7

Production Designer Hugo Luczyc-Wyhowski 15

Composer Stephen Warbeck 26

Costume Designer Charlotte Walter 35

First Assistant Director Lisa Janowski 43

Production Auditor Salvatore Carino 51

Production Sound Mixer Tom Nelson 60

Script Supervisor Angela Allen 68

Camera Operator/Steadicam Peter Cavaciuti 81

Set Decorator Carolyn Scott 88

Post-Production Supervisor Stephen Barker 97

Second Assistant Director Christo Morse 103

Prosthetic Makeup Designer Mark Coulier 108

Storyboard Artist Jane Clark 117

Visual Effects/Miniature Photography Paul Wilson 124

Clapper Loader Susan Jacobson 134

Grip Dennis Fraser MBE 141

Boom Operator John Gutierrez 151

Gaffer Larry Prinz 157

Costume Assistant Helen Blackshaw 166

Best Boy Electric Kenneth Dodd 171

Special Effects Supervisor Peter Hutchinson 175

Special Effects Dental Technicain Chris Lyons 185

Contact Lens Technician Jemma Scott 193

Mouth/Beak Replacement Coordinator James Moore 199

Location Scout James Cosper 204

Greensperson Will Scheck 210

Casting Associate Meredith Tucker 217

Foley Artist Diane Greaves 223

Stunt Performer Richard Bradshaw 229

Unit Nurse Karen Fayerty 239

Animal supplier and Trainer Jim Clubb 243

Location Caterer Beccy Tiller 253

Introduction

The director Francis Ford Coppola said, "In a movie, when you're lucky, every element comes together. In *The Godfather*, we had this wonderful cast, this wonderful composer and music; we had a great photographer, wonderful production design, wonderful costume person and a great book to base it on. And I remember in the old days people would say, 'Well gee, what did *you* do?' and I said, 'I chose them.'"

This book celebrates film crew — those people involved with the production of a movie who do not appear in it. The term refers to the often unsung heroes of a production team, as opposed to filmmakers — directors, producers and screenwriters. As the credits roll at the end of every film, many viewers have no idea what all these people do. This book reveals the mystery behind the job titles as crew members on different films explain what they do, how they got to do it, and their contributions to movies.

The *Oxford English Dictionary* defines "crew" as "A company ... a number of people classed together; a set, a gang, a mob ... A squad of workers under an overseer ... with some particular duty ... A body of people manning a ship, boat, aircraft, spacecraft, train ... A team of people concerned with the technical aspects of making a film."

It is appropriate that the word "crew" most commonly applies to the people who man ships. In fact, stagehands on early films were often beached sailors or longshoremen and there still exists some overlap in terminology. When films first started, they used mostly natural light, which stagehands controlled with large tent cloths using long poles called gaffs — a gaff is also a type of boom on a sailing ship. This seems a likely derivation for "gaffer," which used to be the word for the head of an organized group of laborers and has come to mean a chief lighting technician or head of the electrical department on a film.

In both ships and films, crew members are essential individually, and a hierarchical structure exists where each person performs a specific task,

1

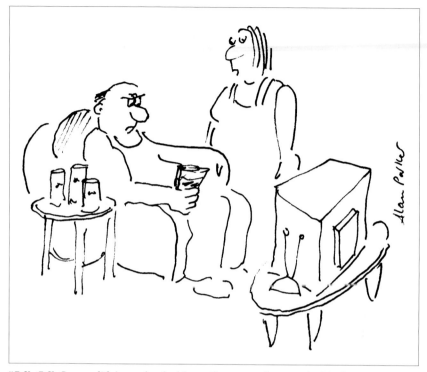

"O.K. O.K. So you didn't get thanked in an Oscar speech yet again. Maybe not everyone knows you oil the sprocket pins on the cameras."

but they are also members of a team. Charles Drazin, author of various books about film including *In Search of the Third Man*, writes of the process of film development as starting with just one man, a writer, but then the people who become involved with the project "multiply like cells under a microscope."

First, the director works with the screenwriter and the producer; more writers may be brought in and actors will be hired. The script is passed on to a production designer, a cameraman, an editor, a production manager and so on. Drazin continues, "In the process of collaboration, the original story changes and takes on a new form, like an embryo becoming distinct from the cluster of cells out of which it first grew. ...The final film turns out not as any of its individual contributors had planned, but according to the interaction — or aggregate — of their egos, and according to countless other circumstances beyond anyone's control."

The individual members of a film crew possess myriad skills: creative, artistic, technical, administrative, interpersonal. These talents require scope for expression but it is also true to say, and was evident in the writing of this book, that crew members are happiest and work most efficiently with strong leadership from the top. They require a director who is supportive, appreciative, approachable and challenging, but above all, one who knows what he or she wants and is able to express and communicate that knowledge.

In many respects, different crew members share similar concerns, attitudes toward work and lifestyles. There are, however, a few differences between British and American film crew. Some job titles differ slightly and these are discussed in the text where appropriate. Additionally, in the U.S. unions require a very strict interpretation of duties, whereas in the U.K. things are more lax and more overlap in job specification can occur. Finally, it was very apparent as I talked to American crew that joining a union was difficult and important. In Britain, joining a union is a much simpler and easier procedure.

As for getting into the film industry, it does appear that the old adage is borne out: It is not what you know, but who you know. Very few of the people I interviewed went to film school. Most got their jobs by chance — happening to know someone (not necessarily in a top position) who gave them their first break. It is also the case that there are more men than women in the industry — not only in the jobs where the physical nature of the work (of electricians, for instance) might dictate gender. There are few women at the top and in general they still perform traditional roles: costume, wardrobe, hair, makeup, script supervisor, casting, catering. Moreover, it seems that women often take on an extra, unspoken role: that of confidante and therapist to everyone else on set.

With the huge numbers of people involved in film production nowadays, it would be impossible to include interviews with all categories of crew members within one book. I have necessarily had to be selective. I have attempted to include someone from each major department, but my choice for inclusion in this book has inevitably been somewhat subjective. Interviews were restricted to crew living in Britain and America who have worked mainly on feature films and in television. Preference was given to crew members with jobs that are generally less known about and that I found interesting. I chose some crew that are well-known in their fields and some who are less so. Together they have worked on a wide variety of films; each explained their craft and had interesting stories to tell. It is my hope that these interviews will be informative and also entertaining.

I have arranged the interviews in the approximate order that the credits might appear on screen. Credits are acknowledgments of a contributor's services. On a film, they also act as a form of advertising and in this respect they are of more significance to other people in the business than to the general public. In the past, the list of credits was shorter partly because fewer people were involved in making a film but also because only heads of departments were credited.

Nowadays it is usual for about nine people (other than the stars) to be credited before the film title: the director, producer, screenwriter, editor, production designer, composer, director of photography, casting director and costume designer. These people are often known as "above-the-line" and are arguably the most creative people involved in the making of a film, the most expensive, and the ones with agents.

The rest of the production people are credited at the end of a film, "below-the-line," the order being decided by the producer so that in no two films is it exactly alike. Often, all the heads of departments are credited first, and it is usual for the people considered most important and the people who work the duration of the film to be given preference in the order. Sometimes credits are ordered by department, with the most senior within each department appearing first. Occasionally crew members will negotiate with the producer for their credit placement. However, there are rarely the fierce battles in which stars engage. It is said that in 1969 Steve McQueen dropped out of *Butch Cassidy and the Sundance Kid* because he wouldn't give up top billing to Paul Newman, which his replacement, Robert Redford, did.

Another story which I like involves a remark supposedly made by Alexander Korda to David Selznick. Throughout the making of *The Third Man* (1949), the relationship between these co-producers was strained. Finally there was a battle over whether the film should be a "Selznick picture," a "Selznick release" or a "London Films production." Eventually it became "A London Films production distributed by British Lion Film Corporation. Presented by Alexander Korda and David O. Selznick." About two years after the movie opened, Orson Welles recalls Korda saying to Selznick: "You know, David, I hope I don't die before you do." "Oh!" said Selznick. "Why?" Korda replied, "I hate the thought of you sneaking out at night and scratching my name off the tombstone."

"Now regarding your new film, I'd like to start by asking you some superficial questions to augment my smart arse article I've already written..."

I have had a very long-standing interest in film, but my interest in the smaller, stranger jobs connected with the industry grew when I spent eight years casting film extras. It was after I was made redundant from that job that my work turned to editing and writing. Researching and writing this book has been enjoyable and interesting but it has not all been easy. Unlike film stars or directors, the majority of my interviewees do not have an agent through whom appointments can be made, and so even making contact can be difficult. Nor is visiting a film set simple (particularly in the U.S. where I have fewer contacts). Film personnel are suspicious and secretive whilst shooting.

In the U.S., my experience was especially frustrating. I had been in contact with the publicist on Steven Spielberg's *Catch Me If You Can* seeking to go on their set in Los Angeles but she had informed me it would be impossible. So I decided to give up the idea and go to New York instead, having first researched in industry magazines and on the Internet what would be shooting there. Throughout my stay in New York, I joked that a certain lift in the hotel, which one could hear but which seemed to go nowhere, led to Spielberg's film. It was on my final day in the city that I learned that *Catch Me If You Can* had been shooting in New York for a week and that the whole crew had stayed in the same hotel as me, leaving the day before!

Nevertheless, I got to meet some absolutely fascinating people both in the U.S. and in England, and I learned a lot. Crew members have certain things in common: together they are an indispensable part of any film. They work extremely long hours and lead unpredictable, unsociable lives, seeing more of each other than their families. Almost without exception they are dedicated, committed and enjoy their jobs enormously, and they are full of eloquence for what they love – for what Charles Drazin calls "the hidden alchemy of the cinema."

Teddy Darvas
Editor

On most films, the director will shoot between 10 and 20 times more footage than is seen. For each scene he/she may shoot at least three different "setups" or "angles," which have different focal lengths, camera positions, amount or type of camera motion, etc. For example, in a two-character dialogue scene, coverage might include a long shot of both characters in their environment, a two-shot of both characters' heads facing each other, and close-ups on each character's face. Additionally, several "takes" of each angle may be shot in order to get the best possible acting and technical performances. Each day the "rushes" (film straight out of the camera after it has been developed, printed and synched with the production sound) are viewed by the director and editor.

The director will tell the editor his/her preferences, and the editor will put together the film, scene by scene, taking account of the acting, lighting, pacing, dramatic tension and emotional charge. Until quite recently, all this was achieved by cutting actual film, or occasionally electronically, by transfer to videotape. Now the majority of films are edited digitally, using computers, saving in time and facilitating experimentation. But audiences are generally unaware of all this.

Teddy Darvas, a veteran editor who still retains vestiges of his original Hungarian accent, is kind, proud and gentlemanly. He worked as assistant on classics such as The Bridge on the River Kwai, *directed by David Lean, who had the reputation of being the best editor in Britain (as well as having six wives and numerous mistresses). Darvas won the Guild of British Film Editors Award for editing* The Railway Children.

SELECTED CREDITS

Cry the Beloved Country (Zoltan Korda, 1951)

Hobson's Choice (David Lean, 1953)

The Bridge on the River Kwai (David Lean, 1957)

Heavens Above (Roy Boulting, 1963)

The Railway Children (Lionel Jeffries, 1970)

Tales from the Crypt (Freddie Francis, 1972)

The first film I was credited on was the third film I worked on as a sound editor, because the whole point was that in those days the only screen credits were for heads of departments, like editor, cameraman, art director, that sort of thing. If you were an assembly cutter, you very rarely got a credit. In those days, you would start as a second assistant sound editor, then be a first assistant, then an assembly cutter, then often a sound or dubbing editor and finally an editor.

But the very first film I worked on was *The Last Days of Dolwyn* [1949], which was written and directed by Emlyn Williams and starred him too, as well as Edith Evans, and it was Richard Burton's first film! I was second assistant trainee sound editor on that. When the film is fine cut, all the effects tracks are laid in synchronization and the dialogues are stripped so they are on a different track so the recording mixer can balance them out more easily and then the music is added. In those days, the editor always laid the music. I used to love laying the music and working with the composer. Nowadays they always have a music editor but very often there is absolutely no need for it.

Next I worked as second assistant with David Lean on *The Sound Barrier* [1952, U.S. title: *Breaking the Sound Barrier*] and I became his "blue eyed boy." Incidentally, David Lean hated the word editor. He said, "I'm a cutter" and I think David was the world's finest cutter of all time. The editor on *Sound Barrier* said to me, "Wait 'til we're off the floor and David comes into the cutting room. That will be the most exciting time of your life." And it was. It was quite, quite fascinating. He made your mind work better than you ever thought possible, and you were never afraid of giving ideas. I went straight from second assistant to assembly cutter. I said I never wanted to be a sound editor and the general manager of the studio said, "Well, you're going to do it!" and that was *The Heart of the Matter* [George More O'Ferrall, 1953]. But again I didn't get a credit on it.

Then I worked with David Lean again. On the big films, David had a sound editor apart from the assembly cutter, who was normally a chap called Wyn Ryder, who was brilliant, although a terrible "old woman." But he didn't get called in on *Hobson's Choice* [1953] because David didn't think it an important enough film! So I worked on it and it is one of my favorite films, though I still didn't get credited. So my first credit was the first St. Trinians film, where I was assembly cutter. I think the present system of everyone getting a credit means there is no sense of achievement. The chief electrician on *Summertime* [David Lean, 1955] and on *The Bridge on the River Kwai* [David Lean, 1957] did a fantastic, absolutely marvelous job so David gave him a credit, which was like getting a knighthood. No chief electrician had had a credit then. But now, a trainee from a film school expects a credit.

On *River Kwai*, the editor, Peter Taylor, wasn't free so I went to Ceylon and had the second-best suite in the hotel, with my cutting room built into

Teddy Darvas editing *The Bridge on the River Kwai* with his assistant (left) Don Ranasinghe in his suite in the Mount Lavinia Hotel, 1957. (Courtesy of Teddy Darvas)

the sitting room which, considering I was really a senior assistant, was fantastic. David Lean wanted to be away from his unit in the evenings so we were in a hotel eight miles away. My suite was next door to his, and in the evening he would come back and have a shower and come into my suite in his dressing gown and we would work on things and I was allowed to do quite a bit of the cutting. I learnt an awful lot because David taught me a tremendous amount. He helped me because I was obviously pretty inexperienced then. I would say something and he would answer, "Well that *sounds* very good but if you did that it would affect the end of the film" or whatever. He always had time to explain why your ideas might not work. But then if you said something which he *happened* to agree with, he would thank you.

David changed editors when he changed wives, but I was never his editor so I lasted two wives! He would look at a girl, and you would see the girl's knees beginning to tremble and he had more affairs than I've had hot dinners. On *Summertime*, when we were recording the music, he had the Italian publicity lady in bed with him for 48 hours and then left her as abruptly! So I had to take her to dinner to let her cry on my shoulder. Then in Ceylon, the restaurant manager of the hotel, Inge, ditto. When the Siamese girls arrived, he dropped her, so she would come into my bedroom at about two in the morning, crying, and I thought, "He has all the pleasure and I have all the pain!" Nobody was allowed to see a frame of the film without the producer or director's permission, but at the hotel in Ceylon David said to me, "Teddy dear, if it helps you with any girl, you can show them anything you like!" – I was a bachelor then.

David was a fascinating man. Afterwards, from *Lawrence of Arabia* [1962], which I didn't work on – that was one wife too many – he got this megalomania that he was everything and the editor was not allowed to cut anything, so everything was held in rushes 'til he came off the floor. The first assistant on that hated him. It was a different David Lean from the one I knew. And on his last film, his credit was "Produced, Written, Directed and Edited by" and the girl who he had in as an editor only got a credit as an assembly cutter, and I thought that was a bit mean. But until then he was very approachable and nice. *The Sunday Times*, when reviewing a biography of Lean, wrote that he never listened, never took advice from any crew, nor did he socialize. So I wrote to *The Sunday Times* and said I was his second assistant and he did listen and ask everybody's advice, and as for not socializing, I lived with my parents, and he used to come to dinner!

I got into the business originally because my father went to school in Hungary with Sir Alexander Korda [the Hungarian producer-director who worked in Paris, Berlin and Hollywood before settling in London in 1930 and forming London Films], and they and a third friend were like brothers. Well, Father and the other friend were both journalists, with a reasonable amount of money, whereas Korda had none and they paid for his coffees and everything, and my father took Alex to see his first movie. Anyway Korda asked my father to come out to England when he first started here, but Father was doing frightfully well with the equivalent of W.H. Smiths in Transylvania and places like that. Anyway, of course he did eventually come and they met up again and so if I wanted to get into films there was always a job for me. In fact, that settee which you are sitting on was given to us by Alex when we furnished our first flat in 1942 because he said he had all his furniture in store because his house had been bombed.

I was very interested in photography from when I was a child and I started work in the BBC European Service as a news typist and they gave me time off to study photography. Then I worked as a photographer for about 18 months. I wanted to get into films but not even Korda could get me a union ticket. So in 1946 I worked in publicity as an exploiteer and in 1948 I heard that there was a vacancy for a trainee so Alex got me in on that, but the union kicked up such a fuss that there was nearly a strike! The unions were ridiculously "closed shop" and wouldn't even give me an appli-cation form even though in fact my father was Secretary of the Hungarian Fabian Society in 1917 and knew the General Secretary of the Labour Party and all that sort of thing. Anyway, I decided to stick it out (although if there had been a strike I would have left immediately), and at that time a new Shop Steward took over and he had a committee meeting and instead of advising strike action they recommended that I be given my card.

It was the Boultings, really, who gave me my break on *Heavens Above* [Roy Boulting, 1963] with Peter Sellers. That was the first big film I actu-ally cut. Then I did lots of fairly small films, and then in 1966, out of the blue, my agent got me a job cutting with Vittorio de Sica in Paris. I have the distinction of having cut de Sica's worst movie, *Woman Times Seven* with Shirley MacLaine! But he was the most wonderful person and wonderful director – tremendously nice – a real gentleman. Actually my wife had had two miscarriages after the first baby and she had just been ordered to bed, and off I went to Paris – but that's show business, you see. One film of which I am quite proud, although it has always had terrible write-ups, is *Assassination Bureau* [Basil Dearden, 1968]. In the '60s it was all hand-held cameras, but this was a 1911 period piece and I think it is a lovely film.

Noël Coward said that there are three creative jobs in filmmaking: the writer, the director and the editor. They are the storytellers. You can have the world's greatest cameraman, the most fantastic art director, and they contribute an awful lot but it's the storytelling which is vital. The editor

Teddy at home in London, 2002. On the far right of his mantelpiece is his award from the Guild of British Film Editors.

and director watch the rushes, and the director chooses the shots and the editor cuts each scene into a "rough cut" and the film grows while it is being shot. Then you do a "first cut" which you show the director and that is the most exciting part because that's when you really make the film. I was very lucky because I was second assistant on *Cry the Beloved Country* [1951] directed by Zoltan Korda, so I worked with him, David Lean and the Boultings: they were all tremendous editors. Even in those days they were so flexible about changing sequences that it gave me ideas of what to do.

On one Lionel Jeffries film, *The Amazing Mr. Blunden* [1972], the end scene didn't work, and realized that by switching the second part of the scene to the front, the surprise was delayed, and it worked. So these sorts of things happen. I cut quite a bit for Don Sharp, who directed lots of the Barbara Taylor Bradford mini-series, and because we are old friends, I knew the way he directed, and he directed because he knew the way that I cut. It's like a marriage. It's a very, very close relationship.

Occasionally there are directors who are difficult to work with, like Richard Donner on *Salt and Pepper* [1968]. That was really quite a nightmare because things were hours long and he wouldn't take any advice, and the producer, who was Peter Lawford's business manager, said, "Look he's making such a mess of it, just keep me informed about how you can put it right, and I'll give you three weeks to do it." The big thing about being the editor is that if there is conflict between the producer and the director, the editor cannot get out from under. You are the only one there. Anyway, the head of United Artists came to see the rough cut, which was 25 minutes longer than it should have been – it was dreadful – and went off to lunch and said, "That's the worst rough cut I've ever seen," at which the producer said, "Yes, we've lost confidence in our editor," and I was fired that same afternoon. So that was a very, very unpleasant period.

The funny thing with Dick Donner was that on the next film he directed, the editor was Reggie Beck, who was a doyen of editors, who co-directed *Henry V* [Laurence Olivier, 1944] and was Joe Losey's editor – he got fired! Then the next film Donner directed, Ralph Kemplen, who cut *The African Queen* [John Huston, 1951], resigned before he was fired, because he was under contract. Both films were disasters, and the third film they thought was another disaster and it turned out to be *The Omen* [1976], which made a lot of money even though it was twice over its budget. Donner went on to direct *Superman* [1978], although all the flying stuff in *Superman* was directed by other directors. But then I think he must have learnt because he is now an exceedingly good director.

Stars don't get involved very much. They look at themselves by and large, though there are some actors who can be constructive. There are very few actors who are rude to an editor! If you direct *and* star in something, then there might be conflict of interests. It didn't happen with Lionel Jeffries, an actor I knew who starred in and directed *The Railway Children* [1970]. He had never directed before, so when he asked me to edit, I said to him, "Li, when I show you something which I have cut and you don't like it, don't scream and shout. That is what it is for, just tell me what you want and next day I'll show it to you a different way." And we became very great personal friends. I mean, he is a bit mad but he is a genius, really.

So every morning I used to go on the floor and Lionel would draw me little pictures of what he was going to shoot, and sometimes I'd say, "Well, you've landed three children in a line so it's difficult to cut" and he would say, "Oh, what a good idea, it would be better for me to bring one of them round the other side" – that sort of thing – it's very exciting when you do that. I got the Guild of British Film Editors Award for *The Railway Children*. The award [which is V-shaped, and stands on his mantelpiece] is known in the trade as the two fingers of scorn to the producer!

Lionel was a bit difficult and, although he was one of the great hopes of British film directors, he only directed three films. Nowadays, because it is accountants that have the say and they can't handle temperamental people, they'll take someone else who is less of a problem. The last work I did was an American television series called *Covington Cross* [1992], which was meant to go for five years but only lasted a few episodes. In the past, whenever there was a lull in feature film work, I would do documentaries, which I enjoyed very much. It's very different, with no real script, so it was a nice change in discipline, but now I haven't worked for nine years. I have never mastered computer editing, although now one can do everything you could do on film. But I think a lot of editors feel a bit remote from the film now. David Lean and all those, used to love the feeling of the film running through their fingers; it was sort of sensual.

Hugo Luczyc-Wyhowski
Production Designer

Hugo Luczyc-Wyhowski lives in a strikingly modern conversion of a Georgian house, "designery" in its predominance of glass, wood and metal and its muted colors. Being open-plan, his desk is adjacent to the kitchen-dining room, which is another strange combination of a vast sculpture mounted on the wall (a prop from a bar scene in When Saturday Comes, *Maria Giese, 1996) and the typical detritus left by young children.*

Hugo, too, seems a mixture. Assured and confident, he also modestly claims to be always learning. He got into the industry by chance, yet his appreciation of the craft of filmmaking is palpable. His job is huge, justifying its credit before the title, but he spent the longest time with me, and was immensely kind, looking up names and numbers of other people I might wish to interview.

SELECTED CREDITS
My Beautiful Laundrette (Stephen Frears, 1985)
Prick Up Your Ears (Stephen Frears, 1987)
Nil by Mouth (Gary Oldman, 1997)
Madeline (Daisy Mayer, 1998)
Snatch (Guy Ritchie, 2000)
Birthday Girl (Jez Butterworth, 2001)
The Truth About Charlie (Jonathan Demme, 2002)
Dirty Dancing: Havana Nights (Guy Ferland, 2004)
Mrs. Henderson Presents (Stephen Frears, 2005)

I'm the head of the art department and I'm responsible for everything you see on a film apart from the actors and what they're wearing, although some production designers are even responsible for that. So I'm responsible for any locations (the location manager looks for locations and services them but reports to me with pictures of them). I am also responsible for the design, construction and dressing of any sets built or adapted in the studio or on location. All the optical effects, and special effects also come under my umbrella. It's an enormous job. I mean, on a film I'll have upwards of 80 to 100 people working with, under, me. In actual physical terms, I'm accountable for about 20 percent of the total budget.

I am appointed by the producer, usually on the recommendation of the director. I get sent a script and then I meet with them and talk about it and any ideas I might have about the film. There is a lot of idea-stealing that goes on at that stage because you are always going for interviews and splurge out lots of really good ideas and then you don't get the job but you go and see the film and find your ideas have been incorporated into the film! There may be several interviews and it's also quite a personal relationship at that stage – an interesting collaboration concerning the film, but also in terms of individuals and how they get on. There has to be a mutual interest of some sort because if you don't like the people you're working with or they don't like you, it makes the job really really difficult.

On a small-budget London location film, you would probably start about eight weeks before; on a bigger film, going up to about a $20,000,000 low-budget American movie, you would probably start 10 to 12 weeks before; and going up to about a $50,000,000 movie you would probably start anything up to three to six months before. On something like *Star Wars*, it could be as much as a year or 18 months before.

Being a production designer is a curious mixture of being all sorts of things. It's partially being an artist, partially a draftsman, partially an accountant responsible for a budget which can be very large. A lot of the job, though, is in people management; more than 50 percent of the job really is being good at delegating work to people and then overseeing them do the work. I would love to use the same people on several films, but it's a big freelance pool that one is drawing from and one is obviously working in many different countries, so it is not usually possible.

The first people to start on a reasonable-sized film would be a supervising art director who would bring on one to three art directors and under them there would be draftsmen and various junior draftsmen. Then there is a construction manager who would start that department, a set decorator and a prop master and maybe several prop buyers. I spend a lot of time

Opposite: Hugo at home. The sculpture on the wall is from *When Saturday Comes*.

Hugo shows some of his architectural drawings.

talking to the director at this stage and going through the script and trying to imagine how the characters are and what they do and where they come from and how we want to set the film.

You do sketches of sets and really drawings of a whole range of things from scribbles on the back of a cigarette packet to proper visuals of sets and often scale models. Every single thing is drawn. There may be several thousand drawings done and every last tiny detail is drawn because you have to have it made, or explain to someone how it works and you can't do that unless it's drawn. Any set which has to be built has to have architectural drawings, plans, elevations, details of everything. As the drawings start coming out, we start construction.

At this stage, again there is a lot of discussion with the director, and the producer would also want to see what is going on. Some producers take more interest than others. To some extent, the producer's skill is in bringing together the right people rather than overseeing how everyone interprets what's scripted. As a designer, it is my view that you should not notice the sets. You should go to a film and come out thinking, "Wow, that was a fantastic performance and she looked so great" or "God, that was such a moving film and I wanted to cry." I think if you are sitting in the cinema thinking, "Why is he sitting on that disgusting blue chair?" the designer has failed.

On the other hand, there are films where the set is important. What I'm always trying to do is to work to the script: to interpret the script to make the characters fit in and the sets seem natural. When you have a period film, there are certain constraints on what you can and can't do. With a modern film, the palette is larger, the canvas is broader, and although I love doing period films I'm also very interested in contemporary work because I think its probably harder to make something unique and stylish and interesting if that's what is required.

I am also very concerned (and this is something not a lot of designers will talk about) with the musicality of the whole piece. The film has a flow and kind of rhythm of its own as it goes from one scene to another and it's very much something that a designer can control through the nature of the sets. If there is an action sequence where a girl is being chased down a corridor, you can compress and compress and compress it and make the space smaller and smaller and then *bam*! Just as she escapes, she can rush out into a big open space. So you can use space very much to affect the visual nature of the tone of the film.

You can also use color. The design of a close-up is strangely probably one of the most difficult and in many ways the most important moment in a film. There are several peaks in any film and just at the moment when some wonderful Hollywood actress discovers someone has died and she bursts into tears and its her big close-up, if you put stripy wallpaper behind her head it's clearly going to distract. But if you have a kind of yellow ochre color or a beautiful piece of silk, you might weirdly and very subtly influence the mood and the tone of that one shot.

I see design very much in photographic terms in that sense. For example, one of the reasons why many Terry Gilliam films are, I think, very difficult to look at, is because they tend to use a maximum amount of decoration all the time; like having cream as well as milk with everything. I personally would rather look at a Kurosawa film where the use of decoration is used very specifically to mean something. There might be a calm period in a film where the image is quite restful and you might see someone against a blank wall and then they go into a very decorative state and its very busy visually. So those are the sort of tools one can use in design in the overall sense.

When I read a script, it either comes into my mind as I am reading it, or it doesn't, and if it doesn't it isn't going to. Sometimes you immediately know and can imagine it very clearly and that's exciting. When you work with the director trying to find the overall look, you watch many other films. I am also interested in the design of film in purely photographic terms so I personally would refer a lot to photographers, antique or modern, and find it a very good way to discuss stuff. I would be able to say, for example, "I like this image because of the soft lighting."

So in collaboration with the director and the director of photography, I would ask what type of film stock we are going to use. Again I am slightly unusual because a lot of designers aren't interested in this, but I am madly interested in it, because I believe that my work is merely light; it only exists on the celluloid, and how it is photographed is absolutely crucial to how you design it. The fact that you can paint a wall red, and the way it is lit can make it look pink or brown or white is completely thrilling and brilliant.

You work with directors of photography who are very skilled in using light and that is the absolute essence of what you're doing – the purest part of designing for film. In the end, you can make an architectural background for the actors to work in front of, but what matters is how the photographic image looks. And it is incredibly complicated because there is this massive range of film stocks and then there are a lot of different types of photographic hardware, like the difference between a Panavision camera to an Aeroflex. Now after 20 years of doing it, I can see the differences, which are really subtle.

Then there are questions like the quality of light, hard or soft? How do you light people, natural or theatrical? Do you make them look romantic? What do you do with skin tones? Do you get rid of all the blemishes, or see

Opposite: Lights set up for filming by the Thames in Hammersmith. "Using light is the purest part of designing for film... it is absolutely part of my job and I love it."

all the lines on their faces? So there is a whole essence of where you position the camera in relation to the viewer. I personally think that is absolutely part of my job and I love it. I love to do tests with directors of photography to get the particular quality we are seeking.

There are so many people involved in the making of a film from the beginning to when it is finally shown on screen that any idea at all that is written down on a page by a writer gets changed, diffused, deflected and subtly varied in a weird snake-like way all the way down. The more I can do to present a clear, cohesive, simple idea for everybody as to how the film will look and what is important to leave out as well as what is important to include, the more the end result will come nearer to our original idea.

I have worked on films where we have managed to get really close to what we wanted, but it happens on about one out of ten films. It's very hard because there are so many people and so many compromises have to be made. One I worked on which was very satisfying was *Nil By Mouth* [Gary Oldman, 1997]. It looks like a film where someone has just rushed into a room with a few actors and picked up a camera, but it is the most designed film. We worked so hard on making a particular look. I referred particularly to one photographer, Paul Graham, whose work I kind of aped in the look of the film.

It was useful because it gave everyone a very clear image of what we were trying to create and we were able to work hard on the look. We suspended the camera on bungee rope and did lots of strange things that still look quite natural. So we invented a sort of realism that was fresh and new that was cinematic and yet referred to documentary style. It was different from a Ken Loach film and from a Mike Leigh film; it was different from an Alan Clarke film but it was a new interesting realism and it looked extremely close to what we started out with, and in all of film design that is really quite rare.

The films that get recognized for their design are period ones, with lots of flashy costumes and lovely baroque interiors with fantastic miles of fabric and everything covered with brocade and silk. In some ways that's fine, but then film design is very much looked at from the point of view of its decorative nature and there is an awful lot of other good work which goes unnoticed – very subtle work. I work very hard at going to look at all the "dailies" and you try all these new surfaces and you look at hundreds of hours of "rushes" and you build up a vocabulary of stuff that you learn works well or that doesn't work well.

Disasters are usually to do with other people letting you down. This is the sort of thing which happens: We're shooting a war film in Poland, in 1990, just after the Wall comes down, and I have a very nice chap trying to find vehicles for me. (Vehicles often play quite a large part in filming.) The protagonist (an American actor) is a bad guy into trafficking black-market goods and in bed with the Nazis as well as being involved with the French resistance, and this man wears a camel hair coat, smokes cigars and would drive a really flashy car.

So I say to the guy, "Can you find me a 1937 Renault, or something like that?" He goes off, comes back with a picture of this fabulous car, lovely white-wall tires, gleaming headlamps and everything, and I say to him, "Is it period?" He says, "Yes." I ask about the inside and he says, "It's all beautiful leather," and I ask, "Can we have a look at it before we use it?" and he replies that the only problem is that it's in Posnam, another city, and we can't get it to the set until the day of filming. I say, "Well, okay, I'll trust you. You promise it's a wonderful period car?" and he answers, "Yes."

Then, on the day, for some reason I am in my office and get a phone call asking me to come down to the set because the director is a little bit upset. So I go down to the set and there is this group of film people standing round (as they do) this beautiful gleaming car. But they're all looking rather glum. So I walk up to the car and see that the whole of the interior is covered in white fun fur, including the steering wheel! That sort of thing happens the whole time because someone lets you down. Every designer will have dozens of stories like that. Sets blow over, and you find yourself in the middle of the night driving across a desert trying to get some polystyrene, or an elephant tramples and eats the garden you just made in Africa or whatever. And inevitably when you put it all together again the director just walks on with absolutely no idea of all the effort that's gone into it. The job is very much about anticipating all of the things that can go wrong.

The other thing people don't always realize is that you have to have a tremendous wealth of technical information of how films are made. You have to know how wide a dolly [a trolley to put a camera on] is with its wheels and everything. You can't build a door and not have the camera go through it. I have done that. I built a door and forgot to check what size the actor was and he came on set — it was Charles Durning and he couldn't get his tummy through the door! It was like a secret panel in the door about two feet, two inches or something and he couldn't fit through!

You also need a reasonable idea of how much things will cost, which is only really something you can get with experience. And then people never believe you. You say, "If you want to do that, it's going to cost this," and they look at you with daggers drawn. Or you say, "We can do that, but it's going to cost *this*, and I don't think we can afford it so I think we should do something else instead." I do a lot of that. A lot of altering even the whole idea of a scene to save money.

But I had no idea of all of this when I started. I was a painter originally, with a degree in fine art and had no thoughts of working in film. Then I got a job, in a way by mistake, driving a truck for the art department on a film and sort of enjoyed it and managed to get some jobs in the art department and was then just very lucky. I met someone who worked at a rock video company who said, "Okay, come and be an art director on this rock video," and the director of the video was Nicolas Roeg! And Nick was very sweet to me and said *[imitating a plummy voice]* "You're my boy now. I'm going to teach you how the industry works!" So I did a whole lot of stuff with him and I was "his boy" for a bit and I did various other rock videos and then Stephen Frears asked me to do *My Beautiful Launderette* [1985] – that was the first film I ever designed.

This is a very untypical path. Normally one would start off as a junior draftsman drawing horrible full-size sections of Corinthian-pillar capitals. Instead I was working with Stephen, and he was a very generous director to work with. He allowed me a lot of freedom and expected exciting and innovative solutions to the design tasks that were required. He always exploited the sets to the maximum with his intuitive direction of the actors and camera.

I was also lucky that I started in the industry at about the same time as Channel 4 started on TV so there were all those Channel 4 films that were a springboard for people like me. It was still hard, though. The trade union was quite strong so you couldn't just walk in and do it like you can now. So I also see it as a very important part of my job to pass on information and I try to encourage and teach young people in the art department.

I also go to films madly. I am often disappointed, and also thrilled, by design work – from mad science fiction to very intense drama. I'd love to direct a film eventually. I am getting a little bit better at it. I have done 22 films and I still know very little but maybe I'll know a bit more when I've done 40 films. Every single film you learn a whole new lot of stuff about some new subject. It's very, very interesting from that point of view. I go to all these countries, seeing parts of them that people never see and meet lots of really extraordinary people. Hundreds and hundreds of people every year, which is quite difficult because you form quite brief associations with them and then you never see them again except for a few that you maybe keep sending Christmas cards to.

But it is endlessly fascinating. One day I will be researching 1950s bubble gum wrappers and I'll find some guy in North London and I'll have to go to his house and his house is full of 3,000,000 bubble gum wrappers. Or you're in North Carolina working with hillbillies, working with raw stone, or up a mountain with people from the Polish army blowing up a whole area. It never stops being completely intriguing.

Stephen Warbeck
Composer

Stephen Warbeck is soft-spoken and self-deprecating (evident in almost all he says, from his first sentence on), but he has the power to transform films with his music. He can conjure moods of romance, fear, suspense, excitement and despair. He can help speed or slow the action; enable the viewers to immerse themselves in, or question, what they see; create climaxes and subtle nuance.

The recipient of several awards, Stephen won an Oscar for best original score for Shakespeare in Love. *Four years later, at the 2002 Oscar ceremony, actor Ben Kingsley eloquently described the effect a good score can have on a movie: "In a film, it's the music that's the wind, which gives the picture flight. When a film is over, the music is a perfume, which remains after a particularly enchanting encounter. It is created to underscore moments in the dark, and to bring us back to those moments again and again — every time we hear it."*

SELECTED CREDITS

Prime Suspect (TV series I-V, 1993-96)
Mrs. Brown (John Madden, 1997)
Shakespeare in Love (John Madden, 1998)
Billy Elliot (Stephen Daldry, 2000)
Captain Corelli's Mandolin (John Madden, 2001)
Charlotte Gray (Gillian Armstrong, 2001)
Secret Passage (Ademir Kenovic, 2002)
Pour le plaisir (Dominique Deruddere, 2004)
Proof (John Madden, 2004)

Similar to my own children, who seem to make up lots of songs and bits of music as soon as they can talk nearly, I always did too. We had a piano in our house and so from as far back as I can remember I wrote bits of music and would often improvise on the piano, before I had lessons. I started piano lessons at four which I stopped again quickly and then started again at six. From the beginning, music was a huge thing; I don't know if it was the *biggest* thing or not, but it was a big part of my life.

My mother played the piano; my father played the drums; my grand-father, before arthritis, played the penny-whistle and the tenor banjo; my brother plays the piano and used to play the cello – so there was a fair bit of music about. All through my childhood, there was a lot of music happen-ing, and at school, I *think*, it would be fair to say that I was prepared to be a musician – that was the way everyone thought I was going, anyway. But I reacted against it in my teens. At least I reacted to "straight" or classical music and got much more interested in rock music and, parallel to that, started to be interested in theater.

I studied drama and French at university, but I was still writing music for a lot of the plays in the drama department at Bristol. My first job after university was as musical director and performer in a play at Theatre Royal, Stratford East in London. In fact, I did both things together until 1985 when two things happened. First I realized that I was getting more satisfac-tion from composing – possibly, although this is contentious, because you have more artistic control as a composer than an actor. Secondly, on a more practical level, my agent at that time said, "I can't work with this!" Actually the word he used, which is a bit unpleasant, is "sell" – he said, "I can't sell you as either one thing or the other. People don't know what you are."

I was working fairly constantly, but what happens in that position is that theater companies sometimes get you for two-for-the-price-of-one. The other attractive thing about *not* performing is that you can sit or stand outside the piece of theater and be a little bit more objective, whereas if you are playing the piano and jumping up and putting a hat on and play-ing the wicked landlord, and then going back and playing the piano again, you are very heavily inside it. So I began just to compose for the theater, and then for film. It is not that uncommon a career path – Patrick Doyle and George Fenton both also started as actors and then composers first for theater and then film.

All the way along I *loved* film. I was particularly keen on European film. There was a teacher called Mr. Voigt at my school in Lewes who ran a film club on Monday nights and he used to do a term of Truffaut and a term of Spanish films – so there was a big European film interest. And around 1985, Mike Bradwell, who now runs the Bush Theatre, but who used to run

Stephen Warbeck (Photo by Lynda Mamy)

a theater company called Hull Truck, made a film, which ended up on television, called *Happy Feet* and because I was a composer who he'd worked
with and we got on well, he asked me to compose the music for that.

Then it was not long afterwards that *Prime Suspect* [TV series I-V,
1993-96] cropped up and luckily it was one of those things which people
thought, "Oh, this is good!" and I think it *was* good, but I also think there is
an element of luck and it being the right time for a particular style of
drama. So what essentially happened was that from being a theater composer who had done a little television, suddenly I was a composer who had
been involved with something that most people had come across. So when
things cropped up after that I was at least in the running for them as a
television and theater composer.

The first feature film I did was *O Mary This London*, directed by Suri
Krishnamma [1994]. On that, and also on *Mrs. Brown* [John Madden, 1997],
I only started composing after the film was shot – not at the absolute end
of editing but quite near to it. I think on *Mrs. Brown* I had nine or ten days
with the film – quite a short amount of time – maybe three to four weeks
actually knowing I was going to do it. That is one extreme, where you are
involved right at the end, when most other departments have finished.

In contrast to that were *Shakespeare in Love* [John Madden, 1998] and *Captain Corelli's Mandolin* [John Madden, 2001], both of which have some integral music in the films – the Elizabethan-style dance music, for instance, in *Shakespeare in Love*. Sometimes they might employ a different composer or different set-up for music before the filming, but in both those cases I was involved with the music well before filming. In *Shakespeare in Love*, we decided that the music within the film should be thematically important because we might want to use some of that material in the score – although in fact we didn't. So a composer could well be involved early on simply for those practical reasons, like Captain Corelli has to play the mandolin.

Really, there are no hard-and-fast rules about when the composer starts work on a film. I shall be doing the music for a film called *Love's Brother* [Jan Sardi, 2003] which starts shooting in a couple of months' time and although there is no music to be performed in the film, they decided they wanted to know who was doing the score in advance. At that point you can't talk about what you are going to do based on the visual images; you have to talk about it based on the script. So you would say, "This script suggests *this* kind of thing to me." And they would say, "Well, that sounds lovely," or "That sounds horrible," or whatever it happens to be. And possibly after you had gone they'd say, "Oh my God, he's not coming from the same angle as us at all – we'll have to think of someone else!"

Your response to the script in those cases can be significant, or it might be your response to the film. You might go to the cutting room and they"d say, "What do you think of this?" and you'd say, "Well, it's got to be banjo and penny-whistle" and they'd say, "Um – I don't think so somehow." Then either there would be a negotiation to try and find common ground, or you would be so far apart that you wouldn't work together.

So when I first start working on a film, I try to think what it is that I would like to hear. Is it strings, or a full orchestra, or is it guitar, bass and drums? I like to imagine it rather than play anything first of all. Then, having established what the musical vocabulary is, both on my own and in conjunction with the director, I would next start to sit at the piano and, looking at the film, try out some ideas. But some of it I might do without looking at the picture. For example in *Shakespeare in Love* I might be thinking of Viola and Will falling in love and play around with different themes – at that stage not quite certain where they would be useful, if at all.

I think each film should have its own particular voice and color and sound – although sometimes that is simply an orchestral texture – but it should have something particular and distinguishing. So for instance, in *Captain Corelli's Mandolin*, although I was very conscious of the Greek setting in terms of visuals, most of the music springs more from an Italian point of view. I have always loved Greek music, but in my background research I probably listened to more Italian music, because Corelli, an Italian, was the new musical influence coming to the island. There were also a few Greek dances, a couple of which were traditional, and one of which I wrote.

If there is an emotion in the film – like two people falling in love – music can deepen or heighten it. Equally, the music could run in counterpoint to the emotion, so it could be reminding you of a danger that you have seen in the past, or that lies ahead. So you could be working *against* what you are seeing on the screen to provide a tension. People quite often feel that music also works thematically in linking various things together. I personally think that things link themselves together perfectly well without music, so when people ask for "Doris's theme" or "Derek's theme" or whatever, sometimes I think it is a bit literal and music can be a bit more abstract than that.

It varies from director to director as to how involved they get in deciding where to add music and for how long and all of that. Some directors, although a minority in feature films, would say, "Right, the music starts here, as he comes through the door, and ends as she falls off the cliff." Some would even say, "As her foot passes the top of the turf sticking over the edge." However in *most* cases when the director says, "Well, I think we should have some music when he comes in through the door and she falls over the cliff," you would then say, "How about if the music actually started earlier as he got out of the car?" and he would say, "You try that and we'll see." So then you write a bit of music and look at it together and say, "Actually, it was better when he came in through the door." Or the director might hear the two cues that you have written for two bits in a sequence and say, "It's too bitty, let's join them together." Or *you* might say, "What would happen if the music just went right the way through?" So it is a negotiation.

Quite often a director will feel sensitive to the fact that the music is not quite working, or there is not quite enough emotion or whatever it happens to be, and he will ask you to do something to increase whatever it is. Sometimes they are just worrying unnecessarily and then I'll say, "I really,

really don't think we need music here, it is playing very well without." Generally when you meet with the director and play him or her the music, both of you will suggest ideas and you will try out different possibilities.

You still do end up having to compose a piece of music to an exact length, say one minute, but you arrive at that minute after a discussion – it is not "And here you will write a one-minute piece." You have what is called a "spotting session" where you talk about where the music is going to be. Then you go away and write it and usually, as you write it, you change a few beginnings and ends. Then, when the director hears it, you change some more. Depending on how many meetings you have and how often you go through it, things carry on evolving. And then when you are recording it, the director may well say, "Just give me a little bit more so that I can take the music out as you start to hear the waves, so it doesn't end so abruptly." So most likely you will be extending or altering cues a little bit even at the stage of recording.

I probably enjoyed composing for all the films I've done in one way and another, but definitely, *Mrs. Brown*, *Shakespeare in Love* and *Captain Corelli's Mandolin* would be high up on the list of favorites. It is a particularly satisfying relationship with John Madden and he directed all those. It is like when you have friends or you meet somebody and you think, "Oh, I like you," and you get on well together and make each other laugh and all the rest of it and the fact that socially things are easy. One way of judging how well you are getting on with a director is how gleefully you look forward to their ring on the doorbell. Occasionally, with some people, you think, "Oh, no, oh, here we go again!" And you know that you are in for four or five hours that are going to be difficult.

What happens when John rings the doorbell is that there is a sense of excitement, because in the time you are going to spend together (probably slightly longer than with other directors because he is very thorough) you are going to turn some new corners. I also like working with him because he has got a terrific musical memory: You play a tune once and he will remember it, and four hours later he'll say, "You know that second tune you played me..." and I'll often say, "Well, no, I don't remember which one it was." And he will tell you which one it was and he will say, "Can you try that as she is getting out of the boat?" And you think, "My goodness, I hadn't thought of *that*." So it feels like a real dialogue and a real collaboration.

The other thing is that when you get to know someone and have worked with them a number of times, your conversation ranges right across the *whole* project. You don't only talk about the music; you talk about other aspects of the film as you would in the theater. In the theater, a director assembles their creative team who generally have something to say about the lights and the set and the music. It is nice when you don't have to button your lip and keep quiet if you have a particular worry about a shot or about the way something looks. I think it is important for a composer to be able to ask, "Is there any way that could be different? It has always bothered me." Or "I don't understand that bit of plot."

Winning the Oscar for *Shakespeare in Love* was very thrilling and seemed rather unreal and impossible 'til it happened. I am very proud of the score, but I *do* think that there is a strange phenomenon at work where no score seems to win unless the film is deemed to be successful. So you might write a good score for a film that the public and the critics and the film companies don't go for in a big way, and then you don't stand much chance. I might not necessarily say that *Shakespeare in Love* was my best score; I don't know. But there is an element of going on a lovely ride with a lot of other people when you win an award.

To begin with, after the Oscar, I was offered a number of inappropriate projects just because people liked the idea of having an Academy Award-winning composer. I turned a lot of things down in the first couple of years. I think probably now, that wave of getting the last Oscar-winning composer has died down. I suppose realistically it does increase your prestige amongst certain people, but it is equally possible that it puts some films out of your hands. If there is a young, rather daring, experimental filmmaker, they probably think, "Oh, an Academy Award-winning composer is too established."

So, in a way, although most of us will still be as interested in doing peculiar, unusual projects and trying out new things, and doing an entire film with a chair leg and a gong or something, the people making those kind of films won't come to me first, although maybe ten years ago they would have. But I have been lucky and enjoyed working in many different ways. For example on *Quills* [2000], the director, Philip Kaufman, allowed me, and provoked me, to write music as odd and as mad as I wanted to. So if I was treading a little carefully in our first meetings, he said, "No, no, no, really go, go, set off!" So he kind of freed me in a way that maybe some directors wouldn't. So I enjoyed working with him in a different way that

was absolutely thrilling and sent me in a direction which I didn't think I
had been in before.

Another good experience, apart from the fact that there were various
frustrations along the way, was working with Udayan Prasad on *Brothers in
Trouble* [1996] and *My Son the Fanatic* [1997]. That was a wonderfully stimu-
lating collaboration because he is very particular and specific. He likes the
music to be quite understated so it is sometimes a question of reining in
your wilder fancies and keeping it under control. Composing is different
depending on whom you work with and that is one of the really great things
about working for film.

I think if you are a sociable, collaborative person, which I feel I probably am, there is something a little bit solitary about going over to my piano
or manuscript paper and writing concert music. It is a real challenge when
I have done it, but I do like the fact of talking to someone about how the
music is developing. I also *love* the fact that film music is an incomplete
thing – it needs the visual images to complete it. I like it because I like
mixing different people's imaginations. I know that in a concert piece, obviously the imaginations of the musicians and the composer and the con-
ductor all come together. But in a film you have a whole extra layer of
dimension of people's imaginations.

A film is the sum of an awful lot of different people's feelings about a
world or a place or a story. At its best, that whole sum of people's imaginations, with the director at the apex, reaches a lot of people. So in fact one's
music is heard by more people than it would be in a concert hall. And the
other practical thing is that to make a living as a concert composer is something that very few people manage to do. There are not that many oppor-
tunities and the world doesn't seem to have room for that many concert
composers.

But having said how lovely it is collaborating and everything, one reason why I, like several film composers, have a band, is that you also need to
be able to write your own thing without anybody saying, "Oh, no, no, no,
not like that. Too fast. Too slow. Can't we have it more dangerous?" So it is
nice when you can write a song or whatever independent of all that. And
often if I am sitting looking at the piano or the television thinking, "Oh my
God, how am I going to write this score?" I'll write a song for The Kippers
band just to take my mind off the problem and get going again. Most of the
musicians in the band are jazz musicians, but there are rock influences and

French chansons, and the influence of Kurt Weill and all those things are there in the music, as well as a degree of silliness!

I still do about two to three plays a year as well as my film work and I would like to continue more or less in the same way. Actually, I would like to increase the concert bit of my work, both in terms of concert performances of film scores but more significantly, of concert pieces, of which so far there are very few. Realistically, if people want to do a concert they are more likely to choose my film scores than, say, a piece for bass clarinet and orchestra I've written. Just in terms of the public, they are going to say, "That is not what we think of him as doing." They want Pelagia's song from *Captain Corelli* or the bit on the beach with Viola at the end of *Shakespeare in Love*.

But I hope to write some more concert pieces. I think it is important to feel you have your own voice and that you are not just blowing this way and that depending on the project – that you have got something individual to say as well. It is lovely that I can do both. I am incredibly lucky and it is a very privileged thing to be able to do.

Charlotte Walter
Costume Designer

I talked to Charlotte in her wardrobe truck, placing my tape recorder on her ironing board. It was a little like being in a narrowboat, with everything stowed to give maximum space. Two washing machines were placed above the cab at the front of the wagon, a tiny sink below, balancing bottles of Stergene and Comfort. To one side were drawers holding accessories, and on both sides, stretching the length of the truck, were clothes rails divided by tags with names such as "Ian Richardson" written on them. Frock coats, waistcoats and trousers hung beneath.

The truck was warm, matching Charlotte's personality. Her passion for her work was emphatic, as was the importance she placed on a good team. Charlotte unfolded her story gradually, and unhurriedly gave.

SELECTED CREDITS

Damage, Assistant Costume Designer (Louis Malle, 1992)
Demob (TV Drama, 1993)
Remember Me? (Nick Hurran, 1997)
North Square (TV series, Tim Fywell, 2000)
Murder Rooms (TV series, 2001)
I Capture the Castle (Tim Fywell, 2003)

I don't design costumes; I design clothes that people *wear*. That's how I feel it should be, and so that is really my starting point. First of all, I get a script and break it down from each character's point of view – what they are doing each day, and I visualize how they will look, whether it's a period or contemporary piece. After that, I have a meeting with the director and say, "This is how I see this character, is that how you see them?" I take direction from him, but also it is often not until you meet the actor or actress that you run with your ideas of costume. As soon as they walk in the door, you get a very good idea of the actor or actress' whole persona and I base my ideas around that.

The next thing is usually a fitting with the actor at a costumier's, where I will take photographs. The photos are incredibly useful, showing shapes and lines and giving me an idea of what the person might look like on screen as opposed to the naked eye. I can also show the photos to a director who inevitably doesn't have time to go to fittings, and show him the direction I am taking. I might find a suit which I like the look of and then find fabric and have something similar made up, or adapt something in stock or whatever. I decide the color of coat, tie, hat and the whole look of a character, and their relation with other characters – for instance, one might look predominantly dark and another tweedy. Or I might meet an actor and realize that they are a comedian and can take really strong colors.

On *Murder Rooms* [period TV series, 2001], I wanted Ian Richardson, who plays Bell, to have quite a sharp look, with blacks, navies and blues and decided not to go with a Homburg – he needed a top hat. Silhouettes are really important. And you want the person to look as individual as possible so that when they walk on screen you get an immediate image of them. With someone like Ian, who is a very intelligent actor who takes an enormous amount of trouble and care with his whole character, I would also listen to his comments and make sure he felt comfortable in what he was wearing. And I would talk to the production designer and find out what colors were being used in different sets.

What I like to do is color – particular looks. So earlier this week we had two different set-ups in a theater, using the same extras. One was an evening out with people enjoying themselves watching a hypnotist, and the other was an audience watching a spiritualist healer. So for the first one I used rich reds and greens and blues, and then took all those rich colors out and replaced them with grays and browns for the second scene. The whole image completely changed without changing everybody.

The female lead's costumes were designed from scratch, because I had a very definite idea of how I wanted her to look and the chances of finding period originals to fit anybody in this day and age is impossible. I decided on the colors and fabrics I wanted for her character first. She plays a medium and I wanted her to look like a blackbird, and use velvety bluey red colors with original buttons and trimmings. Then we tried on shapes in a costume house and saw what necklines suited the actress [Claire Holman]. Then I used the shape of one bodice, the skirt of another dress, and took photos of them to my costume-maker who used our fabric and omitted various details of lace that I didn't like and embroidered it all.

I don't do any actual sewing, but I am forever placing beading and trimmings on fabric and seeing how they look and moving them around and even turning fabric inside-out to get it less bright. I'm obsessed about color coordinating and I'm obsessive about details. Claire wore original Victorian jewelry and my mum's gold earrings. Another of her costumes I had made up from an original 1880s drawing and had the fabric dipped and dyed to just the right green that I wanted.

You need to make decisions fairly quickly, and if you don't like something, elbow it and start again. Your ideas evolve and grow with each fitting and with the breakdown, when you decide when the character will change their colors and whether it is a colder or a more passionate scene. The first morning an actress goes out onto set in her clothes, if she feels really confident in them and doesn't have to worry about them, she can go out and do *her* job and it is really satisfying for me. I can stand back and go "*Yes*" and it's brilliant. It has taken maybe four weeks to get to that point, but it's so worth it, and you think it's lovely and all the details and everything come together.

Sometimes modern films can be even harder than period. I did *North Square* [TV series, Tim Fywell, 2000] up in Leeds and they wanted very high fashion, modern clothes where there are no tight guidelines for the actress. So an actress can say, "Oh, this doesn't suit me" or "I don't look like me." There are no boundaries, but a huge wide palette. Your idea of a character might be someone who would present herself in smart business clothes and at your first meeting the actress might say, "I see this character as someone really quirky who would buy all her clothes from a charity shop," and you think, "Oh my God, on screen that isn't going to work."

I don't fight with actors, but in a way you become quite manipulative. I have three daughters so I have learnt that art! You don't hit them head-on and take all their confidence away – I am not there to fight with an actress, I am there to make her look as good, or as right for the character, as I possibly can. I would never make someone wear something they absolutely hated and didn't feel comfortable with. I just gently persuade them. A fussy man, or one that is unsure of his looks, can be far worse and more needy of reassurance than a woman. But if you are well prepared, and know what you want, and are definite about it, things go fine.

The most satisfying film is always the last one you've done, because you grow. You want each production you do to be better than the last. I did a film for Granada called *Seeing Red* [2000] that was set in the early '70s, which Graham Theakston directed with Sarah Lancashire. It was about Coral Atkins, who is an actress who opened a children's home. I really enjoyed it because it was a special team of people. The director, the production designer, the director of photography – we all liked each other and respected each other's work.

Sometimes I walk out and I think, "Oh God, this set is just fantastic, it's just how I imagined my costumes would be well set-off against" and then

Charlotte Walter checks costumes in the wardrobe truck on *Cambridge Spies*.

you see the director of photography lighting it beautifully, and you see the whole picture coming together. And if the director of photography and production designer come up to me and say, "Charlotte, it looks fantastic!" that for me is the *best* moment because they are my peers, the people I respect, and it is a wonderful feeling.

When an actor appreciates something, it is nice too. Last night Claire Holman (my leading lady in *Murder Rooms*, who was actually an absolute pleasure to fit from day one) phoned me up and asked if she could borrow something I had made for her. Her boyfriend is up for an Olivier award today, so she has borrowed an 1880s jacket from me and is wearing it over a black pair of trousers to the award ceremony, and that's just lovely.

I started in this work when I was at Art College in the Midlands, and we were sent to work in industry. I was put to work in a trouser factory and it was a nightmare and was awful and I lasted a day! I completely screwed up this machine because they told me you had to put the interfacing shiny-side up, and when I pulled the machine down it stuck to the interfacing. They all thought it was hysterical because there I was, this art student in red elephant 'loons and a T-shirt with stars all over, looking, I suppose like a typical 17-year-old art student. Anyway my tutor said, "Where are you going to get a job?" and I phoned my father all upset. He worked at the BBC in Birmingham but nothing to do with the drama department, but he said he'd ask the head of the wardrobe department if I could go and do work experience there.

So I did and I thought I had arrived in Heaven. It was brilliant and I was incredibly lucky. Actually, it wasn't that easy – I was a dresser, and in those days it was like an apprenticeship and you were really put through the hoops. In the '70s as a dresser, you were very much bottom of the rung and that was it. You didn't even get a script to read so you had no idea what was going on and sometimes you weren't treated very well. And I remember thinking, "If I am ever a costume designer, I am never going to treat people like this," and sometimes I really do bite my tongue for that very reason. I do remember times of feeling really unhappy then.

Next you become an assistant, and it depended on how generous the designer was as to how much responsibility you were allowed. I was still quite young, about 27, and had just got to the point where I might have been a designer, when I decided to have my first daughter and left the industry. In those days if you had a baby, you were unemployable. They thought you couldn't be relied on any more, to go away for seven weeks, or to do anything really, even if you had someone to look after the baby. That has changed now. I am very grateful to the BBC for lots of things. The discipline is always useful, but on the other hand there were some awful witches, and no room really for artistic license.

At that time I thought my career was over. I had my second baby two and a half years later, but then I got a job at Central in Birmingham. They were very generous there and it was a completely different attitude. In fact, it was a bit frustrating in the opposite direction in that it was all a bit lacka-daisical and they were all a bit sloppy. I did the last six months on *Crossroads* [TV series, 1960s-80s] and actually it was a pleasure to work there because you felt you were valued, which is essential in this industry. I also did a futuristic soap which took a year, and I got to know a lot of fashion design-ers in London, and on the strength of that I set up a contemporary depart-ment in what was then the costumiers Bermans and Nathans.

I did that for a year, and went straight on to work as assistant costume designer for Milena Canonero on a film called *Damage* [Louis Malle, 1992]. Milena had won two Oscars for costume design. She had done films like A *Clockwork Orange* [Stanley Kubrick, 1971], *The Cotton Club* [Francis Coppola, 1984], *Out of Africa* [Sydney Pollack, 1985], and I thought I would work with her and find out what her recipe was. Also, to work with a director like Louis Malle was lovely and actors like Jeremy Irons and Juliette Binoche who were both a joy, although it was not a particularly happy shoot. Maybe I found it difficult because I didn't get the buzz from it because it wasn't *mine*. But I wouldn't have missed it for the world and I learnt an awful lot from Milena. She would say things like, "This is the *movies*, Charlotte," and I would think, "Yes, you're right!"

I often remember that when I think I may have gone a bit too far. We are *entertaining* people. Milena was fanatical about detail and had a wonderful eye and I liked her enormously. And some fairly extraordinary things hap-pened on that shoot. Like when we were filming in Manchester, a black guy came up to me in the hotel when I had gone back to have a breather and a sandwich, and he said, "Do you want to go to a boxing match tonight?" And I had no idea who he was, but another bloke came over with a suitcase and gave me two tickets, and they kept saying, "You will come?" I said, "Yeah, yeah, I'll be there," and it was Chris Eubank and he had given me two tickets for the front row! So when I went back to the set and told them, Jeremy

Irons said, "I want to come!" I said, "Well, I've just asked the makeup artist," so I had to go back and ask for two more tickets so Jeremy could come too. Things like that would never normally happen.

After that, I did something called *Demob* [TV Drama, 1993], set in the 1940s, with a director called Rob Knights, who had done *The History Man* [1981]. It was a hard shoot but I became great friends with Amanda Redman on that. Martin Clunes was in it and he was very fresh to the industry then; also a delight. Les Dawson was in it too, and I remember it was one of the happiest things going to meet him and his wife in their home.

Meeting people like George Melly, too, was really cool. Afterwards he asked me to go for a drink at Quaglino's. You never get blasé about people, and if you treat them well, you can all really enjoy yourselves. In fact, a costume designer's job is all about giving. Giving to the actors, giving to the directors, and it is easier to give to people who receive well. If someone is hostile, you are inclined to do the bare minimum because it is very sapping to be with them. And then people are funny. There are men who come for fittings not wearing any knickers! And women who suddenly don't fit their costumes and finally admit they are now pregnant but don't want the baby, and you find yourself befriending them through an abortion. In fact, you could easily go to the *News of the World* with the stories you see – catching actors red-handed "at it" – but I think as with doctors, there is a kind of code of confidentiality.

Occasionally you have a bad shoot. I did *Mosley* [Robert Knights, 1998], which was a trauma. I didn't have enough crew or enough money, but you learn not to make the same mistakes twice. No one thanks you for nearly dying over something. I ended up having panic attacks, being unable to eat without throwing up, concussion, a cracked rib! I fell from the caterer's steps that weren't strapped down properly. We were down in Portsmouth and I asked Production if they would drive my car back to London and they said they couldn't afford it! So I drove back seeing double white lines, and by the end I had lost all feeling down the right hand side of my body, I had dreadful bruising and total mental and physical exhaustion.

I think the film was cursed. My usual assistant couldn't do it with me and all the people I feel safe with were busy so I crewed it really badly. I had a man called Gary who was a wardrobe supervisor who I chose because I thought he was an authority on uniforms, but he was a complete charlatan. He was a lazy, unpleasant, nasty person. I had an assistant who was too inexperienced and who I trusted and then she just turned on me. My wardrobe assistant was the only person who I could rely on. I was doing it all through Angels, a big costume house, and they stitched me up too.

They are very powerful and they said our budget wasn't big enough for all the costumes we wanted, so they got the producer to agree a two-weekly turn around. This became a whole snowballing nightmare. Then they booked out a whole lot of underwear and belts which were just junk and we put them back in their boxes, and the lady at Angels said not to bother to return them at the moment. We were all so tired we just left it, but Gary, my wardrobe supervisor, decided to leave after two weeks, and took with him the booking-out form for that particular consignment, and took it to Tim Angel saying, "Charlotte has been using your costumes and not paying for them." I don't know to this day why he did it. I felt like I was playing a game of poker and had a really bad hand and I swapped it for five even worse cards.

But in the main my job is lovely. I absolutely love it. And to have my team is a joy. Since *Demob* I have tried to always work with Caroline Waterman as my assistant. She has the same passion that I have. She cares enormously and agonizes; she doesn't get angry or upset. And we will go together on set and go "Wow" – there is a sense of pride and achievement. Not always; sometimes you feel disappointed, but nine times out of ten, after all that hard work, there they all are looking brilliant – it's like a drug. A complete Grade A drug. The more you do the more you want, so it is desperate. And when you don't have it and you think you are never going to work again, you go into mourning for it.

We all have periods of not working, but I don't know how to do anything else. We sit around thinking, "Maybe we should get a proper job!" I love my garden and home and being with my family, but I need that shot of adrenaline and the panic and the waking up feeling sick wondering if the director will hate it when he finally walks out on set. I also like when you are in production and the director might see a new character for the first time and say, "It's brilliant." It reinforces their own feelings and it's nice that you have given them that bit more. It's totally addictive. And it is not about money. Even if I won the lottery, I'd still do it. I'd still need the drug!

Lisa Janowski
First Assistant Director

In Halliwell's Who's Who in the Movies (edited by John Walker, HarperCollins, 1999), an assistant director is described as "more properly assistant to the director, being concerned with details of administration rather than creation." One of the main duties of a first assistant is to implement the director's vision in practical terms and trace the progress of filming versus the production schedule. There are usually three assistant directors, with different though related responsibilities. In the U.K. these are called the first, second and third AD; in the U.S. they are the first, key second and second second AD.

Listening to Lisa was intriguing because, unlike most crew members I spoke to, she has reservations about her job. She candidly acknowledged sexual discrimination in the industry and the immense importance of the director to the mood of the actors and crew. She criticized the way in which certain directors work – in complete contrast to the happy experiences of another interviewee, auditor Salvatore Carino, Lisa did not enjoy working with Woody Allen.

Selected Credits
Good Will Hunting (Gus Van Sant, 1997)
Cop Land (James Mangold, 1997)
Rounders (John Dahl, 1998)
Witness to the Mob (TV Feature, 1998)
Sweet and Lowdown (Woody Allen, 1999)
Happy Accidents (Brad Anderson, 2001)

Someone once explained filming to me as being like a bull's-eye. The director, cameraman, key grip, gaffer and first assistant director are in the center of the bull's-eye. And in the next ring out are all their seconds, like the best boy, and the second assistant director and it spreads from there. But all the information always comes from the center and if any of those key people in the middle don't do their job and don't spread the information, then the people on the outside have no idea what is going on. So when the first AD does his or her job well, everybody knows what is going on. The downside of being an assistant director is that you get all your information from your director, and if your director is not prepared or ready to tell you what they want to do next, then you can't tell anyone and chaos ensues.

The job of an assistant director depends on how collaborative the director is. I think in the past, even around the '70s, an assistant director was really integral to the creative making of a film. Along with the producer, they were relied on heavily and got to be very involved with everything a director was doing. Now, more often than not, directors want you to be more managerial and administrative. They just want you to run the show maintaining the set and the schedule and getting everyone into the right place at the right time. So if you work with a director who is not collaborative, it can lean towards just telling them how much time they have for lunch; how much time they have to get a shot; what they need to do the next day; what they need to do a week from then, and it is a less interesting kind of job.

A first assistant director is at the camera with the director and the director of photography, the gaffer and the key grip. When they figure out their shot, it is up to the first assistant director to disseminate all that information and make sure that shot can get made. It might mean, for instance, notifying people to move equipment, or telling wardrobe that they are doing a different scene. The director might say, "I would like the sky to be red and for there to be green clouds scudding by," and it is up to you and the other department heads to figure out how to make that happen.

There is a lot of setting up to do, making sure all the production assistants have cleared pedestrians and if cars have to go through you figure all that out. Then when everything is ready, you yell "rolling" over your walkie-talkie which all of your department should echo. So all the production assistants yell out "rolling" and everyone knows to be quiet. Then you wait to hear from the camera that they have speed, and you say "background action" to get the extras moving before the actors start, and then the director yells "action." I have worked with a director, Brad Anderson, on *Happy Accidents* [2001], who wouldn't say "action" or "cut" so I would have to do it, which is quite awkward, like trying to be in his brain as to when he wanted to cut, but normally you echo the director when he says "cut."

I got into the industry about ten years ago. First I went to NYU and did a degree in art history and a friend of mine was working in the film business and called me from North Carolina, and she said, "Do you know anyone who would want to rent my apartment? I am doing a movie." And I said, "Can I come down? Can I get a job?" And so I went, and I worked in the admin office on *The Crow* [Alex Proyas, 1994] and I met an assistant director and I saw what they were doing. It seemed like it would suit me because it was so organizational but you also got to be involved with all the other departments. It was a time in New York where there was very little union work and I got jobs as PA then a TPA then a second second and then a second assistant director. It just clicked for me.

Different colored tapes are always found on film sets: here used in a cross on the floor [upper right] to mark an actor's position.

Then I was on *Basquiat*, which Julian Schnabel directed [1996], and after I had been on the job for about a week they said Julian was going to join the Directors Guild. So I had to either join the Directors Guild or leave the job. I said, "Health benefits and more money? I guess I'll join!" It is normally very difficult to get in and this was a complete back door, so it was wonderful. But I was about 24 and I hit a dry spell for a little bit because I had cut off all my non-union contacts and nobody knew me and I was a very small fish in a very big pool. So it took me a little while.

A lot of assistant directors work with one director for ever, like Anthony Minghella's AD has worked with him for ages and Woody Allen has had the same first assistant for a long time. When I worked for Woody Allen I was actually his second assistant, but I realized even then what a huge difference the director can make to the job. Actually, I got that job like none other. I got a call six months before the work started, which is not how it *happens*. In New York, you usually get the job the *day* before. First Richard Patrick, the first AD (whom I had never met) called out of the blue and said he would call back. A month went by, and then he asked if I could go and meet and it was a done deal.

Then working on *Sweet and Lowdown* [Woody Allen, 1999] was unlike working on any other film because of the way Woody works. For instance he won't shoot outside if it is sunny or if it is raining; it has to be overcast and gray and flat. So, because the assistant director is responsible for the call sheet [a list of which actors, crew and props will be needed for which scenes, and when they will be required], you are working according to the weather forecast and always have to have a Plan A and a Plan B for the next day! You are constantly running parallel schedules and then about one P.M. they make a decision as to which schedule they are going to go with in the morning, so you need to execute the call sheet that is going to happen and tell everyone on the other call sheet that it is not going to happen.

That's one thing. The other thing is that Woody looks at dailies [often called rushes, this is all the day's shooting on film when it comes back from the lab unedited and is ready for viewing for the first time] every day, like most directors. However most directors, if they don't like what they see, will say, "Okay, when we have done filming we will come back and fix it, or maybe I'll cut the scene." But Woody will go back the next day or certainly within the week and re-shoot it. So not only are you working on your call sheets A and B for weather problems, you suddenly might have to go back to a location because he wants to re-shoot. It is an incredible scheduling job for both the first and second ADs. It's all about scheduling.

Woody arrives in the morning, sets up a shot, asks when he needs to come back and shoot, and then leaves. I personally think he likes writing and editing better than shooting. So he leans towards shorter days, and the solitude of writing and editing rather than the camaraderie of shooting. The decisions that his production designer and cinematographer make, without him there, are amazing. I found it very odd because as an assistant director you normally stand next to the director for 14 hours a day for 50, 60, 70 days. So not having a director there to work with for a lot of the time was really strange.

You never had meetings with him. You never worked *with* him. I just felt I was doing this massive scheduling job. If I hadn't been as experienced, it would have been awful because it was really difficult. I didn't do it again. He has had the same crew a lot of the time and they expect to work short days, they have August to December blocked out each year, and I found it all a little numb. It was a bit like a long-running TV show where everyone knows how it is, and they don't really care that much.

Also for *Sweet and Lowdown* we scheduled 50 days, and because of his re-shooting he usually goes over by a week, but we did 71 days, and there is something about the last few scheduled days on a film when you should be getting to the end and everyone gets really anxious to finish, like at summer camp when it is coming to an end! But every added day we had this feeling of despair like it would never end – it was difficult – and Sean Penn got very unhappy. Actually, Sean Penn was *great*. He didn't live up to the nightmare that everyone thinks he is. I found him really talented and professional and I feel he was also disappointed in Woody to a certain extent. I think actors like collaborating with directors – I mean it's what they *do* – and Woody is not interested really.

The antithesis to Woody Allen is probably Jonathan Demme, with whom I did *Subway Stories* [1997]. It was a film for HBO which had 11 different directors, so it was a really test tube environment for finding out how movies work. I remember thinking, "This is the most schizophrenic job I have ever worked on!" It wasn't like a TV show, where you would have a couple of weeks at a time: we had five days with each director. We had Spike Lee (whose piece didn't get used in the end because it was too long and he wouldn't cut it) and Abel Ferrara and Jonathan Demme – huge clashing personalities, so one day our set would be really mellow and another day it would be frenetic with yelling. And that is when I realized that the mood of the crew and the mood of the actors is completely governed by the director.

It was six weeks of nights in the subway in summer. But Jonathan Demme, who was also an executive producer so he was around a bit more, genuinely worked *with* you. He would come up to you and say, "What do you think of that? Do you think it's good? Isn't this great? Isn't this fun?" He really seemed to be enjoying himself and wanted to be there and know you and talk to you and *work* with you. So you really got that great feeling, that you were making a movie, not shuffling someone's paperwork or babysitting a director who doesn't know what shot they want to do next. You got the feeling that he loved making movies and that he loved that you were making his movie with him.

Actors can make a difference to your job, too. I remember *Witness to the Mob* [TV Feature, 1998] was a horrible project to work on – even the weather was awful – but the *actors* were great. It was about the Mafia and the guys playing those parts would give me this whole thing of "Hey, baby! Hey, sugar!" but the FBI guys were genuine stage actors who were happy to be working and were professional and on time and courteous. So we would make jokes like "When's the next FBI day?" We *craved* those days.

Robin Williams on *Good Will Hunting* [Gus Van Sant, 1997] was amazing to work with because he liked talking to *anybody*. He would be talking to the people who were staring at him and go up and totally entertain them. But then I would go up and tap him on the shoulder and say, "Robin, we're ready," and he would say, "Okay, I'll be back, guys" and he would go right to work, so he was like your *dream*: He had fun while he was waiting, which a lot of people complain about, and he would also snap right to work.

When we made *Good Will Hunting*, we had no idea we were making such a huge film. It was $13 million, like a really comfortable budget, and I think it took everyone by surprise. Gus, the director was actually very interesting to watch. He never used a monitor. He always looked straight at the actors. I think some directors use the monitor to kind of distance themselves and keep themselves separate, but not him, he was always right in there. As a second assistant director too, you need to put yourself in the position of being accessible to the actors, producers, crew and teamsters [unions], whereas the first AD is sometimes the "bad cop."

Although this might sound sexist, I think being a second AD is totally suited to a woman because it is an incredibly nurturing role. If you do it well, you are really taking care of everybody. But it is also incredibly organizational and you have to be able to do ten things at once and remember them all. That suits me. There are more men first assistants, but I think that is more a state of the film business. When I was a second assistant in New York, I got called for every job, but after I had done Woody Allen I had done the hardest job in New York so I wanted to move up. There are second assistants who stay doing that for 50 years, but I wanted to keep moving and not do the same job. But being a first assistant director is totally different: You need to work more closely with the director, and most of them are men, and I found a lot of them didn't want to work with women.

A lot of directors expect their first ADs to be yellers and screamers – the strong one – while they can be the nicer one. I don't really fit that mold. Some people would like my different approach but it was not stereotypical. A first AD normally shouts a lot and is a jerk. But I also ran into women directors who didn't want to work with women. I found that amazing. In New York there are virtually no women first assistant directors [and there are not many in the U.K. either]. Because of that, and because the job is so thankless and seems to me to have got too specialized and less creative and interesting, I am unsure whether I want to continue.

Lisa (right) working on *Dead Dog*. Lisa's husband, director Christopher Goode, (center) discusses a shot with the director of photography, Eric Schmidt. (Courtesy of Lisa Janowski)

Recently I was first AD combined with co-producer on *Dead Dog* [Christopher Goode, 2001], an independent, low-budget film. I always think of Michael Hausman, who was an assistant director and a producer and a location manager and has had a career with Milos Forman his whole life; that image of an assistant director is so much more interesting than what it is now. So I am now working with my husband, director Christopher Goode, going back to the olden days, making films for half a million dollars and being totally creatively involved, pre- and post-production. It can be enchanting making movies. It is really hard work, but when you hit that fiftieth day, you feel like you have accomplished something. When you are a first assistant and you are that involved and that close-up, it is a rewarding job; it is just a monotonous job.

Maybe now I will move on but hopefully use the skills I have learned. As an assistant director you always panic that certain things aren't going to work, like it's going to rain, or you're not going to have your schedules ready, or a featured car has a flat tire, but actually I found that it always worked out. It's kind of like the miracle of moviemaking in a way: If you are good at your job you figure out the problems before they happen as opposed to putting out fires. That can be rewarding. Also, you see things you would never normally see. You see the sunrise because you are going to work so early or you are going home so late. You can stand in the middle of Times Square with no one there, or you can ask for the Brooklyn Bridge to be shut down and it happens!

Salvatore Carino
Production Auditor

When an auditor told me he would like to be interviewed, I did not think it would be particularly interesting; but I was very mistaken. A production accountant or auditor knows everything that goes on, including how much money a star or director might be spending on, say, prostitutes.

Sal was not dry and boring; he was funny and enjoyable to talk to, peppering his conversation with humorous indiscretions. He is very enthusiastic about his job which, although stressful, he views as challenging, creative and a part of the artistic process. It combines a knowledge of production and of people management with business skills, diplomacy, detective work and juggling!

SELECTED CREDITS
Bullets Over Broadway (Woody Allen, 1994)
Everyone Says I Love You (Woody Allen, 1996)
Beloved (Jonathan Demme, 1998)
The Sopranos (HBO TV series, first aired 1999)
Men in Black II (Barry Sonnnenfeld, 2002)
Prime (Ben Younger, 2005)

I can get very creative with numbers – as creative as a director can be in his vision. You don't really think of that when you think of film production, but it is really all about numbers, and ultimately everything to do with the production comes through my hands. I like to be called an auditor rather than an accountant because I give people advice, supervise spending, and am also a watchdog: I turn numbers into other information.

I didn't go to school for finance or accounting or anything; I went to film school (graduating in 1987) and I learned what I know from working on productions. Back then I wanted to be a writer or director – all that crazy stuff – but when you finally work in the industry, you realize how difficult that is and that it is really not what you know but who you know. Also I now feel that I would rather produce sometime, than direct, because I really like the business side of it. I like my job because of the responsibilities of having a lot of information that other people don't have, and my responsibilities to the studio and the producers.

I kind of sit on the fence; I tell the studio good news and the producers bad news, giving alternating stories to people to protect my position, protect the show, and protect the producers from the studio and the studio from the producers – it's an exacting position to be in. I get hired by the studio to work with a bunch of producers on a show. Most times the producers will dispute the hire because they feel that I am really the watchdog for the studio and that I will report back any bad news or anything the producers are doing on the sly. But because so many of the producers in New York know me now, they are happy with me on board and I try and be their friend right away and say stuff like, "We don't have to tell the studio this, and we don't have to tell them that..." And I tell the studio that the producers are really good guys who know their stuff and that kind of thing.

To begin with, I work on the budget. My biggest responsibility is to present them with how much a show is going to cost. A lot of times a budget has already been made in Los Angeles for a show that is shooting in New York but they don't have a clue. So I take the budget and completely redo it and add about $1,000,000 because there are a lot of positions in New York that they don't have in Los Angeles, like a Parking P.A – someone who shuts down a street so the trucks can come in and park. It takes about two months to put a budget together, but normally when I am hired the movie is already "green-lit," going ahead; it is not dependent on the budget numbers.

I am responsible for all the production costs. Salaries are about 70 percent of the total budget: both above-the-line, which is producers, writers, directors, actors; and below-the-line, which is working crew. Say for example your movie is $10,000,000 and your above-the-line is $7,000,000 you know that you are not going to get a good movie out of it because you are paying such high salaries above-the-line. Anyway, the producers and I would look at a schedule and work out how many days are needed for shooting. Then we would budget the hours of the day, penalties, equipment, locations, construction of, for example, a stage, hotels – all of that.

We put it all into a budget and present a number. And the studio, without even looking at it, will say, "Take $2,000,000 out." So as we put the budget together, we add money that we don't need – like a little savings account here, there and everywhere that only we know about. Then I also add little pads of money in that the producers don't know about. There are a lot of places where I can hide money so that when the producers don't budget enough, I feel safer, even if I don't have as much as they do stashed away.

When the budget is approved, my job is to supervise its spending. I make sure that the crew is paid according to their union rules with overtime and penalties; that the actors are paid according to Screen Actors Guild rules; directors are paid according to Directors Guild rules. For instance, directors have a certain number of prep days before they start shooting, and go into overtime after a certain number of hours, and I have to be very aware of all the rule books of film production. I don't have it memorized – I have a shelf of books behind me in my office which I refer to all the time. If I pay something incorrectly, I know when I get a fine in the mail from, say, Screen Actors Guild, saying you paid someone who isn't an actor, who isn't in our union, so you owe $500 penalty! We try to dispute it but we end up paying it anyway, particularly on a high-budget show.

Apart from supervising the spending, I also tell them how much they spent in a day. Each morning I get a breakdown of the overtime for the cast, and of how many extras worked and when they broke for lunch, and I analyze all these sheets of paper and come up with a cost of what that day cost. Then I take that cost and compare it with what we budgeted for that day and keep track. So our overage for the week might be $25,000 which I have to report to the studio and they will either have me add it to the budget or find that money somewhere else and offset it to bring us back to zero. What is good is that on high-budget movies we are allowed to book 16-hour days. Now anyone seeing that will realize we can't really want our crew to work 16 hours but it gives us two extra hours to offset anything crazy that might happen.

It is a headache, especially if you are over-budget, because you kind of feel responsible for it. But I will tell them every little thing that happens just to protect myself. I'll say right away, "You want to go *here* tomorrow, and you want to shoot *that*, and do you realize how much it's going to cost?" What I love best is giving good news. I love telling a producer, "You saved $20,000 yesterday because you decided to wrap the crew an hour early, because you got your shot, because the director was doing his job." I like to

Salvatore Carino (Photo by Robin Baker)

put a dollar amount on it because it makes them feel so much better. Like if we have saved $100,000 at the end of an episode, I can say, "You can pay for an additional day of shooting with the money you saved from this episode." It feels so good — like I feel that I had something to do with it, even though I didn't.

It's very challenging to come up with how much everything will cost and to keep track of it. Sometimes you have to wonder how other people find out the stuff I know. Like on *Men in Black II* [Barry Sonnnenfeld, 2002], the lead, [Tommy Lee Jones] got paid $20,000,000 and the second-lead [Will Smith] got $20,000,000 too, which he had never got before. Nobody knew about it and everything was stamped "confidential" and then I read in the newspaper that he got paid $20,000,000 and I'm like, "What? How do they know that, when I'm sworn to secrecy?" Sometimes I think the studio leaks it out as publicity for the show.

But what the papers don't have, is their expense account – what they get paid above their salary – their entourage costs. These are all additional costs that will bump up the budget incredibly, especially when you have a big-name talent and you want to make him extremely happy. They live expense-free so long as they are on the movie. We pay for their housing, their food, their cars, their assistants, their travel – even if it is not work travel and even if it is to fly home at weekends on a $10,000 chartered flight so that the actor doesn't have to fly commercial with all the other people – whatever – so long as they are happy throughout the shoot.

Men in Black II was the largest budget I have ever done. I was one of two accountants, which is very rare. *Titantic* [James Cameron, 1997] had a number of accountants but I don't think they all worked at the same time; I think they just all kept getting fired! I am actually the third accountant on The *Sopranos* now, which worried me a bit. But the usual reasons for firing someone are not keeping straight, or not giving enough information to the producers about what is going on. Then there are some accountants who act as though *they* were the producer. They will think that every single dollar is their own money and they will be really tight and make it really difficult for people to do their jobs and it stresses out the crew and the producers.

For instance, if a prop master comes to me and says "I've spent $3,000 on this," I'll say, "That's fine, is it in the budget that you gave us at the beginning of the show?" Then you look at their expenses and it is usually in cash because you spend money so fast that the vendor can't wait for a check, so you have to approve these expenses. I'll approve it, pay it out, and then look at it, because I know that person is in a rush. But then if there is anything weird, I'll talk to them about it later on. There are some accountants who will look at that expenditure for *days* and meanwhile the person is spending their own money out of their own bank account because her job is in jeopardy if she doesn't have that prop on the set the next day. I'm not going to be the one to hold up production because of the money.

Although occasionally, there *is* no money. When *Illuminata* [John

Turturro, 1998] was two days away from shooting, we still had no money in the bank. It was a low-budget movie with a lot of big names in it [Susan Sarandon, Rufus Sewell, Christopher Walken] and we were carrying on with production and cutting checks. But we would cut that check, put it in an envelope, stamp it, seal it and pin it to the wall! And we did it for three weeks. So we had a huge wall full of checks. We called it the Wall of Shame because we were producing a show without any money in the bank and we had paid all these vendors. The money was coming from foreign sources and it finally hit the bank two days before we started shooting. So we took all the checks down and mailed them. For two or three weeks I had to tell stories to the vendor, like, "It's waiting for approval." I never used the line "The check is in the mail" because they would know it was a total lie.

Generally, though, I try to make it very easy for people to approach us in our department. Crew are afraid to ask for money and to spend it so I make the lighting and the way I decorate my office very comfortable and people will come and sit and relax and open up about other things that have nothing to do with work, and I kind of enjoy that. I also try to avoid unnecessary arguments about stupid stuff, like if somebody spends $10 on lunch when their limit is $7. Who has the time for that? I'm not that type of accountant. Especially when a producer or writer or director will go out and have lunch with a couple of friends and spend $1,000 on the restaurant bill and we will pay it right away. That upsets me a little bit.

I know that everyone has a job to do and it's all about the money and I'll give them what they need and then I will do my job on the side. But when you do catch someone doing something really sneaky, then you are playing detective. On a show I did once I had a set designer who made between three and four thousand a week salary – a huge amount of money, but she was putting in bad receipts to get extra money.

When you get a cab receipt, the serial number is printed on it, but sometimes, when a cabby is in a rush, 20 receipts will come out of the machine and the cabby will rip it off and just say, "Here, take it." What she did was cut up all those receipts and separate them all on different sheets of paper and put them each into different petty cash envelopes. I was anal enough, and had the time, to look at them all, and put them side by side and compare and I had ten cab receipts in sequential order! The total was maybe $60 and I just wondered why she needed to steal that.

So the bad part of my job is that I have to talk to people like her first, and if they make a really big deal about it, then I will tell my production manager. This time it didn't go any further. She excused it saying she had lost a lot of receipts and was trying to make up the money, and I said, "Well, this is not the way to do it." She didn't talk to me for the rest of the movie. We both knew I had caught her doing something, but what is good about it is that I know she won't do it again.

If I suspect something, I will not accuse someone straight out of stealing but I may say, "This receipt looks pretty bad, I don't think I should accept it. Can you get something better?" They won't say anything, but if they take it back really fast, you know that something is up. I have been doing this job so long that I don't know of any irregularity that is unusual any more. But I look for the really unusual to make my job more interesting. So much of it is cash. On *The Sopranos* we spend $130,000 a day – much more than most people make in a year! Most of it is salaries, but it just costs a lot of money to make movies. And it takes a lot of time to spend a lot of money. Think about the amount of paperwork to equal $2,000,000 spending a week! Sometimes it is like playing Monopoly, but other times I step back and think, "My father never made this much money in his life, and we just spent it last week."

On any given day we have $30,000 in cash in the safe in my department. Sometimes someone who is paying out money takes the petty cash box and puts it in his or her drawer to save keeping on going to the safe. My rule is when you are not using the box, it is in the safe, and it is locked. I have had assistants who have had the box in their drawer and gone to lunch and while they were away I would steal the box! They would come back to the office and the box would be missing and I would never see so many shades of white in their faces. Finally, I would say, "Okay, Okay, I have the petty cash box" and I would ask, "But did you learn your lesson?" and it would never happen again.

We have about two to three hundred time cards every week that have to be in on Monday night to be paid out by a payroll company who make out the checks so the crew can be paid by Thursday afternoon, which is a union rule. I had a girl once who would take some of the payroll with her on the weekend because there is so much of it. I was totally against it, and said I would rather pay her to come into the office at the weekend. Anyway one week, she took the payroll home with her and didn't tell me, and came into the office by train on Monday and was completely white and very upset and was getting mad at me because I kept asking what was the matter. She just answered, "Nothing, nothing. I'll deal with it."

At the end of the day, I go, "What's wrong?" and she says, "I left the payroll on the train. I've been trying to phone all day to retrieve it. It's in a bag, with my calculator and everything and it's lost!" So I said, "Well, you will have to do it all over again." It was very difficult, but now we joke about it. When she calls me to give her a reference for a job, I say, "Shall I mention that you left the payroll on the train?" It's so tough that it's funny.

I used to go home and worry about my job, but not any more. Once I overpaid a person by $140,000! I really thought I would lose my job over it but then I knew it could be fixed. I was on a show that was running all the time so the person was going to make way more than that eventually and I could just take it back, slowly. I can only keep my eye on so much and sometimes you just get overwhelmed and let the stupidest things slip through.

I like what I do, and I have been doing it as the head of my department (there are five people working under me) for about seven years now. I would hire someone with film experience before I hired anyone with financial experience. Film production has its own lingo, and you need to know how and why money is spent rather than how to balance a ledger. Ultimately I would like to take the next step and produce my own stuff. Having a financial background by learning it on production, I think I could be a pretty good producer. The producer I work for now actually has the same background that I do, but somehow she left me in the dust and accelerated so fast that I look at her as my kind of idol and know it can be done.

I had a goal that I would be doing my own movies when I was 30, and now I am 36! But it will happen when someone is willing to give me a chance. The trouble is that I make a great living at what I am doing now, so it is hard to take a step back and make no money to pursue a dream. But holding on to the dream keeps me going.

The job I have enjoyed most as accountant, was when I worked with Woody Allen for four years. I didn't realize until I had gone, but it was by far the best company I have ever worked for. It was like a family. We were together so many hours a day and Woody kind of controlled the roost. He hired the same people from show to show and every year he would do a different movie and it was very close. It was like you were spending your family's money. You really cared about production and keeping the budget down. I really respected Woody and the producer, Jean Doumanian. To watch Woody put a movie together with his team of creative people made me really feel I was in film production – and that's what I went to school for.

Most television, compared to features, to me, is like a business where you are trying to impress sponsors. Feature films – it's an art. But in my position, as a freelancer, if you are in the same company for too long, people forget about you. You have to work for as many people as you can, because it is networking. I have turned down work because of the people involved and also taken work because I wanted to see how certain people worked. Accounts aren't considered an important department by some people, but every job is important on a movie. You need every single one of those people to put the final product together. And I pay them all!

Tom Nelson
Production Sound Mixer

The first successful methods of synchronized sound on films used gramophone discs and cylinders, making editing very difficult. In 1926 the first soundtrack was recorded directly onto the film next to the picture and this system is, for the most part, still used today. Sometimes, in a reversion to the past, modern systems feature soundtracks recorded onto compact discs in order to improve quality.

The person responsible for operating the audio recording equipment on set, adjusting volume and equalizing individual reels of sound, is called a sound mixer (or sound recordist). Tom Nelson has been mixing sound for films for over 20 years. He is erudite and sensitive and views his work as an art rather than just a technique. After talking with him, I shared his view.

SELECTED CREDITS

Slaves of New York (James Ivory, 1989)
Reversal of Fortune (Barbet Schroeder, 1990)
Wayne's World (Penelope Spheeris, 1992)
The Mirror Has Two Faces (Barbra Streisand, 1996)
Beloved (Jonathan Demme, 1998)
The Thomas Crown Affair (John McTiernan, 1999)
Analyze This and Analyze That (Harold Ramis, 1999 and 2002)
Eternal Sunshine of the Spotless Mind (Michel Gondry, 2004)

I have played the violin all my life and so I think of myself as a listener, and if I had to say why I am still recording sound after all these years, I would say that sound is the most psychological of your senses. We have a whole culture in our society that is visually oriented and very little analysis of how sound affects us. On the television, for instance, the images come at you, but you will react to sound without knowing the mechanics of why you are reacting or why it is evoking emotions in you.

There are some directors who really understand how sound works in the human psyche. For example, Hitchcock made a film in London where a man walks through a street market where there is a lot of noise and commotion and he goes up into a second floor flat and has an argument with a woman and murders her. Then he comes back down the stairs and returns to where he came from through the same market. From the moment that he strangles and kills the woman, for three minutes or so, there is no sound, and then gradually the sound returns. I saw the film a couple of times, and at first I

Tom Nelson (Courtesy of Tom Nelson)

didn't realize that there was no sound, but it instantly puts the audience into that man's head because the man has committed a murder and has completely shut out the world.

The Day of the Jackal [Fred Zinnemann, 1973] was also a fascinating movie because it had no soundtrack. All the sound is within the movie itself, there is no music. You get your sense of geography when the Jackal is trying to assassinate de Gaulle from how near or far the sound of the band is at the ceremony de Gaulle is attending. Sometimes, in my job, I can make suggestions to a director and that is what is exciting and important to me. For example, I did a film called *Reckless* [James Foley, 1984] which is set in a steel-mill town where there are two classes of society: There are the rich who live up on the hills and there are the workers, closer to the mill, where it is dirtier and noisier. The mill goes 24 hours a day so it is always noisy in the workers' part of town and when you are away from the mill in the pristine, manicured homes of the bosses, it is very quiet and you can hear birds. So you can suggest a sound environment to a director.

There was another film I worked on years ago where one of the characters loses his leg and gets a replacement wooden leg and you could just put that character into the movie by the sound of the clunky walk. Those are things you work out with the director. The picture shows one thing but it is all happening within an environment of sound – some things near, some far. This is the way I think of it. I try to create that environment and sound works in a more subtle way than the picture does. If you study film over the past decades, you see the way changes have happened in picture, but sound is not as obvious; it is more psychological. Sound effects nowadays, particularly with digital sound, are much more sharp with more punch. Films like *Star Wars* [George Lucas, 1977] are completely made with sound effects. Whereas a film like *Out of Africa* [Sydney Pollack, 1985] is done very naturalistically with a totally different feel.

I prefer the naturalistic. If you look at a film set, you have camera, lighting, grip, costumes, wardrobe, art department and they are all connected to the visual. You have two or three people responsible for the sound. So the whole medium is really visually oriented and all the energy goes into the visuals with very little encouragement of the sound. But there are directors who understand how crucial sound is and they are conscious of it while they are shooting. Others who come from a more visual background realize that they could replace all the sound afterwards so they don't think about it while they are shooting. Each film has a different relationship.

At present I am working on *Analyze That* [2002], and the director, Harold Ramis, is fantastic, a joy to work with. The spirit at the top affects the whole organization. Jonathan Demme, on *Beloved* [1998], was also incredible; that ability to have a vision and impart it, and your enthusiasm, to everyone who works for you, makes each film unique and each one very special – I think that is what keeps people in this business. Because for technicians, the hours are incredibly long and it is a very draining process sometimes and it becomes a question of stamina, but each production has its own flavor. It is a very complex and layered process, and American films seem to have a different flavor from European ones. When I worked in France, we did shorter days. You would do a three-month film and shoot it over four and a half months – so there is less stress.

There are people nowadays who go into the film business by heading along a direct path, but around 20 years ago, when I started, it seemed that everyone backed into the business. In college I ran a radio station, which was very successful. I was also a combat cameraman in the Marine Corps, so my interest was really camera and photography to start with. Then I came out of college and fell in love with a girl and followed her to New York and I started shooting for a couple of years. It was then that I ran into another cameraman who wanted to make a film about two farmers and he needed a soundman. So he shot it and I was the soundman and did much of the editing and we spent a couple of years doing films about farmers and doing documentaries.

Eventually I bought my own sound equipment and started working on features, which are to me the most creative part of it. Basically I am the sound recordist on the set while the film is being shot, as opposed to people like the re-recording mixer, who handles the sound during the editing and post-production period. During editing, the sound is all taken apart and reassembled and remixed back together again and, after editing, more sound is added and rebalanced. There are essentially three elements to sound on film: dialogue, sound effects and music. Generally I try to give them all of the dialogue and as much of the effects as I can produce on set.

Sound on set really follows the camera, sharing the perspective with the camera from shot to shot and the sound mixer has to keep the camera and sound in synch. You also try to record the sound in such a way that you can edit in a different way from the way it was shot. A scene might be shot in a certain order with a certain pace, and when they edit it they may reorder the entire scene. If you have recorded the sound with overlaps which prevent them editing as they wish to later, you have done them a disservice. I want to give them as much control down the line as they could possibly use. To do that, I split the actors from the effects as much as possible and split each actor onto different tracks.

Essentially you try to get as clean a soundtrack as possible without getting any equipment into the picture, and sound mixers are responsible for the sound from the microphone all the way to the final media that they are recording on. Originally sound was recorded on stock that was the same length and width as the film. Then they went to quarter-inch tape, which was the standard for decades, and then digital [Digital Audio Tape Recording] started to come in, and occasionally some multi-track studio-orientated recording is used. On this film [*Analyze That*, Harold Ramis, 2002], I am using quarter-inch and DAT – analogue and digital, but there is now a tendency to record on hard disc, which is recorded digitally for the entire process, and from which you can make a DVD. There is still controversy whether digital or analogue is better, but what we do on the set deter-

Tom at work (Courtesy of Tom Nelson)

mines how the entire film is edited. So what the post-production people prefer to work with may determine what you do on set. The sound editor makes these decisions.

I am employed by the production manager or the director, but then I work most closely with the director and the cameraman. The logical way to get the best sound is to get the microphone as close as possible to the actor, because that is the most important part of what you are recording. But that always conflicts with what the cameraman might be wanting to do, so there is negotiation between the camera and sound and lighting and grip departments while you are shooting. This is because you can't put a microphone, for instance, on the end of a boom, into a shot which will create shadows all over an actor. Generally the microphone is boomed, or it might be hidden, or occasionally body mikes on the actors are used with a radio link back to you. The boom mike is held over, or in front of, the actor and is the most natural-sounding way because that is the way your ear is most used to hearing something. A body-mike is placed on the actor's chest or some part of their clothes, which is a slightly unnatural way of listening.

As a soundman, you have to deal with the actors in order to put mikes on them. You have to be intimate in a way, dealing with hiding mikes under clothes, and actors react in a great variety of ways. I did a film with Bruce Willis and you'd do the first "take" and then go to do the second "take" and I'd bring up his microphone and there would be nothing there! He took off his microphone between every "take" and it drove me crazy. Some actors just hate wearing body-mikes because it means people can listen in, and they might be revealing something rather intimate. So part of the soundman's job is to protect the actors and that confidentiality. You keep it so nobody can hear when they go to the bathroom and stuff like that! Some actors don't really care and some are gun-shy because they have been burned, and Bruce was one that I guess at some point in his career must have had someone who left his mike open. He just abhors the things.

Sometimes actors become angry, but that's just part of the finesse of trying to do your job. I look at a job as trying to record and enhance a performance in any way I can. I've had some films where I have put little earpieces on the actor and played music to them throughout an entire scene

Sound mixer

because they felt that the music motivated them to act in a certain way in a scene. One actress asked me to do that for the whole film, and no one else was aware of it. The story is that Jack Nicholson likes to have his lines read to him in an earpiece!

You devise all kinds of tricks as to where to place mikes; it becomes a challenge. For example, I worked on a film called *Coneheads* [Steve Barron, 1993] where all the actors had three-feet cones on top of their heads, so you couldn't hold a boom above them and in the end we had mikes sown into all the costumes. So in that case, wardrobe became involved. It is a very cooperative enterprise. Another difficult movie was one I just worked on called *Basic* [John McTiernan, 2003] in Florida where the entire film takes place on one night in a hurricane. There was wind and rain and slogging through the mud and it was a real struggle to get to the actors' voices.

Some actors love to loop or ADR [automatic dialogue replacement], because they think it's a chance to change their performance. They come in and phrase by phrase they replace what they said on the set, which is the way Italian movies are done. I did a film with Meryl Streep and Liam Neeson [*Before and After*, Barbet Schroeder, 1996] and Liam finds it the most painful thing in the world to replace his own voice, whereas Meryl Streep loves to loop because she feels it gives her a chance to improve upon her performance.

The entire sound for a movie can be added in afterwards in a studio, but there is nothing quite as nice as the original sound when you shot it. So your struggle is to record what is done in front of the camera, and the voice is the most important. You can add in wind and rain, so that when they edit the movie it doesn't jump from cut to cut; the challenge is to break the different elements apart. Interiors also have their problems because of the acoustics of the space in which you are shooting. Your eyes and ears will automatically adjust, but a microphone will record it the way it actually is. Outside you are dealing with things like traffic and airplanes. In sound it is much easier to add than to cut things out, so it is a question of trying to coordinate everyone so you can shoot between, say, airplane noise.

A film I enjoyed working on particularly was called *The Long Walk Home* [Richard Pearce, 1990] where the British composer George Fenton and I went out before the film started and recorded the entire music track. The film was set in 1956 in Alabama in the middle of the Civil Rights Movement, and churches were the center of the real Gospel music and the music track was essentially all gospel music. So we recorded many of the songs before we started shooting, which was fabulous. Then we played them back during shooting, adding in the congregation of extras singing and organ and a few other instruments. Generally the music is an element that is added later, but on this it was thrilling the way we did it.

There is really nothing as nice as the original sound. And for me, sound is very important. I ask myself what would happen in a movie theater if the picture blanked out and the sound kept going, versus what happens if the sound cuts out and the picture keeps going – I would like to know how the audience would react. What I always say is that nobody ever leaves a movie whistling a "two-shot"!*

* *A "two-shot" is a camera angle with two people in the frame.*

Angela Allen
Script Supervisor

Angela Allen has worked on some truly classic films, including **The Third Man**, *and one of my all-time favorites,* **The African Queen**. *Stars with whom she has worked include Humphrey Bogart, Charles Bronson, Richard Burton, Robert De Niro, Ava Gardner, Mel Gibson, Katharine Hepburn, Rita Hayworth, Robert Mitchum, Marilyn Monroe, Gregory Peck, Elizabeth Taylor and Orson Welles. Yet Angela is quite unfazed by celebrity. After my meeting with her she was going to have dinner with "Franco" (Zeffirelli), of whom she spoke in affectionate, almost motherly terms, saying that last time she had visited him she had been shocked to find that he didn't have properly laundered pillowcases, so she had ironed them for him.*

Angela amazed me in several ways: first, in her youthful appearance and energy (she was off to play tennis the next day). Secondly her modesty — she wondered if I had chosen to interview her because her name appeared early in alphabetical listings of script supervisors; she didn't mention her Member of the Order of the British Empire, nor the BFI award for a career in the industry; and her photos, far from being framed on the wall, are not even in albums. And Angela's untidiness surprised me. We met in her pretty garden flat in West London, but every table was strewn with papers — letters, health insurance documents, airline ticket stubs, **The Garden** *magazine, BAFTA programs — it was all there. But Angela's job consists of being totally organized and meticulous about detail and placement.*

Angela is a script supervisor, an American term now used universally, replacing the British title "Continuity" because of lobbying by Angela! Script supervisors keep track of which scenes have been filmed, and any deviations from the script. They also insure that in each "take," props, hair, makeup and everything else is the same so that the film can be edited flawlessly.

Selected Credits

The Third Man (Carol Reed, 1949)
The African Queen (John Huston, 1951)
Night of the Iguana (John Huston, 1964)
The Dirty Dozen (Robert Aldrich, 1967)
Women in Love (Ken Russell, 1969)
Murder on the Orient Express (Sidney Lumet, 1974)
Hamlet (Franco Zeffirelli, 1991)
Callas Forever (Franco Zeffirelli, 2003)

The old term "script continuity" might perhaps be a better description of the job of script supervisor. The idea is to have someone on set who is monitoring all the details all the time for everything. The title actually changed in England, because years ago when the Inland Revenue decided that everyone should be on Pay As You Earn tax, we all fought it. We are freelance and never know where the next job is, and so it is right that we be taxed with other similar jobs on Schedule D, which you pay at the end of the year and claim back your expenses. I and four or five of my colleagues fought it with the Inland Revenue, and we used the term "script supervisor" mainly because it sounded better.

The Inland Revenue, naturally, thinking you were a woman, thought you must be a clerk or the junior and their idea was that if you work with anybody you are subservient and taking orders and therefore you must be an employee and pay PAYE. But I said, "No, the director may talk to me but he doesn't dictate my notes; in fact *I* tell *him* when something is needed." Another thing they found hard to understand was the need for a car. Now you have laptops, but in those days you had a typewriter to carry, plus your scripts and files, and as you know the film industry does not work regular hours or in sensible places, and a car was a necessity. They refused us at first and then all the papers were sent to the Head of the Inland Revenue, and they lost them! When they accidentally admitted their incompetence to me, I knew I had won. So they finally said my section could stay on Schedule D taxation.

In America, the union would probably have dealt with questions of pay and tax for you. Often in the U.S., people start out non-union and become union members later because if you are not a member of the union you can only work on non-union, independent films. But it is much better organized in the U.S. and you have a pension fund and other benefits. Here the union used to be much stronger. I could not have worked when I started without joining, but now, unfortunately, you don't have to be a union member in any department and the union has no clout, although at least they are not corrupt. When I was asked if I wanted to join the union in the U.S., a condition was that the head of the section's son would work on the film!

Anyway, now we are all called script supervisors, and we are almost entirely female. It is possibly because women are better at detail and men would find it fiddly. I think there was one fellow once who tried, but he didn't get very far. In America they do have male script supervisors. When I was working over there, I was asked if I could go on location and I said, "What do you mean? I am always going on location." But they thought women didn't like being away from home, and might not cope on Westerns in rough places. It was also easier not to have a "honey wagon" [portable toilet] specially for women! They thought you were a nuisance, although I feel sure that makeup and hair were always women. But I think that that is how men started over there and a couple even went on to direct. Men still are promoted much more easily than women.

Script supervisor is a hard job, in the sense that you are the only person doing it, although very occasionally nowadays they give you an assistant. You are responsible for watching where the props are set, what the actors are saying, if they make a mistake, if they are looking the wrong side of camera. And if anything is different, you have to point it out to the director so that the film can be edited together smoothly later on. For instance if an actor picks up an apple on the word "go" in the wide shot and then picks it up on a different word in the close-up, you can't cut smoothly from one to another and it could seem that the actor is picking up the apple twice.

So after every "take" you endeavor to tell the actor, who may or may not ask you, "When did I pick up the cup and what did I do with it?" Some actors are very well-organized and trained and they rehearse their actions so that it is easier for them to do it always the same way. But some cannot do it that way and then it becomes a nightmare because every "take" they do something different. Then the director prints five or six "takes" and you ask "Which one did you really like?" Otherwise you have to do five or six matching, which he won't want to do. Sometimes the set is taken to pieces and moved around and it is my job to notice if they have forgotten to put an ashtray back on the table or if the vase is in the wrong position. You work very closely with the prop man, who usually has everything to hand, and with wardrobe, who check that clothes and jewelry are the same.

It is a detailed job and you cannot leave the set for a minute. It is rather like at school asking permission to go to the bathroom – nobody is going to wait for you if they want to "turn over." When I started, there weren't even Polaroid cameras, which are used all the time now, by both script supervisors and wardrobe, but then, you used to draw. My personal sketching is awful, so I would also have to label the drawings, and you make copious notes. I did shorthand, which all the continuity girls of my era did because you also often had to take down dialogue changes.

Things alter all the time. A director suddenly decides he doesn't like a big bunch of flowers and gets it removed, perhaps between "takes." You are constantly making notes. You also make a lined script for the editor. You draw a vertical line from where the shot starts to the word or action where it ends, and you put a number above the line so the editor can see how many shots he has for any sequence and where each cut ends. I always retype the script before I mark it up because I seem to have worked on films where the script changes a lot, but I don't think many people retype it.

I got bitten by the film bug in about 1945, when I went to Denham Studios as a very young girl as a secretary. I was only about 17 and was not really up to it and I got fired. I never felt I was quite right as a secretary. I don't think I am subservient enough. But, seeing the studios and the life, I thought, "This is what I want to do." First, like most kids, I thought I wanted to be an actress, but script continuity was the nearest. I couldn't have done makeup or costume because I couldn't draw, so I found out about this job and I literally went knocking on doors in London until somebody said there was a film about to start where they would probably take on an assistant. It was called *Night Beat* [Harold Huth, 1948] and it was at an Alexander Korda studio.

So I did a full training at the Korda studios, and Alexander Korda was *the* elite producer at the time. On *Night Beat* they had a second unit after about three weeks, which I got on, in the most freezing cold winter, on a location that was rat-infested with broken windows, but I was young and at that age you do mad things. From that I went on to *Mine Own Executioner* [Anthony Kimmins, 1947] and *Bonnie Prince Charlie* [Anthony Kimmins, 1948]. On the latter, the lady I was assistant to was getting married, and it

overran so I finished it off on my own. It was after that I was assigned to
Carol Reed on the second unit of *The Third Man* [1949]. He taught me all
the important things about my job, and I did two more films for him.

The Third Man was a fascinating experience. It meant going to Vienna
just after it had been liberated, when the rubble was still on the streets. It
was completely dominated by the four powers, and there was only one hotel,
the Astoria, that was open to non-military personnel. Carol Reed was a phenomenon because there were three units: the main unit doing night work;
the group that I was with who were down the sewer (I used to double sometimes as well during the day); and the day unit. Carol used to direct all three
– he used to live on Benzedrine. But he was totally in command and we had
a wonderful assistant director, Guy Hamilton, who then went on to be a
good director himself but he was Carol's protégé.

One of the difficult things about *The Third Man* actually was Orson,
because he was so elusive. He would come one day and then disappear. He
had the production manager chasing him around Europe; he was playing
games. Orson had been signed up by Alexander Korda long before *The
Third Man*, to direct or act in three films. All the suggested projects had, for

The "sewer unit" on *The Third Man*, 1949. Angela, the lone female in a sea of men, is in the center.
(Courtesy of Angela Allen)

various reasons, fallen through and Orson decided to get his own back. First he arrived in Vienna well after shooting had started – Guy Hamilton had doubled for him, wearing a big hat and a black coat with the hanger in to bulk out his frame. Then when Orson did arrive, he would only ever come down the sewer for about an hour. So under the direction of Vincent Korda, the main sewer in Vienna had to be built at Shepperton Studios back in England, for him. Orson wouldn't put up with the smell and discomfort of the real sewer, although Trevor Howard and everyone else did.

And the famous "cuckoo clock line" is the only line Orson wrote.* All the rest is Graham Greene's and Carol Reed's. Orson said he virtually wrote and directed the scene in the Prater on the wheel – but he didn't.

People ask me now, "Did you know you were making a brilliant film?" Well the answer is that you never know. You always hope that whatever film you make is going to be a success, but you certainly don't know that it *will* be; it's in the lap of the gods. It was after working with Carol Reed that I went to work for John Huston. Again I was lucky. I was the youngest continuity girl in the country, and there was a bit of jealousy that I got the job. Actually it was the producer, Sam Spiegel, who interviewed me, in London. I think he thought that because I was young I might be physically tough enough to withstand Africa, which I did.

Most people on *The African Queen* [John Huston, 1951] did get ill. But it was a wonderful and interesting experience. We went to Uganda and Kenya and it was very primitive. The food in the Belgian Congo, which was done by the French and the Swiss, was good, but when we lived on the boat (a kind of paddle-steamer) on the Murchison Nile, and shot everything from there, that was when everyone got sick. The water from the East India Company was contaminated and we had to have a three-day shutdown. The only ones still standing were two or three crew, me, Huston and Bogie – because they said they didn't drink water, they only drank whisky!

I only met John when I got to Africa. He was this enormous character and I was about 21 and it was certainly an adventure. We arrived in what was then Stanleyville and went on the wooden train and then rafts to the camp in Biondo in the Congo and worked with these two rather illustrious

---

* "In Italy for 30 years under the Borgias they had warfare, terror, murder and bloodshed, but they produced Michelangelo, Leonardo da Vinci and the Renaissance. In Switzerland, the had brotherly love; they had 500 years of democracy and peace — and what did they produce? The cuckoo clock."

Angela Allen (left), Katharine Hepburn, Eileen Bates (hairdresser), Humphrey Bogart and Lauren Bacall on *The African Queen*, 1951. (Courtesy of Angela Allen)

stars: Humphrey Bogart and Katharine Hepburn. Bogie was easy – you could deal with him because he was always pleasant. He wasn't a great conversationalist and he didn't joke around, but Katharine was Miss Bossy Boots. She would say, "Tell him to learn that next scene." And I would go up to Bogie and tell him and he would say, "If I learn that one, I'll forget this one." Really, they got on very well although they had never worked together before.

I remember one day we had to do a pick-up shot on a sequence we had shot earlier and Katharine said, "I was wearing so-and-so" and I said, "No you weren't." Now arguing with Miss Hepburn is not easy and I remembered a piece of advice from a wonderful script lady who used to work with David Lean, and she said, "Never dither. Always be positive." So there was I, aged about 21, talking to Miss Hepburn, aged about 46, although you weren't supposed to know her age, and I insisted, "No, you wore this." Of course there was no way of seeing the "rushes" so I remember sending a note saying,

"Please will you phone; will you tell me if I was right?" Well, thank God I was right. But she was so strong-minded that a lot of people would have been intimidated and just said, "I'm sure *you* know better than I do."

John was wonderfully supportive. If I said something, he would go with me rather than her because that was my job. So in that sense John would always defend me, and in the end I did 14 films with him. Of course, if you get on and they like you, they ask for you and you established a rapport with a director and he respects you. Although we used to argue, too. Once, on *The African Queen*, we had an argument about which way the boat was sailing and which way the camera had to be. He kept needling me. He was actually joking but I didn't know and I got very angry. I used to get angry with John sometimes and throw the script down and say, "That's it, I'm leaving!" But I couldn't do this on the boat because there was nowhere to walk off! But this time it backfired on him. When we finally finished the scene, we were meant to sail back and be in Sorrento in about an hour. Anyway, the journey seemed to be taking ages so I asked the captain when we were getting to port. It turned out that the cameraman, who had been turning the boat round for the sun, had forgotten to tell the captain that we had finished shooting so we were sailing for Africa instead of back to Sorrento. So we didn't get back for three or four hours.

But I seemed to get on with John; I was never frightened of him. He could be incredibly lazy at times. But anyone could make a suggestion to him – if you didn't like something, you could tell him and he would always listen. He might not use your suggestion, but it would distill something in his mind which might give him another idea. Anyone could ask John a question, which is not true of a lot of people today. For me, starting out, what was important was doing everything right. Then with experience, and watching and learning, you can make – and I have a lot with Huston – a big contribution. You can suggest something to make a scene better that just possibly the director hadn't thought of. They take the credit, but if they take your suggestion it is still rewarding. Nowadays you would probably call some of the things I did at the end of *The African Queen* second unit direction. I got left behind with the cameraman when everyone else had gone back to America, and I was really in charge because I was the one who knew how the shots were to go.

I also did doubling. In the scene where Bogie has leeches all over his body, they were mock-ups. But when we did the inserts with real leeches, it

Angela discusses a script with the young John Huston. (Courtesy of Angela Allen)

was my fingers that you see flicking them off. The first time we tried to get them to stick to a double's body, they wouldn't because they had been too well fed, so we had to starve them! So I got that lovely little job with the leeches. I also had to double taking the boat down the river steering round the crocodiles. I wouldn't do it now!

On *The Roots to Heaven* [John Huston, 1958], I was sent to another part of Africa with a cameraman to do lots of pick-up shots. I didn't get a credit or any extra money, but there I was, getting cables from Darrel F. Zanuck and John, "Get me so-and-so, get these shots!" And I doubled on that, too. It was funny. We needed five white men and we would be driving in a village with the French cameraman and I'd see someone and say, "Stop, look, go and ask that man if he would like to be in a film." And the cameraman would say, "*I'm* not going to ask him!" And I'd say, "But you're French, and so is he!" But I would have to do it and try to persuade some tall man that he would be brilliant as a double in this film.

Anyway, I couldn't get a double for all five men so I had to double for Eddie Albert. So I was wearing his boots, trudging in the sand and dust and my wonderful French cameraman shouts, "Your bottom looks female." And I replied, "Well, I'm hardly surprised!" And then the boots were so enormous I stepped right out of them. I did some mad things in those days. Nowadays I personally wouldn't work on something if I really loathed the script. I am not into violence or semi-pornography. When I first started, up to a point, you could pick and choose, because there was more work around. Now it isn't that way – it's a kind of battlefield out there. In my day there was no such thing as a résumé – people knew of you.

I have traveled to lovely places on films. I enjoyed *Moulin Rouge* [John Huston, 1952] because it took me to Paris for the first time and I fell in love with it and have not fallen out yet. *Beat the Devil* [John Huston, 1954] took me to Italy and I met Truman Capote [whose lovers were said to include Errol Flynn and who went on to write screenplays such as *Breakfast at Tiffany's*] and all those characters – Peter Lorre, Robert Morley. It was hysterically funny. It used to be one beating the other to the punch line, and although Bogie was in that film too, he wasn't really in that group. He didn't have that kind of wit, but he was very efficient and professional.

I have got on well with most of the actors I have worked with. I was friends with Ava Gardner because I met her on *Pandora and the Flying Dutchman* [Albert Lewin, 1950]. I remember even having to double for her one night and go swimming in the sea. Ava was very beautiful, but she was a character, too. She certainly used to imbibe quite a lot, and when she drank she could be difficult with some people. I had evenings with her in New York, London and in Mexico when we did *Night of the Iguana* [John Huston, 1964]. Lauren "Betty" Bacall was also a great character. She wasn't in *African Queen*, she was there as a wife, but she used to throw her weight about a bit if she could.

Elizabeth Taylor is marvelous about continuity. I remember her on a film with Franco Zeffirelli, and he said, "Turn the other way, Elizabeth." We were up in the gods in the theater and she was on the stage performing and she shouted back through the megaphone, "Ange, I didn't turn that way, did I?" and I said, "*No*, you didn't, *you* did it the right way, but match-

ing is not something we do around here!" So Franco screamed back, "You
two bitches!" Elizabeth was marvelous. She always did the same thing because she was trained as a child. The one who you *can't* tell anything to is
Mr. Robert De Niro. He's not allowed to be told anything, because he must
feel free....

I do find that some young directors think they know it all and you can't
tell them anything either. I've been on commercials where I have had an
idea how something could be better and told the director, and the director
will say, "You tell the actor," and then I'll say, "I *can* tell him, but you're here
as the director, and that is what the actor is expecting you to do. Don't shout
at him. He wants to be told what he's meant to be doing and feeling." Or I
might suggest something and the director will say, "No, no, no," but in the
end I will notice that it got used.

I have worked with many directors with very different temperaments.

Angela and her portable typewriter on *Pandora and the Flying Dutchman*, 1950. (Courtesy of Angela
Allen)

I enjoyed working for Richard Eyre because he was so good with his actors. It is a pleasure to see a director who talks to his artists and gets something special out of them, as opposed to ones who are only interested in the camera. I also did *Theatre of Blood* [Douglas Hickox, 1973], which is about the only proper horror film I have done. That was great fun. Vincent Price was lovely to work with and shooting used to get funnier by the day. Now I work mainly with Zeffirelli. We have terrible rows but we love each other.

The last film I worked on was *Callas Forever* [Franco Zeffirelli, 2003]. It had Fanny Ardant in it, who is terrific. I was going to do another film for John Frankenheimer but unfortunately he died. They probably call me the "Doyenne" now. Next month I believe I am getting the Women in Film Lifetime Achievement Award, and I think in a way I have to say thank you on behalf of all my fellow colleagues who I'm sure deserved it more than I did but who have now either retired or passed on. It is difficult to recognize everyone, and most awards are given because of the visual content: You can see the actor's performance, the art direction, the costumes, the photography.

But no matter how good you are at your job, when they edit films and take large chunks out, it does look like you have made a terrible clanger occasionally. Today, they don't care. Some directors say, "Matching is for wimps!" But actually people *do* notice. Strangely enough there was something on TV about a man who goes through films picking out the bloomers and they asked me, even though I had nothing to do with it, why these things happen. One clip was from *The Wizard of Oz* [Victor Fleming, 1939] where the person changed position. So I said that very likely the director changed his mind after a few "takes" and said, "I don't like him there, I want him *there*." And no matter what the continuity person says, the director has the final word. They also had a clip from *Gladiator* [Ridley Scott, 2000] where you can see the prop man or someone running off wearing jeans. I did say that they had six cameras running on that, but with the amount of digital work on that film they should have taken it out digitally, which of course you can do today.

In many ways things are easier now, with Faxes, computers, walkie-talkies and mobile phones. And I'll continue if the phone rings and I like the subject. Some younger ones are scared if you've got too much experience. They are a bit wary of older people. But I had a good time on the whole. I have been very lucky with the men I've worked with. Directors and producers nowadays do not seem to have the same charisma or charm.

Someone like Alexander Korda would come up to any member of the crew and ask if some relative was feeling better now. He would seem to take such a genuine interest in you that although you knew you were being manipulated, you would not hesitate to work that extra hour for him. John Huston could make the ugliest woman in the world feel beautiful. And if he told you that he had just lost more money gambling and he really had to finish this film in a hurry and get started on the next one, who could refuse?

Peter Cavaciuti
Camera Operator/Steadicam

Getting to interview Peter Cavaciuti was like chasing a rainbow; it took many attempts and much determination. I wanted to talk with him because few camera operators have worked on such an impressive list of films with so many interesting directors. In the end I thought maybe Peter did not want to be interviewed, but I was mistaken, and he finally arranged to see me while enjoying a few days off between films, at his north London home. His wife and children were charming and welcoming even though they rarely get a chance to be with him and Peter was forthright and helpful. Nor did he disappoint with his description of his work and the anecdotes he told.

SELECTED CREDITS

Aliens (James Cameron, 1986)
War Requiem (Derek Jarman, 1988)
The Secret Garden (Agnieszka Holland, 1993)
The Full Monty (Peter Cattaneo, 1997)
Kundun (Martin Scorsese, 1997)
Eyes Wide Shut (Stanley Kubrick, 1999)
Captain Corelli's Mandolin (John Madden, 2001)
Harry Potter and the Philosopher's Stone (Harry Potter and the Sorcerer's Stone)
  (Chris Columbus, 2001)
Finding Neverland (Marc Forster, 2004)

In a camera crew, the director of photography [who is credited before a film and sometimes called cinematographer or cameraman] is the head of the department. Under him is the camera operator who actually works the camera in accordance with the concept and lighting design of the cameraman. Next is the first assistant or focus puller who adjusts the focus of the camera. In the U.S. there are two more crew: the second assistant who loads the film and clapper loader who slams the clapperboard. In the U.K. there is traditionally just a clapper loader, but the guild of British camera technicians is trying to push towards the American system because the job is becoming more demanding, with equipment such as remote camera heads and Steadicams.

A Steadicam is a body-mounted stabilization device. Instead of operating a camera on a tripod, you wear a vest which is strapped tight to your body and there is a mechanical arm which has springs in it and supports the weight of a camera sled – a metal tube with a TV monitor on it and some batteries which act as a counterbalance for a camera that sits on top of the sled. Steadicam is a specialization, but I always do both – camera operating and Steadicam.

I went to art college first; I wanted to be a painter or a sculptor. But I got a bit disillusioned with that and so I got a job as a trainee in a film company. I spent two and a half years there and was very fortunate because during that time they bought a Steadicam and I practiced a lot on it before I left in 1984. At that time, there were a lot of pop videos being made and I worked on hundreds of them and really cut my teeth on those, and in that way met cameramen who were shooting commercials, and they went on to work on films and that's how I got my introduction to films.

This was quite an unconventional entry. Usually in Britain you are a trainee, a loader, a focus puller, before becoming an operator. I missed out the two middle stages, which tends to happen more in the U.S. – there are some American Steadicam operators who have had a very similar path to me. When I started there were only three or four Steadicam operators in the country and I had an ability for it and off I went! I was very fortunate.

The camera operator's job is to synthesize the story in a visual way. It is my responsibility to insure that all the shots cut together and make visual sense, and that the visuals enhance the script. I also "frame" the shot which involves deciding exactly what is visible and how it is composed. It is a precise art, planning out each shot in advance, with the director and the director of photography [DP]. And because the camera is much heavier-duty than, say, an amateur camera, it is less likely to be hand-held, although since the advent of TV series like *Hill Street Blues* and *NYPD Blue* it has become more fashionable to see camera moves and be aware of the camera. In more classical filmmaking, the camera movements would be far more difficult to detect.

Under the guidance of the cameraman, I also have to organize my department and make sure everything runs smoothly. Ideally I like to work with the same camera crew, because I have built up a relationship with them. Years ago, teams of people went from film to film, but that happens less now. Cameramen work abroad a lot more these days and you have to be flexible about who you work with, which keeps everybody on their toes. Every cameraman works in a different way so as an operator you have to change your role. Sometimes you have complete responsibility for framing, especially if you are working with an inexperienced director, who may rely on you completely.

In England, there is a tradition that the director and the operator work very closely. In America, the cameraman will decide the shots; where the camera starts, what tracking there might be, what lens to use, where the camera ends up, and the frame. The first way is better for me because there is more responsibility and you can be more creative. Some American DPs want that; it just depends. And it depends on the director too.

Kubrick stands out amongst the directors I have worked with. I learnt a lot from him on *Eyes Wide Shut* [1999], particularly about framing. His framing was quite unconventional. He would give people a lot of head room so the actor would appear quite small in frame and you would notice the environment more around him so there was an oppressive nature to his framing. Kubrick was incredibly demanding. He would do 30 or 40 "takes" and was an absolute perfectionist, which was physically demanding for me because I was doing Steadicam.

I admired his bravery because you have got to stick your neck out to give yourself that amount of time. We also did very, very, long "takes" on exteriors and I would have to use things like gyroscopes on the Steadicam because sometimes it would be windy and I would need as much technical backup as possible. The level of steadiness that Kubrick demanded on his shots was very tough. I really felt I had to go up a notch with my work with him.

I remember the first day on the shoot I was quaking in my boots because I had heard so many stories about people departing very quickly on his films, but I got on really well with him. Now and again the actors would get a bit frustrated with doing so many "takes" and one day I asked him why he did so many, and he replied that it was "pinball theory." I said, "What do you mean?" and he explained: "It is like a pinball on a pinball machine ricocheting everywhere and something unexpected might happen. You can do things one or two times and actors get bored but when you push it to 30 or 40 times that boredom could turn into anger or frustration or whatever, and something unusual might happen. That's why I do it." He was very open. I was prepared for him to be a very dark, distant figure, but he wasn't like that at all. You could ask him a question about anything, at the right time, and he would always be very forthcoming, and to *me* he was incredibly kind, so I had a very good experience with him.

That is, except when he asked if I could roller skate! He sent me off to the best roller skate shop in London to buy some skates and his idea was to get the grip to push me around the actors on skates, but it didn't work. In *Eyes Wide Shut* there is a scene at the start of an orgy, and all these people are in a circle and get paired off with partners and one by one they go off into different rooms to get up to the antics they get up to, and Kubrick wanted to get the camera as far back to the edge of the wall as he could. So he had this idea that putting the Steadicam on me, and me on roller-skates, would be the way to do it, because I would occupy a smaller space than a

Tying a shoelace is an impossible task whilst wearing a Steadicam vest. Here Bill Geddes, key grip, (left) ties Peter's shoe while Rawden Hayne, focus puller, (right) steadies the Steadicam on *Eyes Wide Shut*. (Courtesy of Peter Cavaciuti)

dolly [a trolley, often mounted on rails]. Unfortunately my roller-skating wasn't up to it though!

In total contrast to this ideal of a perfect shot was when I did a film last year [*The Hunted*, 2002] with William Friedkin, the guy who did *Cruising* [1980], *The Exorcist* [1973], and *The French Connection* [1971]. He wasn't interested in technical perfection; he wanted you to use your intuition as an operator. It was like the opposite end of the spectrum to Stanley. You had one or two "takes" if you were lucky and no rehearsals. William wasn't interested in making pretty pictures; it was capturing the moment and the dynamic of the situation. And if the frame wasn't quite as good, it didn't worry him. Physically that was very demanding too, and quite nerve-wracking because you *had* to get it right. It was demanding for everyone – the focus puller, the grips, everyone involved, knew they might not get a second "take."

Harry Potter [Chris Columbus, 2001] was also interesting. Of course the kids were pretty lively, and John Seale, the DP, wanted us to use zoom lenses and fluid camera heads so we could accommodate them. Because although the kids had worked in films before, it was their first big film, so they couldn't hit their "marks" [position] like an experienced grown-up. It was particularly hard on the focus pullers. I worked on the first unit, but the second unit did a lot of the "green screen" where, for example, Dan [Daniel Radcliffe, who plays Harry] would be dangled on a broom on a wire with a green background for the Quidditch scenes. There would be little white crosses on the screen and Dan would move across frame and they would use the crosses as reference to put the background on afterwards.

Another thing I remember were the shots we did of owls dropping mail! What the animal trainers did was amazing. They were mainly real owls, although there were some that were computer-controlled. There is one scene when Dan has his owl on his arm in the snow and it takes off and you follow the owl up for a bit and then it turns into a computer-controlled owl.

There are always different demands as a camera operator. When you are inside, you are always looking where the cameraman has placed his or her lights, so you frame for the lighting. In a studio you are always fighting for space, so you have to be aware of mundane things like lamps in shot, yet when you are outside there is also always some kind of lighting. The cameraman will either bounce natural light or enhance the light – so there are not great differences other than weather (when you might have to protect the camera) when shooting inside or out. Outside you do have to have a

Peter Cavaciuti working on *The Hunted*. (Courtesy of Peter Cavaciuti)

good eye for landscape; you have to be aware of the reason that you are shooting outside and relate all the shots to the script. It is all script- and atmosphere-driven, in fact.

    I really liked the way Caleb Deschanel worked. He was the director of photography on *The Hunted*. He worked in the American style, so he set your shots, but he was an intelligent man and open-minded and so if I had a suggestion I could put it in. The speed of Caleb's work impressed me and he lights beautifully. Plus he's a great man to hang out with – a nice man. I also learnt a lot from John Toll, the DP on *Captain Corelli's Mandolin* [John Madden, 2001]. He came up with some very interesting shots – both in his framing and lighting. For instance, we were shooting a scene after the massacre where Corelli is brought back to the doctor's house and the doctor is performing an operation on him to save his life and John lit it like a Goya painting. Everything was really backlit and there was very little fill lighting so you just got the outlines of people and it made the colors very rich. He didn't show a lot of detail, which actually gave it a lot of atmosphere.

Sometimes lighting can be compromised if you use more than one camera because you are lighting for all of them. If it were an action film, though, that would lend itself to several cameras. Cameras have changed a lot in the last 15 years. They are modular now and you can do more things with them: you can put the magazines in different positions, you can add speed and shutter controls, so they are more versatile and also much smaller and lighter than they used to be. Dollies are still much the same, but telescopic cranes are a recent development, allowing you to squeeze into spaces you wouldn't have got into before.

But you cannot just be a technician to be a camera operator. You have got to be able to compose a shot and it helped me to have studied painting. I have a sense of composition and where to put people in the frame and an understanding of how something is being lit. I wouldn't have wanted to do it any other way. I loved my time at art college. But now, the job I have is incredibly exciting.

Every day is different. The great thing about going to work for me, is that anything could happen. It's completely unpredictable, which is alluring to me, and also I find it extremely creative. I love helping to frame a shot. I really like the artistic nature of it. Also the interaction on a film set makes it a communal effort and it is great seeing it all come together: you have a chaotic scene that gradually becomes controlled and there is a beauty to creating the shots. It's like painting or drawing for me. Ever since I was a kid, drawing was a passion of mine, and now, what I do is still positioning things in frame. Sometimes I work in very volatile situations and it can be nerve-wracking, but you've got to get through it. It is always exciting and creatively demanding, and eventually I would like to be a director of photography, which could be even more so.

Carolyn Scott
Set Decorator

Carolyn Scott chose to come and talk to me at my house on a day when builders were ripping out my old kitchen. She arrived, immaculately and smartly dressed and I proffered a dusty hand. My tape recorder unaccountably kept turning itself off and required to be hit repeatedly, but my back-up machine failed to work at all. Just as we were about to start, an increase in dust set the smoke alarm off. I rushed into the kitchen, knowing that the emergency code number to stop the alarm was written on the inside of the cupboard — but of course, the cupboard was no longer there!

Carolyn remained poised, calm and outwardly unfazed by all of this and I realized that she possessed qualities which were essential to her work; for as I was to find out, the job of an Oscar-winning set decorator can at times be very frustrating and quite unpredictable.

SELECTED CREDITS

The Scarlet Pimpernel (Clive Donner, 1982)
Mountbatten: The Last Viceroy (U.S. TV drama, Tom Clegg, 1986)
The Man in the Brown Suit (U.S. TV movie, Alan Grint, 1989)
Nightbreed (Clive Barker, 1990)
The Madness of King George (Nicholas Hytner, 1994)
Some Mother's Son (Terry George, 1996)

I used to work in the Foreign Office and only got into films when my husband, a producer, was working on a commercial when everything went wrong. People weren't available and dates had changed and he said to me, "You can do it! You've got to help us out here, we need..." and then a list of props followed with places I might try to get them from. And the rest came from there. If you do a good job, the phone starts to ring and people give you work. If I could start from the beginning now, I would go to art school and do things the proper way. I wanted to get into decorating and design, rather than remain a buyer, but as it happened I vaguely knew how to draw up a set and get it built and all the rest of it.

Now I'm a designer and set decorator, which in England used to be called a set dresser. In England we don't use that term any more, although in America a set dresser is a prop man. The first thing I do as set decorator is to read the script (sent by the production office who has hired me and done the deal) and do a massive breakdown of it, which is vital. So I find out how many sets there are, what is required for each one, and then the arguments begin!

If there is a designer on the job, they will often see to the studio design and build and then the set decorator will come along afterwards and dress it, but on location the set decorator is often in charge of the construction crew. Really, the whole art department works together but the set decorator is responsible for all the props and dressings that go onto the set. Sometimes the set decorator will have a say regarding costumes, too. In any case the set decorator, with a great deal of help from the production buyer, will be expected to source all the special props that might be required for a production from among the hundreds of specialist suppliers and services that there are.

Items needed might include period vehicles, calligraphy services, medical equipment, animals, drapes, fruit machines, firearms – on and on, really. Wherever possible, we hire props but occasionally various props become so well-known that you cannot go on using them so you have to find sources elsewhere or get them specially made. The buyer runs the props budget and will find things for you, but you decide what is wanted. Some buyers are extraordinarily good and can do a lot on their own, but others won't, and want to be told exactly what you want.

I happen to have worked on a lot of location stuff, and a lot of it "period" films, but just lately I worked on a film set more recently in Ireland at the time of the death of Bobby Sands and all the hunger strikers and we needed to know what the Maze Prison was like. In an instant you have to know how to do whatever is put in front of you. Often I find it is just general knowledge, and I kind of have a feeling for things, or I do research.

You also work closely with the location manager, because they would always have to check with the art department. Most of them know their job and are absolutely ace, but some of them aren't so hot. Anyway, on this occasion we tried to get into the prison to see what it was like, but we were chased away in no uncertain terms. Then our producers had the idea of hiring an airplane and flying over the prison, but that idea didn't go down too well either! In the end we built it from photos and there was kind of enough reference.

The set decorator has to pick things out of the script. For instance, it might say, "George comes in and he kicks the cat as he goes past the window." So you have got to have a door, a cat and a window. It can be as literal as that, but having got those elements, you then decide on, for example, their style. I think if you can get the spirit of the time or place, I don't think you need to slavishly copy everything,

Patient Carolyn

and usually you don't have the time. It's the essence you need to capture and not have anything which sticks out as looking wrong or irritating. Once I was on a TV series called *Cadfael* [Ken Grieve, 1994-96] starring Derek Jacobi, where we built a whole cathedral in a studio and whenever anyone went on that set they started whispering!

On the whole, actors don't usually get involved, except once we were doing one of the Hammer films, with Sian Philips, delightful lady, no problems, except I put some peacock feathers on the set and she *freaked*. She was so unhappy about it, and I said, "Okay, Okay, we'll take them away," but she said, "No. That's not good enough. It doesn't work that way. I know that peacock feathers were there." Apparently they are unlucky – I didn't know –

I thought they were rather lovely! So we hurriedly had to change the whole location to find another similar room somewhere else because she refused to film there because she knew the peacock feathers had been there!

Sometimes it is less dramatic but equally frustrating, and as often as not, crew rather than actors are the culprits. You can't be there while they are shooting all the time, so sometimes you think to yourself, "Why on earth have they moved that from there to there?", which is why now you very often have an art department person there on the set who can stop that happening. In *The Madness of King George* [Nicholas Hytner, 1994] there is one scene where a blue and white vase containing daffodils appears on the mantlepiece, when he is ill and virtually in prison, so it would never have been there. You shouldn't let the camera department out by themselves, really!

But if they had really wanted it, I could have hired something more appropriate from a specialist props company and I would have put more appropriate flowers in it. Every time I see the film now I cringe at that bit, and because the vase had been established, we had to see the same damn pot again with roses in it to try to mark the passage of time. But the script will do that, not a vase that looked as though it came from the fairground-awful.

For that particular film, apart from knowing what interiors should look like, we had to find out about all those remedies for illness, like cupping and bleeding, so we could give them the real gear. I now know that there are several medical leech farms in Wales! In fact, they have gone back to using leeches because they work very well. You can put a leech on a wound and it will clean it instead of using antibiotics. You end up knowing a little about an awful lot!

It may sound odd, but the design work is the easy bit, compared with all the peripherals – like finding locations and scheduling so that you don't go from one end of England to another in an afternoon. Then as well as dressing the set you have got to pull it down and leave the location clean and tidy and get everything back to the right places. You have got to know how to run a department and keep hold of it and you've got to do small things like load the truck with everything you could possibly need – that sort of thing.

An example is when we shot at Syon House [an eighteenth century stately home in Isleworth] on *The Madness of King George*. We could only shoot on Monday, because that is the day they are closed to the public, which means you have to dress the set on Sunday night. In the big room where we were, the first thing that we had to do was take down all the picture lights. Lo and behold, we discovered they were the only lighting source in the room. So happily we had boxes full of candles which we needed for shooting, so we did the whole thing by candlelight!

But at daybreak the following day, somebody had to be outside the candle shop in Camden in London to replace the candles we had used and get them onto the set as soon as they could. That's the kind of nonsense that goes on. But that's reality. It's a bit nail-chewing. The director and cameraman come wafting in and say, "What've you got for us, darling?" And you say, "Well, it's fine, but can you hold off anything with candles in for the moment on account of..." "Why aren't they here?", and then you have to explain – but I've never held up shooting.

Some directors are very understanding and really like what you've done, while others don't know what they want and therefore they don't know whether they like what you've done or they don't. Some are prone to a lot of whispering in their ears from their cameramen. Always they will look to the art department for an excuse, because cameramen take an inordinately long time to light the set, and they are always looking for excuses so if they can land it on the art department, so much the better for them.

Nick Hytner, the director on "Mad George" was a joy and a delight. First, even though he had not directed a film before, he knew his stuff – his subject – and he liked his actors, and happily he liked what we did. He had no reason not to, but at least he appreciated what we were doing and would always just ask if something was really right, saying, "Did they really have those?" People often expect period films to be all beautiful with nothing strange and look like something out of *House and Garden* magazine or Osborne and Little furnishings.

Winning an Oscar for *The Madness of King George* was wonderful. The production designer and set decorator get the Oscar for Art Direction. But I didn't realize that the first nominations come from your peers, your own chums, not the whole Academy – which makes it lovely – and not like BAFTA or anything else. At first they vote for their own group and best film, and then in the next round, everyone votes for everything. But oh goodness me!, what they don't tell you is that you should not go to any of the pre-Oscar parties, because by the time Oscar night comes you are knackered. Sam Goldwyn paid for us all [Nigel Hawthorne, Helen Mirren and Alan Bennett were also nominated] to go to LA about a week in advance. At first you think, "Gosh, this is lovely" and "Ooooh," but then the days wear on and you can barely keep your eyes open.

But you really don't know who will win. When we were standing in our queue on the red carpet, the guys who came along behind us in the line were two men with guns and a briefcase and we were just chatting and asked who they were, and they said, "We're from Price Waterhouse, and we've got the envelopes!" And they sat behind the stage, so when the presenters went onto the stage, at that point only, they gave them the envelope. To be quite honest, I just had no idea that I would win, so I just saw what I had in the wardrobe to wear. If it ever happens again, which is doubtful, I would do it differently. I would get them to give me a frock. I'd get them to give me jewelry and all the rest, which they do if you ask them. About three or four people in front of us in the queue on the red carpet was a man who told me he was from the official jewelers. "We have an interest in this production," he said.

When they called my name, I thought I was going to be sick, it was just so unexpected. I hadn't prepared anything to say, but Ken Adam, the production designer, had a long prepared speech so it didn't really matter. But it really was amazing. You are given this car, which is twice the length of this room, and your driver, and you can go anywhere and do anything. But when you've *won* your Oscar, you have to carry the damn thing round with you all evening and it weighs eight and a half pounds. And people are terribly reverential about it! Lots of people come up to you and say [Carolyn puts on good accents, this time American], "Oh, may I touch it?" I mean they don't just say, "Ooh, let's have a look." It is something very special for Americans. But the Brits hate you for it.

There was a very nasty piece written in *The Times*, based on absolutely nothing. It was full of mistakes, and basically asked why did we get an Oscar? So I phoned up the lady who wrote it and asked why she had done it, and she said she thought it would make a good story. There *is* resentment. When we got the nominations, two English people phoned up who had both got Oscars in the past for Set Decoration, and they both said, "Don't think this is going to do you any good. You won't work for 18 months!", and they were damn nearly right. I should have worked in America afterwards, but I didn't know about all that then. Most English people have the same experience. The English don't like success. When Prince Edward had just come back from New York, I remember he said what a change it was to be somewhere

where everyone was pleased about people's success. He said you come back to England and there is this great "Monty Python foot" crushing you. It's true – but then that's the English way.

After that there was a long period when we were going to do a film about Byron which kept on biting the dust, partly because the script wasn't good enough. That happens quite often. There were also two American productions that were meant to happen after the Oscars, one about stealing the Mona Lisa and one about the Hunchback of Notre Dame, and we got very far along the line but they folded. In fact, Ted Turner [owner, amongst other things, of New Line Cinema and Castle Rock Entertainment] was going to put in the bulk of the money for the Mona Lisa film and the producers had got Sean Connery, Ian McKellen, all the British stalwarts to be in this film.

Anyway, time went on and I found a lot of locations and we had a start date and the producers went to see Ted Turner to tell him it was all ready to go. So out came the golden pen and he started to write the check and he said, "By the way, I never asked you, who is your star?" And they said, "Well, it can be whoever you want, they're all equal, Connery, McKellen ..." and he said "No, who's your *star?*" And there wasn't an American in it and he said he couldn't finance it. That's probably the closest I've got, because lots of people were already over here, in the hotels and everything.

Funny things happen in this business – shooting sometimes never starts, sometimes it has hiccups. We were shooting *The Scarlet Pimpernel* [Clive Donner, 1982] at Blenheim Palace in Woodstock, Oxford, and we weren't allowed to close the courtyard where we built a guillotine – I don't know how many people have built working guillotines, but anyway we built one – so we had to do a scene and then stop and let the tourists in. Well, it started with a Japanese party seeing the guillotine and wanting to be photographed with it, in it, holding a head from the basket, and it just dominated the day. Everyone who came in after that was the same. It became an absolute nightmare. But that's one of the joys of shooting on these fancy locations; it's not plain sailing by any means.

Then another time, I was shooting an Agatha Christie story in Spain, *The Man in the Brown Suit* [Alan Grint, 1989], and the script called for a dead rat. So I got onto the animal hire people in Madrid and they said it was no problem, they had brown ones, gray ones, and we agreed the cost and the handler, the time and everything. Come the morning, I saw the driver of the rat van and I asked to look at the rat, but at that moment I was called away to do something on the set.

As events turned out, I didn't get to see the rat. That should be rule number one. Whatever you want to go on your set, you see it first. Anyway, then they called for the rat. A few minutes later, "Where's Carolyn? Get Carolyn here!" and the walkie-talkies and mobiles were all going, because you are not usually on set while they are shooting. When I arrived I saw a cage, and in it were two rats, cleaning their whiskers, all

Carolyn Scott in conversation

smart and lively. I said, "Oh my God, we wanted dead rats!" and they said, "Yes, which one?"

Well, the English unit just freaked out. They said we couldn't shoot the scene and would be behind schedule and lose lots of money. In the end, the only compromise was to get the RSPCA. There is a branch in Madrid, and we asked them to give the rat an injection to make it look dead. The director really went berserk at this point and said, "If I don't see these rats get up and walk away at the end of the shoot, you are all in big trouble!"

Now here's another silly animal story. We were shooting *Mountbatten*, a film for TV [Tom Clegg, 1986], and we had to do all the violent scenes that really took place in north India in Sri Lanka instead, because of the political situation, which would probably have set off real riots in north India. Well, apart from the problems of trying to make Sri Lanka look like north India, one of the sequences needed some dead cows, which had been murdered. Again, we got onto the cow people and found someone who had some Indian cows, because Sri Lankan ones look different, and he said the vet would have to give them an injection to make them sleep for about six hours. These cows are terribly valuable, and he said the one thing we must not do was to feed them for several hours beforehand because if they had this injection on top of food, they would die.

We got the cows and built them a little shed which could be locked up the night before shooting. And to this day, I do not know what made me do it, because it was miles away from our hotel, but I said to my driver, "I would really like to go back and check on those cows." When I got there, the cows were all out eating grass, the whole family with granny and babies were sitting in the shed that we'd built for the cows and they were having picnics and singing and feeding the cows little bits of their food, too. So I had to phone up and say, "We've got a problem; we can't do the cows tomorrow." This is the kind of thing which happens. You think you are a designer, but that isn't the half of it!

When you are working on a film, it is my experience that the world could come to an end and you wouldn't know. You are just so involved with the film. You hear stories where someone like a props man will say that when he was home his daughter clutched onto his wife's skirt, shouting, "Mum, mum, there's a strange man in the house!" It's so intense for five or six weeks, and then nothing. That's the time I sit under the apple tree with my nose stuck in a book and a glass at my elbow. Actually, there has been a study done about people who have this kind of working life and it can upset a lot of people and the withdrawal now has a name. It is the time when people get flu, and other illnesses because of the kind of anticlimax.

Torture and fun. It used to be very well paid, but it isn't any more – too many films made which aren't good enough, perhaps. The more I think about it, the less actual design work is involved with my job, but I enjoy it all. I *like* getting things done. It is always possible to do what they want you to. Always. It may not seem so, and some people are lazier than others, but it can always be done.

I'll tell you one last animal story. It happened on one of the Frankie Howerd feature comedies and we were on location somewhere near Elstree. In the film we needed a big mother pig and father pig and lots of little piglets. So we found the mother and father, (which we used in the film first) and a farmer who was expecting a litter of babies at the right time. And the piglets were born just when we needed them, but they were black and the parents we had found were pink. So we got the painters to paint the mother black! And she adored it, and all the washing after. Pigs love being scratched and tickled and she performed beautifully. So it had a happy ending.

Stephen Barker
Post-Production Supervisor

I met Stephen Barker in his busy office in De Lane Lea Studios – a building housing many film production facilities. It is in the heart of Soho in London, an area famous for companies connected with the film industry, as well as for restaurants and strip joints. There are also cinemas within easy reach, although Stephen, working in the industry, stereotypically, no longer goes to see movies for pleasure. But who could really blame him when he works such long hours and is able to spend little time with his wife?

As a post-production supervisor, Stephen oversees the whole of a film after the cameras have stopped turning on the set. In this twilight zone which the punters forget – between shooting and distribution – he will work closely with the director and editor for a minimum of 16 weeks but for up to a year on bigger budget films. His duties include dealing with sound, inserts and re-shoots, whilst insuring finishing on time and within budget.

SELECTED CREDITS
The Van (Stephen Friers, 1996)
Sliding Doors (Peter Howitt, 1998)
Mickey Blue Eyes (Kelly Makin, 1999)
Chocolat (Lasse Hallstrom, 2000)
Possession (Neal LaBute, 2002)
Iris (Richard Eyre, 2002)
Touching the Void (Kevin Macdonald, 2003)

When shooting finishes, the producer of a film is often off doing other things and the production manager usually leaves about a week after completion of principal photography. From then on, the management of the film on a daily basis is done by the post-production supervisor. The job involves creating a post-production budget; arranging facilities (like labs and cutting rooms); managing the equipment, the people (picture and sound editors and their assistants), music, special effects, right the way through to delivering the finished film (the various negatives and soundtracks) to the financiers – in effect, everything that needs to be done after shooting has ended on set.

The budget will have been set when the funding for the film is originally "green lit." In many cases it is good for the post-production supervisor to be involved in this stage so he or she can set the parameters of post-production within the overall budget. So the best way is when, right at the start, I get a call from the producer saying, "Hey Steve, I'm trying to finance a film for such-and-such to do such-and-such, could you put some numbers together for me?" I do that, and then hopefully the producer goes away and makes the film and calls me six weeks later and I get the job and manage it from then on.

Sometimes global figures are used in budgeting at first so the post-production supervisor will later create a more specific budget and schedule. When selecting crew such as assistant editors, he will then take their skills and rates into account and will use the best facilities and equipment the budget will allow. The post-production supervisor will also keep a technical overview of all special effects, lab and sound work. There are times when the crew are too close and miss problems that might crop up farther down the line in the delivery of the picture. This is why a background in a cutting room [editing] or lab [film processing] is important for a post-production supervisor.

I started off at Rank [now called Deluxe] Film labs. I always wanted to work in the entertainment industry in some way. My father was a musician and my mother was a dancer and I must have inherited some of those genes. Actually, when I first left school I went into a photographic company doing stills photography, and then I decided I wanted to get into the film industry and at that time I wanted to be a cameraman. But somehow that never happened and I worked at Rank Film labs for about ten years doing color grading and then liaison with the productions. Then I decided to go into a small company which did documentary filmmaking and which set up a video editing facility up the road here in Dean Street. Then I moved to Cannon Films, which is when I really cut my teeth on post-production.

There weren't really many post-production supervisors around at that time – 15 or more years ago – because traditionally post-production had

Stephen checking figures in his Soho office.

been run by the picture and sound editors. But now it has become more common to use post-production supervisors so that the editors and their crew can do what they are best at – editing – rather than making arrangements and spending hours on the phone fixing things. At the time I worked for Cannon, they were quite a big operation run by Golan and Globus. A lot of their products were shot in Israel and I remember I went to work with them to liaise with the labs and organize printing throughout Europe.

They did a series of live-action fairy tale movies which were shot and edited in Israel and they sent 16 cans over, eight of picture and eight of sound, which landed on my desk, and it was, "There you are, finish that!" It was quite tough because a lot of the original dialogue was no good because they shot in aircraft hangars next to construction sites and it was full of extraneous noise. So we had to get a lot of the original artists back to re-record their dialogue in a better environment.

Each film has its own set of problems, but re-recording dialogue is quite a common one. For instance, there might be a film involving a lot of battles and you need to be aware that you will have to do a lot of re-recording, called ADR, with the original actors, because the production track will have too much noise. So you have to get the artists back when they are often in other parts of the world working on other films. They always provide free time in their contracts but the past production is always on second call to their current production. I have had to fly editors and directors round the world to record the actors. So from a budgeting and scheduling point of view, that can be a problem.

I enjoy it when it is all finished and I am watching a completed film and think, "Hey, I helped do that!" I am proud of making it all look good and finishing it on time. I particularly enjoyed working with Mike Figgis because he is so talented: he directs movies and writes music, and I worked with him on a film called *One Night Stand* [1997] and it was with nice people and it was all a good experience. I have had some bad experiences too, and as I get older there are one or two people I wouldn't want to work for again, but generally I enjoy what I do.

Several people have asked me why I don't produce, and it would be nice, but there are a lot of out-of-work producers who have been doing it a lot longer than me. I make a comfortable living so I am quite happy where I am. I have turned a little bedroom into an office at home for weekends and evenings when the Americans are still working, but in the main I work from my rented office here. At the moment I prefer Soho because it is more active. I could easily have an office at Pinewood Studios which would be much closer to where I live, but I feel in Soho you get a more diverse cut of the industry. You only have to walk out on the street and you will bump into five people involved in ten different projects and you go into a restaurant and meet more people.

A lot of my business is social and knowing who is doing what when — trying to put the square pegs in the square holes. Often I'll be asked to crew movies for sound and picture and you need to keep a handle on who is available. For example, a film might be cut and in the final stages of post-production when they need a pick-up little insert shot of a man's hand, and because the production office for the film is closed, the post-production office has to arrange an insert shoot involving lights, camera, makeup. So although the director of course remains the same, we have to find a completely new crew; in fact, take on a producing role.

The job is very big, varied and difficult to describe because managing post-production is rather a generalization. You have to be a diplomat, a technician, an accountant, a manager and a producer — you have to wear lots of different hats — and you are often the front line of the production office dealing with all the problems, people and facilities involved. I work on more than one film at a time because they get "hot" (stressful and involved) at different times, but some supervisors only work on one at a time. I don't know who's right.

Relationships with colleagues are also sometimes difficult. You have to maintain some kind of authority but also be friendly with the people you work with, particularly assistant editors – you have to be friend and foe. You have to let people go sometimes too. I don't put my toe fully into the social arena because I don't want to be embarrassed when it comes to the nasty bit. But I think it is part of being a diplomat.

So I don't socialize a lot with the people I work with and I never go to the cinema! My journey home is an hour and a half and I work quite long hours so I am never home before 8:30 or 9:00 p.m. and I just want to sit down and spend some time with my wife. And the weekends are so precious, I don't want to sit in a darkened room and watch a film when I've spent the whole of my working week involved with a film and sometimes in screenings as well. I am aware that perhaps this is a failing because I can't enter into conversations with people when they say, "Have you seen such-and-such? And wasn't so-and-so good?" I can't remember the last time my wife and I paid to see a film, although of course we go to screenings and premieres.

My wife doesn't mind my long hours because she is a very understanding lady. I'm sure if she was less understanding our marriage wouldn't have lasted 30 years. She doesn't mind me working at home in the evenings and weekends because I'm self-employed and have to do my accounts and expenses in those times. You have to enjoy the work or you wouldn't do it. I particularly enjoy the music recording and the final mixing of all the sound elements when all the music, dialogue and effects are refined and put together – that is satisfying.

I think the next five to ten years will see much bigger changes in the way pictures are recorded. I think the digital root will mushroom and that digital post-production for pictures will be the next big step, which will affect the whole industry and the labs will need to change because everything will be shot on digital equipment and be digitally post-produced. For the moment, shooting and finishing on film is the best way, but I believe that ultimately we won't have conventional projectors any more. But that is a long way off and will be a gradual process.

At present I actually enjoy working on smaller British films because the post-production supervisor is more involved and has more ammunition to fire than with studio pictures. On studio pictures, you are "their man in London" and you can't always make your own decisions. Generally the smaller the film, the more involved each member of the crew is.

And talking of crew – another responsibility of a post-production supervisor is the end credits! There is no real structure to an end-roller – it is often down to the whims of the producers. Sometimes paperwork is involved, coming from the production during the shooting period, for instance when a location is used and a contract is drawn up between the production company and the people from the location. Often there will be wording in the contract as to how the location is credited in the end-roller, so it is important that those kinds of agreements are passed on from production to post-production.

Sometimes a person, too, will have something written into his or her contract about the credits. For instance, a big composer might have a front credit "composed by" and then somewhere buried in the end credits there might also be a "conducted by." In the U.S. the end-roller sometimes has to be passed by the Writers' and the Directors Guilds and in some cases the unions also ask for certain credits. In England, the end credits are all down to the discretion of the producer.

Usually, the nearer to the beginning that a person is credited, the better, but I am not the kind of person who would ever make a fuss about where I am listed. Some people really mind, although the end credits are only for the people who work in the film industry; 99 percent of the general public have left the theater by the time my name scrolls through!

Christo Morse
Second Assistant Director

Christo's account of his work was fascinating, partly because it directly con-trasted with that of Lisa Janowski, a first assistant director. There is absolutely noth-ing jaded in Christo's approach to his job; he is keen, eager to please and full of praise for directors, especially Steven Spielberg. While Lisa found Woody Allen's minimal direction difficult and numbing, Christo was inspired by the way Spielberg's crew had the ability and opportunity to anticipate his needs.

Some of the work of a second assistant overlaps with that of the first – for example, a second helps the first with scheduling. But there are some jobs specific to a second AD, such as the responsibility for all background artists or extras. Again the job requires a blend of creative and organizational skills, a combination which Christo delights in.

SELECTED CREDITS

The First Wives Club (Hugh Wilson 1996)
Marvin's Room (Jerry Zaks, 1996)
Conspiracy Theory (Richard Donner, 1997)
In Dreams (Neil Jordan, 1999)
Catch Me If You Can (Steven Spielberg, 2003)
Cold Mountain (Anthony Minghella, 2003)
Proof (John Madden, 2004)

My original love and passion was ski racing. I took a lot of still film and photography classes, but I was a political science major at the University of Colorado, and then I ski raced for ten years around the world! It was dur-ing the early 1990s and there was very little money in ski racing and all my friends were getting laid off, and a friend of my mum's got me on a film set and I fell right in the middle of it as a production assistant and really en-joyed the whole process.

It was an American Playhouse Movie and we had 90 Cambodian kids on our set where we had created a Cambodian village with chickens and little fires as well as soldiers walking about creating an atmosphere of terror. I would have two or three children on my back all day and set them into the scene. And it was like a family and we all bonded. When you have a good experience on a movie, everyone comes together and a lot of the normal boundaries in a workplace go away. You spend 16 hours with people, and they are very professional, but there is a familiarity and closeness that evolves, and I enjoy that.

So I worked as a production assistant for three and a half years on different movies. I also worked as Kevin Spacey's assistant for a while. It was at the beginning of his film career, when he was working on *Glengarry Glen Ross* [James Foley, 1992], and I was really impressed with his work ethic. He is truly a method actor and really goes into the details of the character he is going to take on. He did a tremendous amount of study and crafting but he lives a full life too. He lives big. Occasionally he invited me to premieres or we would have dinner with actor friends of his in the community. It was fascinating for me.

But eventually I became a second second assistant and then a key second. The key second [in the UK called just second] assistant director starts to work on a film either at the same time, or a week later than the first — anywhere from two weeks to two months before the film starts shooting. During this time, it is the job of the first assistant to produce a schedule. He or she will work with the producer, director, location manager and production designer, but the second helps with this process and is involved with all the meetings. The script is broken down scene by scene into its components: the location, the number of actors, extras, set dressing, props. With these they create the schedule, taking into account the order that the director would like to shoot (usually as chronologically as possible) but also variables like actors' and location availability.

During shooting, the first AD sets the pace of the day, determining how much can realistically be accomplished, and the second writes everything down on a call sheet with all the actors and props needed for that day. The second AD is also responsible for setting the background actors. So in pre-production I meet with the director and discuss what types of people would be seen in each environment. Then I notify the person casting extras, with a breakdown of people, times and places and what they should wear.

On the day of shooting I make sure the extras are all dressed correctly and in position, and listen in on the rehearsals with the director and the cast, and then set the background actors, giving them some direction – that is one of the more creative parts of the job.

What I find gratifying about my work is being in the middle of chaos, with so many things happening at the same time, and being able to keep calm and prioritize and help pull it all together. I enjoy organizing and also watching and seeing shots being composed beautifully. I would like to direct. One of the main functions of an assistant director is to help create the director's vision. So you need as much information from the director as possible. A film I really enjoyed working on was *In Dreams* [Neil Jordan, 1999] which starred Annette Benning, Robert Downey, Jr., and Aidan Quinn, and it was a dark, psychological murder mystery.

Neil Jordan was an extremely creative director and had some very talented people working on the film as well. His sense of creating a shot that played well was phenomenal. If he was shooting a scene where the actor was lonely, he would often pull back and show this empty space around the actor. There were demands of time and precision, and he trusted his crew to set the scene for him. Some directors don't feel they can do that and then it doesn't bring out the best in people.

I just finished working for a few days on a film with Steven Spielberg, which was fascinating for me as an assistant director – a unique experience He was only here in New York for a week but they were nearing the end of their schedule and they really packed a lot of work in, more like two weeks in four days of filming. The process was very exciting. Scene by scene, everything went very quickly. When we got to each rehearsal, often the scene was already lit. A lot of the department heads had been with Steven for five, six, seven movies and they had created a real shorthand that works together so that without many words, things happen very quickly. The crew anticipate really well, and it was amazing to see such a big production work so fast.

Normally on a feature you watch the process evolve: The scene is rehearsed, and crafted, adding lighting, background, props, set dressing, and that is great to see too. But this was more immediate. It was pretty much all laid out when we got to the rehearsal, and there would be 10 or 15 minutes' tweaking of lighting and then we would shoot. So everybody had to be ready and know what was wanted. Being new to Steven's work, I just followed in step with the other assistant directors and it was a tremendous experience to be part of that. Sometimes you get that kind of shorthand on a TV series, like *Law and Order*, which I have worked on, but it is all much smaller and more contained and manageable. On *Law and Order* we might have 10 or 15 extras working, but on *Catch Me If You Can*, we were working at JFK Airport with 225 extras and we set the scene in ten minutes. So it was a tremendous challenge but very gratifying to see it all come together.

Christo working on an episode of *Law and Order*. (Courtesy of Christopher Morse)

It had a lot to do with Steven's vision of creating beautiful shots, and also with Sergio Mimica, the first assistant director, and his ability to help him. Sergio really had a feel for Steven's work so that when Steven was in rehearsal, walking Leo DiCaprio through the scene, Sergio would intuitively know what else was needed. For instance, there was a scene at the airport where detectives carrying pictures of Leo are running through looking for him and he walks by but they don't see him. So we had to direct the background actors so that this looked feasible, so they were there, but not facing Leo directly. Sergio had an immediate vision of how to make that work, and Dave Venghaus, the second assistant on most of the movie, and I, worked with Sergio to make that happen. It was a really neat process.

Another thing which was fascinating were the shots Steven put together – they were so comprehensive. He didn't do a lot of coverage. For instance, if he was shooting you and me speaking here, other directors might do a master, wide shot to show where we are, then do a medium shot of our setting with closer coverage on our conversation, and then close-ups. Steven found ways to include many of those elements in one or two shots. He managed to show all of it and create the entire atmosphere in very few set-ups, without all the different angles, and that was inspiring.

Steven is very gracious, personable and down-to-earth. I never heard him raise his voice and he trusted his crew to create his vision. He would stand in the middle of the set and create the shot and then sit down and let people do their jobs. That's a perfect environment for people who are good at their work. It was nearing the end of the shoot and everyone on set was very focused on the work, including Steven, but he was also very friendly. After the last shot, he brought in all the New York crew and sat for five or ten minutes and gave a beautiful speech thanking us for making him feel at home and welcome on his first film shoot here. It is not unusual for a director to make a speech at the end of shooting, but his grace and poise *were* unusual and I really felt that he connected with the crew. He loves his crew and the people he works with. I felt that this goes very deep with him and that he is a real gentle man, caring, passionate and not blinded by his own creativity.

We all worked hard, and it was a period film, so the second ADs had to show up two hours early to get all the background actors ready, through makeup and costume, but we also had fun – especially in the scenes with Tom Hanks. He has a fabulous sense of humor and always found a way to get everyone laughing. On the last day we were filming in a laundromat and every take he would do something goofy and different, like crawling right into the washing machine with his entire body inside and then coming out with something silly.

For a few days working with Steven Spielberg I felt part of the family who worked on that film and that was wonderful and I felt really special being there. As hard as everyone worked, they had energy and were happy. There was a glow in their eyes and a light that shone, and connecting with that was great. It was one of the top highlights of my career. It has only just finished, and I wish I could have worked longer on it, and now I feel I need some time to reflect on it and take it all in, but I was completely blown away.

Mark Coulier
Prosthetic Makeup Designer

Mark Coulier is modest and uses "we" a lot rather than "I" – not in the royal sense – but because he is anxious that he is not credited alone for collaborative work. He is also slightly tense, and is clearly driven in regard to his work. To be a prosthetic makeup designer you need to be as interested in the process as the result, for it is quite possible that your work may never get used.

I met Mark at his workplace, on a dismal industrial estate. Entering the room, however, was like walking into a sculptor's studio. At one end, photos were set up of Pierce Brosnan's head, shot from every angle. In front was a partially sculpted clay bust, eventually to be used as the basis of a mask for a stunt double, to protect him from fire on the latest Bond film. Other busts and creature's heads stuck out from shelves and windowsills, while on a long workbench lay two silicon legs. These were amazingly lifelike, with individual hairs applied, and ghastly bloody wounds. They had been made (though actually never used) for Leonardo DiCaprio in The Beach, *molded to fit over his leg and one cheek of his bum, exactly.*

SELECTED CREDITS
Mary Shelley's Frankenstein (Kenneth Branagh, 1994)
Star Wars Episode 1 (George Lucas, 1997)
Babe: Pig in the City (George Miller, 1998)
The Mummy (Stephen Sommers, 1999)
The Beach (Danny Boyle, 2000)
Harry Potter and the Philosopher's Stone (*Harry Potter and the Sorcerer's Stone*)
  (Chris Columbus, 2001)
Harry Potter and the Chamber of Secrets (Chris Columbus, 2002)

Primarily, we are artists. That is the most important thing when designing prosthetic makeups and creatures and sculptures. You have to draw designs and understand anatomy and facial structure, which all stem from

Mark applying makeup to Xavier Keene on *Jason and the Argonauts*, TV, 2000. (Courtesy of Mark Coulier)

an artistic background. Most of the people I know who do this have been to art college or are naturally artistic.

I went to art college. I did my foundation course, and then did a two-year course in illustration because my artistic bent was leaning towards doing something commercially rather than fine art; I was more attuned to gearing my artistic abilities towards a brief. At the same time, I was really interested in the film industry, so I was hoping to be a storyboard artist or a conceptual designer or something like that. Then while I was at college I started sculpting and I realized I was much better at transferring ideas three-dimensionally. Next I found a book about prosthetic makeup in Cambridge market, and I was hooked completely from then on, just from reading that one book!

I had always been a fan of horror and fantasy films and Ray Harryhausen [American trick film specialist and model-maker] and all the other guys. There was a huge explosion in makeup effects at around the time I really got interested in cinema: films like *American Werewolf in London* [John Landis, 1981] and *The Howling* [Joe Dante, 1981] where there were fantastic werewolf transformations which had never been seen before. There were also lots of new makeups that came out at the time, like for *The Elephant Man* [David Lynch, 1980]. It all really inspired me, and I decided that that was what I really wanted to do, and I would single-mindedly try to do it. But it was very hard to find out any information apart from contacting the people who are actually doing it, like Chris Tucker who did *The Elephant Man*. Even now, the film industry is difficult to get into, and only the people who are really driven tend to be successful in getting a foot in the door.

The next step for me was to start constructing latex masks, and trying to sell them at fancy-dress shops, with no success at all! It takes a long time to make the masks, and the materials are expensive. So then I decided I really wanted to know more about makeup, and I decided to go to makeup college for a year, at the London College of Fashion. In fact it was a two-year course, but I left after the first year because I got a job in the film industry! A girl I knew was offered some work punching hair into a werewolf suit for a company called Image Animation at Shepperton Studios. They were looking for college leavers, but she couldn't do the job at the time and passed it on to me because I had done some similar work. So I worked on a film called *Waxwork* [Anthony Hickox, 1987] and that was it, really. I stayed with the same company for five or six years, going from film to film, learning and progressing.

Generally, nowadays, I design, make and apply the makeups. Sometimes there is a conceptual designer, sometimes I employ someone to do some drawings – it depends on the project – and you have to know your own strengths and weaknesses. Big films like *Star Wars* will have conceptual designers that spend two or three years doing drawings and laborious vetting processes where about 16 makeups will be honed down and those will be the ones. Then someone like me is just there to make them. Sometimes, though, I'll have as much creative input in making that design work on an actor. Other times, someone else will have designed and made the makeup and I will be the person who applies it. That is the other side of the artistry, to stick the makeup on an actor, and make it look real, blending the skin colors together. So being a makeup artist *and* a sculptor is really handy.

In my work I might use computers for design and photo compositing but I don't do any computer animation. I work with designers and visual effects artists, and the brief will involve some prosthetic makeup and then maybe some computer-generated effects on top. We work together to achieve the desired result. So, for example, we did a makeup in *The Mummy Returns* [Stephen Sommers, 2001] where they wanted a prosthetic makeup, but wanted the guy's cheek to be eaten away more than it was possible to do with prosthetics. So we put the makeup on, and then the computer animator would put tracking marks, or little white dots all over the actor's face, which enabled the animator to register the removal for each particular frame. So if they wanted to remove the character's eye, they would build a little model of the inside of the eye cavity and then track it onto each frame of footage with a software computer program and composite the two images together.

The actor's mask was made of silicon, which has recently been introduced as a prosthetic material. It used to be unsafe, but now there is medical-grade silicon, which is usable by prosthetic makeup artists. The material is translucent, so it has the feel and texture of real skin. But foam latex is still used in the majority of cases – that is latex mixed with a foaming agent in a mixer and injected into a mold and cooked in an oven, so it is like sponge rubber.

Basically, you take a life-cast of an actor, covering the face with alginate (a powder mixed with water that sets in three or four minutes into a rubbery texture) and back it with plaster bandage (like they use on casts for broken legs) to support it because it is a floppy material. We do that in two halves, front and back, and take it off the actor's head and fill it with plaster so we end up with a plaster copy of the actor's head and shoulders. Then we sculpt on top of that in clay (usually oil-based clay) whatever makeup we are going to make. That is where the artistry comes in.

So you might have a plaster nose, with a sculpted hooked nose on top. Then you would make a plaster mold of that, take the two molds apart, clean the clay out, and there is a gap between the two molds and that's where you inject the mixed-up foam latex. Then you put it in the oven, and when you open the mold again, you can peel out your new nose. The whole head is broken down into its components and each piece is made like that.

A whole face can take a few days or several months. Typically with today's budgetary constraints, an old-age sculpture for a fairly featured actor would take around two or three weeks, liaising back and forth with the director. Sometimes I turn down projects because someone will ring up and say they want a full old-age prosthetic makeup for an actor, by Friday. They don't understand the amount of time and effort that goes into making prosthetics, particularly when you turn up on set with a few small appliances and stick them on an actor, and they are transformed.

I very rarely make people nicer looking. Sometimes I might make a fantasy creature that is meant to be beautiful. But making people look older is a really interesting challenge, using what they have, and imagining what their skin is going to be like in 20 years' time. Most makeup and creature-effects people love sculpting wrinkles! Some actors get quite horrified by the aging process; others take it in their stride and are fascinated by it. The payback is that they look 20 years younger when you take them out of the makeup at the end of the day. On the other hand, you might put a makeup on some handsome extra, and he goes on set, and finds it really difficult to chat up women because you've done some horrendous boil makeup on him, or rotted corpse, or whatever. So he doesn't have the same effect he would normally have, and can be quite disappointed!

I've done some prosthetic makeup on models on a fashion shoot who hated it. One particular girl broke down in tears and had to have the makeup removed. It destroyed her confidence completely because she thought it made her look ugly. For *Nightbreed* [Clive Barker, 1990] we stuck a pair of prosthetic breasts on this lithe, long-haired guy, and turned him into a her-maphrodite. He was painted blue and was near-naked and all the guys on the set thought he was a girl with her boobs hanging out, so he had a whole day of getting lecherous comments off all the stage hands and sparks and chippies – but he loved it. He kept it really quiet and played up to it all day long, pretending he was a girl, 'til the end of the day, when he just ripped them off in front of several shocked faces.

On the same film, I did an aging fantasy makeup for an actor who was always on early. So we were there at about three or four o'clock to do his prosthetics and his beard and wig and contact lenses. One day he had a late call about three months into the shoot and all the other actors were already there, and he said "hello" to them and nobody recognized him without his makeup. He walked down the corridor and people he had spent three months working with turned away and ignored him. That was interesting.

Makeup can help the actor to become the part, and that is rewarding too. You might work quite a lot with the actor, giving them instruction to get the best out of the makeup. Sometimes the prosthetic can look like a mask because the actor is not moving his face enough. They might really have to exaggerate in a way that if they had no makeup would look ridiculous. So we can sometimes give the actor little bits of advice, which the director doesn't even know about. We just work together with the actor if they want us to. Every job is different, so I would be quite happy to carry on doing this for the next 15 or 20 years, by which time I might make a decent living out of it!

Arabian Nights is the work that I am most proud of. We won the Emmy Award for it in 1999. Steve Barron was the director, and he was very coopera- tive, and the actor, John Leguizamo, really enjoyed having prosthetic makeup put on. We did him as two genies, as a fat comical one, with a fat suit, and as the lamp genie, who was bald and tattooed, but was a much more seductive, sexy character. It was really interesting to do both. It is so rewarding when the makeup works, and when the character walks on set, people are wowed by it. That's when you get the buzz from the job. Even though it's really hard work and technical a lot of the time, and you are up at three or four in the morning, applying makeup for about five hours, every day of shooting.

They say that actors only put themselves through a really horrendous prosthetic makeup once – like say *The Grinch* [Ron Howard, 2000], although Jim Carrey has actually done it a few times – a glutton for punishment. I think they applied *The Grinch* makeup 70 times, which even for a two and a half to three-hour makeup is still a lot – for the actor and the makeup artist. People just coming into the industry may have rosy ideas of just sitting down and sculpting every day, but it's not the case.

I've just finished working with George Lucas, which was a lot of fun, although with 600 people working on the film, and visual effects in every shot, I didn't actually have a lot of interaction with him. But it was a fun project. I have worked with the director Steve Barron a lot, and enjoy work- ing with him, because he enables you to use your imagination. Some direc- tors are really specific and even if you think you are hired as an expert and your way is better, they will not budge from how they feel it should be done.

Prosthetics are very delicate to handle, too, and you have to be careful. Luckily I have never had any disasters, but you always tell actors wearing prosthetics to be very careful when they are eating food because the oils in food actually destroy the foam. But you always get one guy who will bite into a double sausage sandwich and get grease dripping down his face. On *Harry Potter* [Chris Columbus, 2001] we did a lot of goblin makeups and some guy got half a chicken tikka lunch in his chin piece, which just pulled the whole

Mark Coulier opens the wound in Leonardo DiCaprio's (prosthetic) leg.

lip off. Then you have to just do what you can – clean everything out with a cotton bud and re-glue it all back together again. Sometimes you do a makeup which takes four or five hours and then the actor will have breakfast just as you finish, and you have to spend another 20 minutes re-touching it. So the maintenance can be quite stressful. Some actors are really good with it, and you don't have to touch their makeup for ten hours and the whole thing works beautifully.

On *Harry Potter* I worked for Nick Dudman, who was the Creature Effects Designer, and there were about 30 of us just working on the goblins for months on end. They are in the film for about a minute! We also spent several months doing designs for the centaur, and at the last minute that was axed in favor of doing it as a computer-generated effect. On the other hand, computers can also create more work for the animatronics and prosthetic makeup side of things. Films get made that would not have without the advances in computers.

On *Star Wars Episode 1* [George Lucas, 1997], I made what I think is my best makeup, for a character who is in it for about a second, and I spent about two and a half months making it! It was a big, fat, blue, tentacled character. When you get the script and the breakdown of all the makeups that are required, you don't know how long they are going to be on screen. A whole creature might even get cut out at the editing stage to keep the story moving along. Sometimes the enjoyment is in actually making the thing even if it never gets seen.

In fact, doing a small TV thing where you get to do one of the main characters can be most satisfying. In a half-hour episode, you might see ten minutes of my makeup, and I get a lot of pleasure in that. I might work nine months on *Star Wars,* and yet much of the time was spent in the desert putting masks on crowd, although that is also fantastic, because you are paid to go to beautiful locations and stay in five-star hotels.

Unfortunately I didn't get to Thailand to do *The Beach* [Danny Boyle, 2000] because I was doing *Arabian Nights* at the same time and I was already committed to apply the makeup on John Leguizamo, so I sent out an associate to *The Beach*, and it was he who put the prosthetics on the "shark attack victims." We used lots of real-life reference to get the wounds to look as realistic as possible. Sometimes the damage to a limb had to look so severe, with huge bites taken out, that a prosthetic could not achieve the effect and a full silicone limb would be used. But while I was in Turkey in torrential rain, hand-painting tattoos, applying a bald-cap, a false pierced nipple, body makeup, moustache, beard, contact lenses, teeth and long black fingernails, my associate was out punching hairs into a leg and lying on a catamaran out in Thailand. I drew the short straw on that one, and it is my company!

I formed my own company four or five years ago, during which time the film industry in England has been up and down. But I have been very fortunate in that I do a bit of freelancing and then I do my own projects. I have been doing it for 15 years now, and it is still interesting. I like the cooperative element of working for someone else so long as there are some rewarding designs to sculpt and apply, but slowly and surely I want to concentrate more on my own company and hopefully get bigger and better projects to do. It is a tough job, and long hours, especially having a family and children. So the idea now, is to run the company, and let all the other keen young innovative artists come in and do the work alongside me.

Jane Clark
Storyboard Artist

A storyboard is a means of pre-planning a sequence of individual shots for a film via a series of drawings, somewhat like a comic strip, which communicate the desired visual appearance of a scene. It is said that Alfred Hitchcock would prepare an entire film in this way. More usually, storyboards are used for action sequences and the artist can play a creative role by suggesting shots or camera angles that the director may not have thought of.

Jane Clark was born in America and started her career there. When she moved to the U.K. and had a child, she made a decision to relinquish ambitions of promotion. For unlike the work of most other crew members, the job of a storyboard artist can be done partially at home. Nor does it necessitate the large team involvement of the majority of participants in the industry – when I left her basement West London flat, Jane asked me what a gaffer did. In conversation, Jane was intense and slightly bird-like as she peered over her glasses to talk to me. She displayed an unusual combination of "artiness" and pragmatism in her very candid interview – although interestingly, her final statement really belies her first.

SELECTED CREDITS

Prizzi's Honor (John Huston, 1985)
Three Men and a Baby (Leonard Nimoy, 1987)
Big (Penny Marshall, 1988)
Last Exit to Brooklyn (Donald Bellisario, 1989)
The Madness of King George (Nicholas Hytner, 1994)
Wings of the Dove (Iain Softley, 1997)
Shakespeare in Love (John Madden, 1999)
Bridget Jones's Diary (Sharon Maguire, 2001)
Captain Corelli's Mandolin (John Madden, 2001)
Harry Potter and the Prisoner of Azkaban (Alfonso Cuarón, 2004)

Let me tell you God's own honest truth: I don't give a shit what movie I work on; I honestly do not care. I really want the money. It's part of school fees now. When I was looking for a career, before I had my daughter, I was looking to be an art director through the usual route of drafting and storyboarding for a while – that's what I would have liked to have done. At the point where I decided babies were in order, it became just money.

I traded ambition for motherhood and it's been really worth it. What I should have done was had the ambition earlier, so that by the time I got to the kid, I had already been there. Maybe then I could have had both. But I don't really see how you can be a hands-on mother and do what you have to do to be an art director. When Sophie, my daughter, was born, I had a nanny until she was four, and actually, maybe I even regret that. But three years ago, when Sophie was four, I stopped going to work every day, and doing really big films, and said, "I am only going to work on things I can do at home," which is mostly commercials, and the occasional small movie.

I have to be able to stop at 4:30, when Sophie comes back from school, and pick it up again when she goes to bed if necessary. A good experience is a nice art department, a long hitch, not too much pressure. Often a film will employ you for a couple of months, and it ends up as three, but you can also work just a few weeks. Ideally, you get a movie, with no pressure on, and you say, "I'm going to do you a four day over five deal." Then you get paid for four days, but do it over five – that's perfect, with no big deadline pressure.

So this is what I do: Before they shoot a scene, especially a complicated one involving lots of different departments – things including stunts, special effects, computer generated imaging, opticals, complicated cutting (like two different locations, pretending you are in the same place when you aren't) – all those things – it's best to plan it out in advance, and think about it dramatically. That way, everyone involved knows exactly what shots are needed to cover the story and when they go there, they are not going to miss something and have to pick it up later. The storyboard artist sketches every shot, cutting the sequences together.

It is often the producer who will ask the storyboard artist to do this, or the particular department involved, like special effects. They need to know up front what the director wants to see. The director might not have time to deal with it, but the producer, wanting everything to go smoothly on the day, wants everything prepared and it might be *him* pushing for the storyboards.

Jane Clarke at her desk.

I would have looked at the location photos or the plans, and know what characters are involved in that scene. Some directors will tell you exactly where the camera will be and what it will do, and will have done their own kind of storyboards. They can be very prescriptive. But some directors ask you to do a couple of scenes just because they want to know what someone else would do with it.

From the creative point of view, of course, it is great to direct it yourself – have the director tell you nothing. That can be really great. On the other hand, it's slower because you have to think, and throw things away, and you worry, "He's going to hate this, just *hate* it" and there's all that anxiety involved. With the guy who tells you everything, you can run through a lot more frames in an hour and from a money point of view I suppose that is best. The less you have to think, the faster you can draw, the more you can turn out, and the more you can charge them.

My real skills are in drawing and in knowing what people want. If someone says a few words to me, I got it. I got it, and I can produce that for you on paper, and make you feel you were there. I remember once another storyboard artist was looking over my shoulder. He was not a particularly personable guy, and my drawings are very nice – I was an illustrator – and my drawings are fairly "arty." Anyway, this guy is more in the line-drawing department and his pictures are not pretty and he said, "I don't draw like that, I'm really more of a director." I heard him say that and felt like slapping him around a bit! But actually, having been left alone a lot, and done it for so many years, and watched newer guys sit around having to think about what is really fairly obvious, I could direct. There is a lot of "How do you see this scene?" and you have to know.

I had been an illustrator – magazines, ads, that sort of thing – and hated it, and I really wanted to be a set designer in the theater. So when I was 30 I jacked in everything and went to drama school, Yale, and learnt set design. So I started doing cheap theater and it was like two or three nights straight with no sleep in a little theater on West Broadway or something and it was quite thankless. There was never enough money to make it look like anything, or enough labor or time.

So I went to California for a few months and made a connection there and it was actually through him, that when I came back to New York, I worked on my first film, *Prizzi's Honor* [John Huston, 1985]. Suddenly people just offered me all this money! It just came along. I paid off my $9,000 student loan on one movie. But I didn't know what I was doing. This guy told me every shot and I just sat and drew it. I had seen storyboards so I made it look like a storyboard and I did my first week on that; just a couple of scenes they were shooting on location in New York.

The other person who helped me was a woman friend, Hilda, who trained at the same time as me. When you come out of Yale, you are acquainted with everyone you need to know, at

Jane drawing a storyboard.

least a little bit, and this woman from another program at NYU who was more confident and better at pushing herself got all this storyboard stuff and passed her niche on to me. She got me jobs and showed me how it was done, and she became an art director and I became one of the two or three New York storyboarders, which didn't please me particularly, but it was a living.

To start with, I bought four or five books and read up on storyboarding and camera angles and stuff like that. Then I stuck some information in an envelope and did a cold mailing, and the next day, on the quality of my drawing I am sure, because I was already a good drawer, I got hired to do *Ishtar* [Elaine May, 1987]. I still didn't know what I was doing and the production designer told me every shot. It was a mess of a movie. They were just dying to spend money. I sat there for a long time doing very little.

Anyway, I did a lot more movies in America and then decided to come to England, looking for adventure, which I found, because I got married and had a daughter. Of course, some work experiences are better than others. I enjoyed working with Stephen Frears, even though I get nothing from him except the "Go home and show me what *you* would do." Really, knowing the director is happy is the thing that makes it good. Like John Madden, who I have worked with several times, and if *he's* happy, *I'm* happy. Like everyone else in this sort of thing, you are really looking for approval. Sharon Maguire, who directed *Bridget Jones's Diary* [2001], was very nice. What is interesting is when the director is not all that sure and is really open for you to give input.

I really know I did a lot on *Bridget Jones*. That was the movie in which I felt like I could direct, because while I was waiting for Sharon Maguire to think of what she was going to do, it would come to me. It seemed clear – this is how I see it – and she was very happy to listen. And everyone, as well as the director on that film, came up to me and said that it was really, really helpful. So that was excellent for me.

On the other hand, a few directors are just not much fun to be around. Some of them just say "Do it *my* way." Peter Hewitt [*Thunderbirds*, 2000] *always* says "Do it my way." Brian Henson [*Muppets Treasure Island*, 1996], too. That's just his way with everyone. He grew up as a puppeteer, and he feels that he knows best, and actually he probably does. I once worked with a new young Scottish director, to all appearances cheerful, but one just knew that he was not half as nice as he was making out. He wanted to storyboard much more than normal, and because he was new he was indulged.

So they wasted a lot of money having me sit in on the conversations with the director of photography, which is unusual. He had an older Eastern European DP. Anyway it became clear quite early on that they weren't all that interested in what I had to say. But occasionally I would say, "Well, what if you...?" and I would get the director along a certain distance, and then just when it seemed as if I had sold him a good thing to do, the DP would break in and suggest something entirely different. I swear to God, not any better, just different, because there are a million ways of doing things. So the director would go, "Yeah, yeah, *yeah*, we'll do that!" So I'd erase all the notes, and take hours and hours, getting pressure from the producer to do this in a short time. And the same thing would happen over and over.

Then one day there was a long pause, and so I suggested something, and the other guy, the DP, cuts me off, and takes over. But he started saying exactly the same thing I had said, and the director said, "Yeah, yeah, that's *great!*" and they slapped each other's hands, and I was saying, "Excuse *me*...." Like if you direct a film, you want the credit for it yourself. But actually no one was unpleasant to me, which is the main thing.

What is nice, is that storyboarding is very much out of the firing line.

Anyone on a set, if they are not fast enough, or something like that, gets yelled at. Nobody, except Brian Henson, ever yelled at me. People are always grateful and nice. You make them pretty little pictures and they are *happy*. And that's lovely. People come up to you and pat you and smile and you never get anything but good feedback.

But any storyboard you do is not exactly what you see on the screen. It's always different when you see it. It will look similar sometimes, and you often get the feeling that that was what you did, but if you look at the actual frames that you drew, and what actually ends up on screen, it is never the same. I never feel I have played an important part in a film because it's never what I drew. When I'm proud, is if I see a set which I have designed, which I've done for a couple of movies, like *The Wind in the Willows* [Terry Jones, 1996], but I'm not proud of my part in the film when I do storyboards. They go through too many other hands and heads, so what you do is never really there. That's just how *I* see it.

For me, the challenge of the job is making someone feel like they were there from a picture, and it's fun getting a lot of little moments into one drawing. I enjoy conveying movement and making one drawing tell you several stages of the action. I might do one drawing which represents one shot or camera movement, where you see five phases. So you might be tracking in front of a man running; he gets close to camera; he fills the frame; as you pan, for a moment it is black; and then the black resolves itself into the character moving off in the other direction.

Again on another shot, you might just see a man running through a door and past a column. But on my drawing you would see that the camera is starting on his feet as he comes through the door, and by the time he is at the second column the camera is focused on his head. My storyboard is what sets the director off, but you can't take any of the credit. Occasionally you dream up some big shot, which is all your idea, and solve a problem, and occasionally you feel emotionally useful – which maybe gives the lie to everything I have said before. You always give as much as you can in your drawing. And the more you can manipulate people's feelings, I guess the more satisfaction you get out of doing the storyboard. If I know the building, say, I can really make you feel you are there. That's what I do better than other people. Every storyboarder has their thing that they do that others don't; their little something extra. That's my something extra.

Paul Wilson
Visual Effects/Miniature Photography

Paul Wilson's job, perhaps more than any other, demonstrates the interdependence of the various departments which together make movies. Paul talks frequently of the "team" involved with his work. In particular, he could not fulfill his brief without the contribution of the director of photography, the art director, the special effects supervisor, digital effects supervisor, painters, carpenters, electricians, grips, gaffers, as well as Paul's own crew.

Paul started his career in film in 1943 and got into visual effects, indirectly, because of the Beatles' lack of acting skills! Paul is a kindly, congenial man whose enthusiasm for his work has never waned. For his job consists of manipulating the audience's vision by means of the camera: almost like using Photoshop on a computer, but on a huge scale, Paul can alter the appearance of reality.

SELECTED CREDITS

Superman, Superman II, Superman III (Richard Donner, 1978; Richard Lester, 1980; Richard Lester, 1983)

Willow (Ron Howard, 1988)

Batman (Tim Burton, 1989)

Cape Fear (Martin Scorsese, 1991)

Tomorrow Never Dies (Roger Spottiswoode, 1997)

The World Is Not Enough (Michael Apted, 1999)

Die Another Day (Lee Tamahori, 2002)

Most people associate special effects with bangs and crashes, whereas visual effects are the magic that we do to change something on the screen. They cover a whole host of things. For instance, if you are sitting in this room in England, but you want the background to be China, then that would be a visual effect: I would shoot you against a green screen and then add in China as a background. An example of miniature photography is if you

The camera crew on *Goldeneye*. Paul is fourth from left; a miniature plane is held in the background. (Photo by George Whitear, courtesy of Paul Wilson)

have a castle which has got to explode: you probably can't explode a real castle, so you build a miniature one and blow that up. Or you might have a miniature plane which crashes, and my job is to photograph that and make it look full-sized.

My work is done with a camera in a studio while the film is shooting, whereas digital effects are done in post-production. For example, on *Goldeneye* [Martin Campbell, 1995] we had miniature jets which were models, with about an eight-foot wingspan, which flew, but we couldn't get them to fly together in formation. So we shot one "for real," and then the digital people reproduced two more so that it looked like there were three flying together. Another advantage of modern technology is that you used to sometimes spend all day building something and then it would collapse and you had to do it all again.

These days, you could take what you had and recreate it digitally. It is a big money and time-saver although the computers need massive memories. You take 24 frames a second, and if the camera is moving, the computer has got to compose a background, which, if it is a ten-second shot, means 240 different frames. All that is different from when I started. When I was a camera operator I worked on *Solomon and Sheba* [King Vidor, 1959] and Tyrone Power died halfway through, and we had to go back and re-shoot with Yul Brynner all the scenes that Tyrone Power had been in. Nowadays you wouldn't do that. Provided you had shots of different angles of Tyrone Power's face, you could put his head on someone else's body.

I decided I wanted to work in the camera department on films very early on. My grandfather was a pioneer amateur photographer: he was a real late-Victorian boffin who made his own cameras and built early radios and it was he who introduced me to cameras and got me interested. Then my father was dramatic critic of "The Star," a London evening newspaper, and when the war started the film critic got "called up" and so my father did two jobs, theater and films. Well one day, when I was still at school, in 1940, he asked if I would like to come with him to Ealing Studios. It was the school holidays, and I said yes. As soon as I walked in, I thought, "This is where I have got to work. This combines photography and films – it's brilliant."

When I left school in 1942, it was easy to get a job because chaps were being called up to the army. They were 18, whereas I was only 16, so I had a couple of years before I joined the Navy and I started as a second assistant cameraman at Shepherds Bush Studio at Lime Grove, which became the BBC. Then I went into the Navy as a photographer, taking photographs of enemy territory and all that sort of thing, and when I came out, I went freelance and carried on with my career, working as first assistant camera-man on films like *Miranda* [Ken Annakin, 1947], *The Sound Barrier* [David Lean, 1952] and *Father Brown* [Robert Hamer, 1954].

I worked my way up all the different grades in the camera department – first assistant and then camera operator for very many years – but I had always been interested in effects. When I worked on *Moby Dick* [John Huston, 1956], that involved a lot of large-scale miniatures of the whale, and the ship going down, at that time it was mainly the Americans who did miniature photography. Even now, it is quite a specialist thing, and actually quite a few of the people who do it in England now are people I trained! It was coincidence, how I got started, really. I was brought in as an extra camera operator on the Beatles films *Hard Day's Night* [Richard Lester, 1964] and *Help* [Richard Lester, 1965] because the Beatles couldn't do the same thing twice — not being trained actors.

In a close-up they couldn't remember that they put a glass down on a certain word — so the continuity would be all wrong when it came to editing. There might be several "takes" when the glass would seem to be put down several times, without being picked up in between. So it was decided to get three cameras in to cover the shot from different angles *simultaneously* instead of one camera doing separate shots in turn. That way we got continuity. And that's how I got to work with the director, Dick Lester, and it was through him that I got onto the first *Superman* [Richard Donner, 1978]. Dick was brought in as an additional director on *Superman* because they were so far behind, and he said he would get me a job on it too, since we had worked together before, and it was on *Superman* that I first got involved with the visual effects side.

I worked with a visual effects director called Derek Meddings and then we just stayed together, going from one film to another, doing visual effects all the time. Occasionally we would hit on a way of doing something just by chance. In the first *Superman*, Lex Luthor [Gene Hackman] captures two rockets and sends them to earth and Superman has to decide which one to chase because they split, one going one way and the other going the opposite way. Anyway, we had to do the shot of them parting at a great distance and we couldn't think how to do it. We had a rocket mounted up on a wall against a blue screen but we didn't really know how to make it look like two rockets had parted and gone their own ways. A canteen trolley came along and one of the electricians got a sandwich and he was a great salt-lover so he got the salt cellar and started sprinkling salt on this piece of bread.

And Derek Meddings said, "Paul, look at that! Could you light a stream of salt?" And I said, "Yes of course, anything." So we got a piece of black velvet which the electrician wrapped round his hand and the salt cellar, and we laid a piece of glass down and cross-lit it from the side and underneath we had a plain blue backing. All we did was run the film and took some salt and threw it so that it went in a little stream which ran out to the right and out of frame. Then we wound the film back and just next to it did another exposure and made the salt go out to the left. On the screen the next day there are just two white streaks (because you can't see anything that is black), and one goes one way and one goes the other. It was down to take three days to shoot and we did it in half an hour!

But the main challenge on *Superman* was making Christopher Reeve fly. Chris is a lovely man and so interested in the way that we were doing things and so cooperative. He didn't make any fuss like some actors do. Sometimes, Superman was a miniature, like a doll, but mainly Christopher was suspended on a contraption which fitted the shape of his body, which he lay on, leaving his arms free. This was attached to a pole placed in front of a screen onto which we projected film which made him look like he was flying through the skyscrapers of New York. You obviously never saw what he was on, and we had wind machines and all that going on too.

Originally films used back-projection, then front-projection, then blue screens and now mostly green screens. Back-projection was mainly used in the '20s and '30s to create a moving landscape while people sat in vehicles. But you could not get a screen bigger than about 30 feet across. On *Superman* we would have needed a screen 100 feet across, so we used front-projection.

Derek Meddings (front) and Paul looking at a large photo on *Goldeneye*. The camera is focusing on a slot along the center through which a real runway at Leavesden film studios is visible. Bond, riding a motorbike will chase a plane along the runway with the appearance of a mountain landscape behind. (Photo by George Whitear, courtesy of Paul Wilson)

When you do front-projection, there is a 45-degree mirror in front of the lens of the camera and the background is projected into that mirror, and reflected down the same axis as the camera. The background is projected onto a huge screen of highly reflective material, made of millions of tiny mirrors, rather like reflective road signs which glare in headlights. You need very little projected light, because the screen is so reflective. So you don't see the very faint picture of the background on Superman's face and body. As with back-projection, the camera had to be synchronized with the projector because the shutters are opening and closing, and if it wasn't synchronized it would all be a blur.

On *Superman* we also used "matting." When this technique was first used, the foreground was filmed against a matte black background and the negative of this film was combined with a separate film of the desired background. Since then, digital departments are able to work on the photographic components later on. You film the foreground subject against a blue screen and separately film the background, like, say, a street scene. These two films are then combined digitally in a process where the blue background is detected and replaced with the background film.

We almost had to change Superman's costume because half of it is blue. If we had photographed him in that pure blue, he would have holes in him where the background would show through. So we had to test colors and in the film his costume is actually a blue-green, not the pure blue it is in the comics. We had to just keep making the blue greener until it was solid and you couldn't see through it. Nowadays we wouldn't have had this problem because green screens have largely replaced blue screens, as they have been found more effective.

When *Superman* came out, I went to see it with a normal audience, not at a special crew screening, and the kids all started cheering when Superman flew, and I thought, "They really believe what we have done. They believe he's flying!" We struggled to get there, and threw so many things away that didn't work, but in the end it was all worthwhile. We learnt a lot and it showed. And I still enjoy the work because you use your brain a lot. You take it to bed with you, wondering how you will achieve something. For instance, sometimes a camera has to be specially adapted to get a shot, so that it can, say, tip over sideways or get into a confined space.

Another challenge was *Cape Fear* [Martin Scorsese, 1991], which was largely brought our way by Freddie Francis, the cinematographer. They

Paul checks his light meter. (Photo by George Whitear, courtesy of Paul Wilson)

were worried about the whole sequence when the houseboat gets wrecked and is swirling about. They couldn't do it "for real" and so Freddie said, "Why don't you do it with visual effects, using models?" Scorsese said, "Well the closest I've ever come to special effects is breaking a bottle over somebody's head!" So he left it all to Freddie to organize it in Britain (they had shot the film in America) and Martin Scorsese was delighted with what we did. He had known that it would be impossible to light and film his location in the U.S. at night, where it was all swampland, so we did it all with third-scale models. We filled half of "H" Stage at Shepperton with a big tank with a model of the houseboat and we had lightning machines and everything – and it was quite an achievement. Scorsese thought it couldn't be done, but when you see the picture, nobody would think it was miniatures.

Now I mainly do miniature photography. In addition to building a whole set in miniature, you might put a miniature painting of, say, a castle, on glass, in the foreground, or a three-dimensional one, and then in the distance you can have mountains or whatever you like. I was asked to come in as a guest and do some miniature work on *Harry Potter and the Philosopher's Stone* [U.S. title, *Harry Potter and the Sorcerer's Stone*, Chris Columbus, 2001] because they had so much to do. They used a miniature castle on that and I also photographed the part where the owl flies away over the rooftops, and the roofs were all miniatures. One problem is to get everything in focus, so you have to close the lens down to a tiny stop in order to get depth of field.

So we try to make models as big as possible, about to one-fifth scale.

They can be very beautiful and expensive to build. Those jet planes I mentioned earlier that we used on *Goldeneye* [Martin Campbell, 1995] were about one-fifth scale and powered by 20 horse power motors and they flew beautifully, even if they wouldn't fly in formation. Once, though, when we were trying them out, on the back lot of the studio, one banged into the other and disappeared over the horizon, now without wings. We thought it had gone into open country. Then a couple of days later, an old chap rode into the studio on a bike, with this plane without wings strapped to the bike and he said, "I found this in my garden. I think it might belong to you!" The planes were all hand built and cost about £40,000 and we thought it was lost for good. One way or another, things work out in the end – we overcome accidents and we achieve the effects.

In each script you come across these tricky shots which can't be done "for real" and you start to talk about how to do them. You might work this out with the cameraman or the art director – filming is all teamwork. With visual effects you often have several camera operators to insure that you get the shot because you don't really want to blow something up more than once. And without a painter or a carpenter and riggers, you couldn't do half these things. On the Bond films in particular, there is a real family feeling amongst the people who make the films. I did some work on the very first two as camera operator and now they always call me. That is why I am still working at my age. I would work for Eon any time because they are such good bosses. They will probably phone to ask me to come and do the next one, and I probably will, so long as I can still get there!

On *Moonraker* [Lewis Gilbert, 1979, Oscar-nominated for visual effects], all the space station was created in the studio and as Cubby [producer Albert Broccoli] said at the time, "When this film is shown, it will probably be science fact." But when we were making it, they hadn't even made the first shuttle take off. Eon got permission to take pictures of a real shuttle and got advice from NASA. For instance, we wanted explosions in space, but if there is no oxygen nothing will burn, so how do you shoot a space explosion to make it look real and yet not have smoke? It is teamwork. The special effects man will create the explosion, but he will know that he has to try and avoid smoke. And then he will say, "There will have to be *some* smoke, but I'll make it black." So then the art department will paint the background black so that when we photograph it, you don't see the smoke.

The clapperboard marks the shot when the helicopter will explode on *Tomorrow Never Dies*. The helicopter and the whole of the far-eastern street scene were built in miniature at the studio in England. (Photo by George Whitear, courtesy of Paul Wilson)

One thing I hated doing was a stealth boat in *Tomorrow Never Dies* [Roger Spottiswood, 1997]. It was black, painted with non-reflective paint, and we had to photograph it at night, and you couldn't see it! I had to get the lamps so they just caught a tiny glint of just the water, but black against black was dreadful! Most recently, on *Die Another Day* [Lee Tamahori, 2002], the main things I was involved with was the end sequence where the big transport plane in the magic ray all breaks up; and the ice fall over the glacier; and all the explosions on the North/South Korean border were all done in miniature.

Sometimes you have to involve an artist. Like in the previous Bond film, *The World Is Not Enough* [Michael Apted, 1999], there is a scene inside a mine where Pierce Brosnan is supposed to be falling down a lift shaft. We built a miniature lift shaft and we had to add him in falling away from us. So we had a camera on a vertical mount that went up in the air and we photographed Pierce just standing there, imagining he was falling, but it was the camera that made him look as though he was. Pierce, like Christopher Reeve, is very cooperative and interested in our work. But to me, there is still only Sean Connery. He is James Bond. I grew up watching him and worked on some of the earlier films, too. The others have been good, but never quite the same. I think Pierce Brosnan comes the closest; Roger Moore was a bit too tongue-in-cheek, and George Lazenby — well, the less said about him the better, really! But in the main, you are not really involved with the actors.

The great thing about my work is that you have an idea in your head, which you can translate, to enable people to help you make it happen on screen. And you can hardly ever say, "Oh, I've done this before." There is always something new and something to think about. It is enjoyable going to work because you think, "How the hell are we going to do it?" And then a few of you get together and try something new and it is always fascinating. I find it much more challenging than being a straightforward cameraman. I wouldn't change it. I would go and do it all again. It's almost like a doctor mending somebody's leg — you can feel that you have really done something worthwhile, that has made people enjoy themselves, or laugh, or even cry. Then you know it has worked; and it is a great business to be in.

Susan Jacobson
Clapper Loader

There are five or six main members of a camera crew, with slightly different titles in the U.K. and U.S. There is the director of photography (also known as cameraman or cinematographer), the camera operator, the first assistant camera, known in the U.K. as a focus puller, the second assistant camera and the loader. In the U.K., the last two jobs are performed by one person – the clapper loader.

So Suzie, working in England, performs two main duties. The first is working on the floor, clapping a small hinged board which synchronizes the audio and visual components of the film and identifies the shot (typically the board records the movie title, names of director and director of photography, date, slate or scene and take numbers). The second of her duties is loading the film stock into magazines which go into the camera. However, meeting Suzie on the set of Cambridge Spies *(TV Series, Tim Fywell, 2003), I saw that these responsibilities form just the bare backbone of her job.*

Amongst other things, she gets out the correct lenses each time the camera operator needs to change them; she marks the floor with tape so that actors stand in the right place; she assists the focus puller; and she looks after equipment and does a lot of administrative work. Suzie is unusual in a camera department, being female, but though she looks petite, she is full of energy.

SELECTED CREDITS

Oklahoma! (TV drama, Trevor Nunn, 1999)
Summer in the Suburbs (TV drama, David Atwood, 2000)
Second Sight: Kingdom of the Blind (TV drama, Jonas Grimas, 2000)
Nature Boy (TV mini series, 2001)
Jeffrey Archer – The Truth (TV movie, Peter Kosminsky, 2003)
Cambridge Spies (TV series, Tim Fywell, 2003)

I am not your classic clapper loader because I don't actually want to progress up the camera crew, I have aspirations to direct. I wanted to be on the camera side because I think it is very important to understand the technical, visual side as well as the acting side – and a lot of directors don't understand the technical side – so that's what drew me in. After university, I got a work experience job in a production office but I didn't like the office at all and wanted to get some experience on the floor. So I got a job as a sound trainee, which was the only opening they had. But I saw the camera department, and knew *that* was the department I wanted to be in. Being a sound trainee, I got to know some camera people and was able to become a camera trainee and then a clapper loader.

Equipment on the set of *Cambridge Spies*.

The way into many film departments is as a trainee. Often you have to be really determined, like the trainee on this film [Gabriel Hyman working on *Cambridge Spies* TV Series, Tim Fywell, 2003], and trawl the Internet for lots of names of people in the department you want to work in because it is not necessarily the head of the department who

Just before "action": Susan claps her board with the microphone above.

hires the trainee. Otherwise it is a "Catch 22" situation where you can't get a job 'til you have some experience and you can't get the experience without a job. Some films build a trainee salary into their budgets now, which is excellent. And at least there are not the same union problems that still exist in America in that here, once you have a job in the entertainment industry you can automatically get an application form and pay your fees to BECTU [Broadcasting Entertainment Cinematograph and Theatre Union] and become a member.

Being a woman in a camera department is tough because it is a very physical job and it is a very sexist industry. There are a few directors of photography who are women and some women do work through the grades, but not many. I despair. Few make it past clapper loader and it is still completely male-dominated even down to the job titles like "best boy" and "cameraman." I often look around me and think, "Wow, there are 20 people on this set and only two of them are women, and it's me and the script supervisor, who always seems to be female." *I* often get tired of having broken nails and feeling grimy and lugging heavy equipment and I think a lot of women have fallen by the wayside. I am lucky that the crews that I work with are very open to helping with the physical stuff, but there are still a lot of old-fashioned, male-dominated camera crews. I always say, "I've got arms like Popeye; don't mess with me" because I know I am strong because you have to be.

By definition, a clapper loader claps and loads. The clapper board

used to be made of wood – the classic chalk boards that everyone thinks of
– but now they are made of Perspex with just a little wooden clap stick at the
top and they are often engraved with the name of the film and then written
on with a black ink marker. Because the sound is recorded separately from
the picture, the board is used to synchronize the two. In the U.S., the board
shows the scene number; in the U.K., the slate or "set-up" number [e.g., a
close-up, which might be the two-thousandth shot but be in the first scene].
The "take" is also written on each time [e.g., however many times you repeat
the close-up].

The camera operator will say "turnover," the sound mixer will say "sound
running," I will say "56, take one" and then dash out of the way! And then
the director will say "action." The board is held before the camera for iden-
tification and in front of the boom so the sound mixer can also identify the
shot. It is clapped to make a starting point in the soundtrack, which is then
synchronized with the image of the closed board.

Additionally, at the beginning of the scene I will speak to my director
of photography [DP] and ask what sort of stock is required and then I will
assess how much will need to be loaded for that scene and go off into my
darkroom which, on location, is on my truck, and put the film into the magazines – the vehicles which allow the film to go through the camera. Then I
unload the magazines, and although it is quite simple, it is very responsible
because you are handling the film and if you do anything wrong, that's the
scene gone! I think the buzz comes from being efficient and working fast.
There is a joke that filming would go much faster if there was no camera.
Of course that is senseless but it has some truth. Changing lenses and magazines should not hold things up too much.

But clapping and loading are actually a very small part of what I do. I
see my job as supporting the entire department and making my focus puller's
life as easy as possible and taking away as many as possible of the other
things he would have to think about, like equipment, stock, stores or production office worries. Then he can do what is most important, which is to
make sure that the picture is sharp – focusing the camera by measuring the
distance between it and the person or object in shot. So I have to make sure
I have enough stock and tape and that things are repaired and that everyone is paid properly – lots of little admin duties.

I always enjoy working on something that has integrity and a good
story and is well-acted and well-directed. You can work in really tough con-

Susan outside the camera truck.

ditions, but if you know you are working on something good, it is worth it. This is great because of its subject matter. The last job I did was very interesting camera-wise. It was called *Jeffrey Archer – The Truth* [Guy Jenkin, 2003] and Guy, the director, was *very* experimental in what we did with the camera. I'm not sure it works with the drama, but from a camera-point-of-view we did some fantastic things like contra zooms – which is when you track in and zoom out or zoom in and track out, so essentially your subject stays the same but the background distorts.

On that job there was a mishap in that the magazine had not been properly closed and we lost the day's "rushes" but it was all a bit awkward because I had not loaded that magazine – I had come in three days late because I was finishing another job. So although it wasn't my fault, I was there that day and we had to re-shoot. They were pissed off, but they weren't angry. But there was one time a few years ago when something awful happened that really was my fault. I loaded the wrong stock, which meant everything was at the wrong exposure. So I told my DP (David Higgs, who I am working with at the moment), and he said, "Fine, just tell the labs to pull it one stop." But for some stupid reason I told them to *push* it one stop. So instead of being one stop over, it was now two stops and it was completely ruined. An entire scene. I ruined it, just like that; in a heartbeat.

But the irony of it all was that I got the "rushes" report in the morning and they said everything was fine, so I thought it was, but my focus puller came up to me at lunch, and said, "Actually we can't see anything; it is totally over-exposed." But it was incredibly lucky because they had over-shot everything and actually had to lose that whole leg of the story and so they never needed that scene. That is my one horror story. Everyone does it sometime. There is a story that there is a Loaders' Wood where all the loaders who have "fogged" their "rushes" go and bury their "rushes"!

Every time you have a really busy day, with three or four cameras and just you, the only thing I have in my mind is, "As long as the film is okay! As long as everything is shot on the right stock and it is all canned at the end of the day." And when it is all manic, *those* days, you feel great, when at the end of the day you have your stack of cans and all the cameras are back in their boxes and it has gone smoothly and you have run it. I have worked with the same team for the last four years or so and it is fantastic and we are like a family. It is such a dislocated industry that departments do try to stick together.

In my department, the two most important people, according to me, are my trainee and the camera truck driver. They are your support. They are the people that you can order around and know that they are going to do the little things *now*. Like I am sitting talking to you, and my trainee is up there running the floor. And good camera truck drivers are worth their weight in gold. Mine helps me carry the gear; he has the truck powered up so you can charge batteries, those little things that always have to get done.

I feel now, though, that I am coming to the end, really. I have been doing it for five years and people are beginning to ask if I am going to go to focus, but I want to concentrate on my directing. I have made a few short films and they have done okay. It is a great opportunity when you are loading! I can go off and make my little films and get all the gear and all the people for free because I know them. Normally on my shorts, I get the actors who I have worked with. And whilst loading I get to watch really interesting directors too. Peter Kosminsky, who I did *The Project* with [BBC TV, 2002], was really good – I find it fascinating how directors pull a performance out of an actor, or how actors interpret what the director says so that the whole dynamic is changed.

Tim [Fywell], directing *Secret Spies* now, tends to whisper his directions to the actors, which is probably nice for them but a shame for onlookers. Which reminds me, I should get back to work. The skills needed to be a clapper loader are "think ahead." You have to know what is going to be required in the next hour or day and have what they require before they need it. You need to be diligent and efficient. It is very organizational and the name "clapper loader" doesn't do justice to the amount of work that is needed for the job.

A clapper loader is the person you never talk to on set, because they are always so busy. And the job is about the little things. Everything has to be in the right place so you know where it is when you need it *now*. It is very anal. I always tell people I am a camera assistant because people never know what a clapper loader is and it avoids so much explanation. Sometimes I say I assist a cinematographer, because people tend to know roughly what a cinematographer does. But now *you* know what a clapper loader does!

Dennis Fraser MBE
Grip

A grip is a technician who builds, maintains and adjusts production equipment, such as dolly tracks (rails for a trolley which holds the camera) or scaffolding, on the set. The term "key grip" is only used in America, and is the title given to the chief of a group of grips; he often doubles for a construction coordinator. In the U.K., grips are specialist laborers working exclusively with equipment that the camera is mounted on. They work with a group of skilled tradesmen (called "stand-bys") consisting of a carpenter, a stagehand, a rigger, a plasterer and a painter. Dennis Fraser explained that the word "grip" is thought to have originated from the times of silent films when everybody did lots of jobs and there was a very small unit which used to keep all the tools in a bag. When someone wanted to do a job, they would ask for the "grip," meaning the bag.

After I had met Dennis, he faxed me a definition of a grip, which he said he had because so many people asked him what it was. A slightly condensed version reads as follows: "A grip should be a master in the art of jerry rigging, an inventor and should be able to build everything when the time arises. A good grip should save the company time in the shooting day and enable the director and cameraman to make shots that would be impossible without the grip's specialist skills. Demands are placed on a grip that would befuddle the average tradesman. He needs to be an instinctive engineer who constructs only what it takes to get the job done and no more. He should be able to work with grace and precision to move a camera dolly, and work in perfect harmony with the camera operator and actors to achieve the shots. A grip has to take the lead and make sure his camera crew and the rest of the unit are completely safe in what he does."

Dennis has worked in the business for 19 years on over 100 films and has been recognized and honored by many organizations as well as HRH The Queen who gave him his MBE (Member of the Order of the British Empire). He is justifiably proud of the high professional standards that characterize his career and is keen to insure that the new generation of grips receives adequate training. I talked with

Dennis at his home in Elstree, Hertfordshire, where framed photos of himself with stars such as Clint Eastwood, Jenny Agutter and Spike Milligan decorate the living room and form a gallery in the downstairs bathroom.

SELECTED CREDITS

The Yellow Rolls Royce (Anthony Asquith, 1964)
Where Eagles Dare (Brian G. Hutton, 1969)
Goodbye Mr. Chips (Herbert Ross, 1969)
Fiddler on the Roof (Norman Jewison, 1971)
Jesus Christ Superstar (Norman Jewison, 1973)
The Man Who Would Be King (John Huston, 1975)
Chariots of Fire (Hugh Hudson, 1981)
Pearl Harbor (Michael Bay, 2001)

I prefer the British system of grip to the American key grip, because in England you can rely on a crew of skilled tradesmen. So when you are building a 50-foot tower to put a camera on, you would instruct a specialist rigger who is health- and safety-conscious, rather than a group of people who are "jack-of-all trades." The grip works very closely with the director and cameraman. They tell him what they want to achieve, and then the grip will tell the stand-bys where the camera is to go and how it will be used, and then they all do the job together. But I have worked the key grip system too, with people like Clint Eastwood and John Huston.

Originally I got into the business because of where I lived. As a child I lived in London in a flat that wasn't very big and Dad was ill so we ended up coming out to Borehamwood, Elstree, to a council estate where we were given a three-bedroom council house. At that time there were seven studios within a mile of Elstree: they included MGM, ABPC, the Rock ... and obviously everyone worked in the studios, so I got a job when I was 17, in 1953, at the old British National Studios. I went in as apprentice laborer, cleaning paint pots and things for builders who were painting the studio building. My first experience with films was when I was asked to go and clean some windows ready for the painter. I went up the ladder and it was Shelley Winters' [Oscar-winning American actress] dressing room. Well, I looked up, and she was in there naked, so I rushed down the ladder again!

Two days later I walked into the studio carrying a load of paint pots, and the film company were doing an outside sequence and Shelley Winters was in a car with Glenys Johns – *To Dorothy a Son*, the film was called [U.S. title, *Cash on Delivery*, Muriel Box, 1954] – and the whole crew was there and I was this raw lad who had never been in the studios, so it was all new to me. Anyway, I had all these paint pots and they were all clattering and I was walking along and all of a sudden she saw me and (you don't mind me swearing, do you?) she said, "There's the dirty little bastard!" And I ran. And all you could hear were the paint pots clattering. And I went red. And there's about 60 crew all looking at me. That was my first experience in the studio!

I was there a year, and in those days you could get transferred to a different studio, so I went to MGM next, starting off as a stagehand. That's where you start to learn your trade. You work with carpenters and riggers and learn all your knots and how to lay tracks and then when they feel that you are capable of doing the job, they start sending you out on films. So I was a stagehand on films like *Anastasia* [Anatole Litvak, 1956] and *The Inn of the Sixth Happiness* [Mark Robson, 1958] and the films they were doing then at MGM. After about seven years, you get your confidence and know your job, and that's when I started gripping.

Nowadays no one has any training at all. Now people ask their friends or relations to take them on a film and after three days they can call themselves a grip, which is outrageous, really. I am trying to stop that and set up a training scheme for grips and grades for grips. I have spent the last two years putting together a document on health and safety on cranes which has just been passed by the health and safety committee of the industry so it is now in place. Cranes are 80-100 foot long these days and more complicated, with two people riding on them. They are all put together on the job and stripped down afterwards, and they swing over people's heads. It's dangerous and a grip has people's lives in his hands, so it is vital he knows what he is doing. If the director and cameraman haven't got good people, they can't achieve the shots. In my day you would go on a shoot and do 25-30 moves in one take. They don't do that now. It's all on rail, and no one wants to really move the camera around. They're losing that, and we need to get it back.

Nowadays grips can get away with murder. If they get it wrong, the computer can put it right. Film is faster, so the cameraman can shoot when it is almost dark and if they don't get it right, they can send it to the lab and they'll put it right for them. In the old days, if they didn't get it right they got the sack! Like with us, if you put a rig up and it was in the picture, you

On *Goodbye Mr Chips*, Herbert Ross directs from the top of the crane; Dennis Fraser (lithe bare back to camera) swings the crane across the train. (Courtesy of Dennis Fraser)

would have to do it all again the next day, whereas now they can wipe it out. Also there is far more equipment now. If I was to put a camera on a car, boat or plane now, I could phone up any rental company and get a rig for it.

One of the most difficult things I have had to do was the opening shot of *Goodbye Mr. Chips* [Herbert Ross, 1969]. It was the first shot we did on location at Sherbourne School and it was a 100-foot tracking shot [a shot taken with a moving camera, often on actual tracks]. It started off on Peter O'Toole's eyes, tracking back as he calls the register and the boys are coming in and walking up the stairs to go into the school, and we are tracking back and tracking back, and as we go we are pulling the tracks out. Then you can see the whole width of the school and the boys are still coming in, and we track back 100 foot and go into a lift and start going up 90 feet in the air. Now you see the whole of Sherbourne School and the boys are still coming in and he is still calling the register. And then you go right over the top of the school and pan round and see the whole of Sherbourne and finally zoom into a classroom and there is a boy sitting at a desk and that was the first shot of the film. I think we got it in three takes. That was one of the best shots.

The Yellow Rolls Royce [Anthony Asquith, 1964] was also interesting. We were doing a shot up a mountain and they had a girl driving who I think was supposed to be Ingrid Bergman, and she lost control of the car and it went over the side with about nine people in it. By luck, they had chopped some trees down which had been there for years and years, and the logs stopped the Rolls Royce, but it looked like it would tip any minute. We were in a tracking car in front, and I quickly got out and I had some ropes and I tied the car off and climbed round and slowly got everybody out. Then they were worried about getting the car back because really it was the star of the film, so I got a truck from the local village and we got it out and pulled it onto the road and there wasn't a scratch on it!

Some of the films I am proudest of working on are war films: Where Eagles Dare [Brian G. Hutton, 1969], Kelly's Heroes [Brian G. Hutton, 1970], Cross of Iron [Sam Peckinpah, 1977]. Peckinpah was fantastic. But the nicest film I ever worked on, which I most enjoyed, was Fiddler on the Roof [Norman Jewison, 1971]. I was out doing Kelly's Heroes with Brian Hutton, a great director and really nice man, with Clint Eastwood and a whole bunch of big stars and I was booked to come back and do another big film for MGM, and the producer, Gabriel Kotzka, told me that MGM was going to close. Well, I didn't believe him – I'd been with them for 18 years and it was a busy studio, in fact the best in Europe at the time, but Kotzka said he would bet me a pound to a suit in Savile Row that it would close when I went back, and sure enough it did. I saw him six years later on another film and I gave him his pound!

When I left, there were not that many freelance people about so I was a bit nervous about what I was going to do. Actually, Brian Hutton wrote a letter to me saying not to worry, and he said if I was in any kind of financial trouble he would help me out! That's lovely, isn't it? A director, to a grip! But I'd worked with a production manager, Larry De Waay, on two small films and he was working with a new director who was coming to England, Norman Jewison, who had made films like The Thomas Crown Affair [1968] and The Russians Are Coming, the Russians Are Coming [1966]. Larry phoned me and said I should come and have an interview with Norman, who was interviewing a load of grips in this country to go and do *Fiddler on the Roof*. He wanted an American-type key grip, and I went, and he liked me, and that was the first film I did as a freelance and it was a great film. I learned a lot from Jewison, and I went on to do all his pictures in Europe. Then he went back to America, and he asked me to go out there and I went with my wife, but she didn't like it, so after about a month we came back and I stuck it here, really. But in the first 20 years of my marriage I was away all the time. And because I was so busy I would walk in after five months and put my washing down and say, "I'm off again tomorrow." My wife brought up the children on her own. She's quite independent. She's a bit special!

Jewison was a director who knew what he wanted, and would involve you, whereas a lot of directors don't really involve you and I think they are the type of directors who are a bit insecure. If you had done a good job, Norman would make sure you knew. He was full of praise, always loyal; he was just such a nice man. One director I didn't like much was Ken Russell. Stanley Kubrick was another who I didn't want to work with after *2001: A Space Odyssey* [1969]. He had so many units on that picture and I worked on one of them. Some directors, and artists, too, think they are "God's Gift."

I didn't like Peter Sellers at all — selfish, spoilt, no regard for others. I did a film called *Ghost in the Noonday Sun* [Peter Medak, 1973] with him in Cyprus and he was a very selfish man. You would be up at four or five o'clock in the morning and build a big track or rig and get it all set up, and he would come in in the morning and decide he wasn't going to do that shot that day, and you would have to pull it all down. No regard for the crew. It was all self. I didn't like him — although I never spoke to him — he was not the sort of bloke who would come and speak to you anyway. Clint Eastwood was my favorite. He spent time with you, talking to you. I could sit and have lunch with him. He was a great technician. He knew what was going on and appreciated what you did; he used to watch you. A nice man. I still go and see him now. He remembers you as soon as you walk through the door and makes a fuss of you.

I enjoyed working with John Huston, too. On *The Man Who Would be King* [1975], the characters played by Michael Caine and Sean Connery had won a battle in the story and were walking up to the castle and John Huston was lining the shot up and he said to Ossie Morris, the cameraman, "I would love to be able to track." But it was a really, really steep hill and Ossie wasn't

A moment of closeness: John Huston (left) with Dennis Fraser (right) on *The Man Who Would Be King*. (Photo inscribed to Dennis by Huston. Courtesy of Dennis Fraser)

sure, but I tapped him on the shoulder, and I said, "I'll do it. Give me an hour and a half, and I'll do it." Ossie relied on me so much, he was lovely. And he said to John Huston, "Don't worry, we can do it, we can track." So I built this big track up the hill and put a big dolly on it and I built another one down the hill, and put it on pulleys, so it was like a lift and pulled by itself, and I did it while they were at lunch! That night I went back to the hotel and the unusual thing was that all the crew, the sound people and everybody, all came up and said they had never seen anything like it in all the years they had been in the business.

We had the same thing on *Jesus Christ Superstar* [Norman Jewison, 1973], where we were working in chalk caves and couldn't get a crane in. Norman Jewison wanted a shot starting on Jesus and then wanted to track back, so I built a track up to the roof of the cave and built another one going down.

Dennis (behind) holding Norman Jewison in his grip as the director lines up the shot for Judas on *Jesus Christ Superstar*. (Courtesy of Dennis Fraser)

Those sorts of things you have to do on the spur of the moment. It's hard to say, and I don't want to put grips down, but I don't think there are many around who do it now because they don't get the training and the opportunity. It may be that the cameramen don't think they can do it, which is a shame.

When I started gripping, Pat Newman, a fantastic grip, took me under his wing. If I hadn't worked with him, I wouldn't have been as good as I was. It's difficult to say it yourself, but people tell you that you were the best. But I still don't know who nominated me for the MBE, or why. It is all a mystery. It was funny really, getting it. I had a letter one morning in 1992 from No. 10 Downing Street, and it was a sort of a nomination saying I had been put up for an MBE and would I accept? I thought someone was having a joke with me because unfortunately, in our business, all the stars and cameramen get all the recognition. I always think that when a cameraman gets an Oscar, that his crew on the picture should get one because he certainly couldn't do it without his crew; I don't care how good a cameraman he is, he is only as good as his crew. So I couldn't imagine anyone giving me an MBE. I had no school education. I'm just a self-taught guy who loved his job and put a lot into it.

So I took the letter up to my wife who was in bed and said, "Look, someone must be having a joke," and she read it and she said "No, it's from John Major, it must be right." So I wrote and said I would accept it but they tell you you mustn't tell anyone until it is announced in the paper. But I don't know how you keep it a secret, really. Anyway, then the Queen still has to make the final decision as to whether you are going to get it or not, so you don't really know if you'll get it.

My old dad had died a year earlier and my mum was getting quite old, so I said to my wife, "I've got to tell my mum and the kids that I've been nominated," and she warned, "Don't tell anybody; you mustn't." But I insisted, "I've got to." So we were all having Christmas lunch here, round the table, and I told my family, but I said, "You must keep it secret, and not tell anyone." Then in January, when it came out, I went to work, and I looked in my paper and there was nothing in it about me getting an MBE, so I gave it 'til lunch time, and I phoned my wife, who was at my daughter's, and I said, "I haven't got it," but my daughter shouted, "You have!" so I asked, "How do you know?" and she answered, "Well, my friend found it in *her* paper." And I said, "How did your friend know about it?" and my daughter said, "Well, I couldn't keep it to myself, Dad, I've told all my friends!" Then my mum, and my wife and daughter and son went up to Buckingham Palace and it was quite a day really. I was quite proud. It was apparently "For services to the film and television industry."

One other thing I did was to form Grip House in 1981. At that time, when you had to build a rig, or put a camera on a car or train, or mount it anywhere really, you would have to build the rig on the day, which took a lot of time. So I thought it might be a good idea to design pre-rigs that people could hire for the day. Then I began to design cranes, camera mounts, tracking vehicles, dollys and everything that the grip uses, which was a whole new concept to make it a lot easier for grips. In the end, Panavision bought the company, and I decided to leave in 1997.

The last film I worked on was *Pearl Harbor* [Michael Bay, 2001], but the thing about it is, I don't really want to go away any more. Physically, I'm good, but the *hours* they do. It was an American crew, and they said the director was really, really difficult to work with, and he was the hottest thing around at the time, but I worked with him, and when I'd finished he came up to me and said, "I'd love to do another picture with you" and he phoned me two months later to go and work with him in Prague. So I was pleased.

Basically, I am working on trying to get standards up now, and I work for Chapman, a big U.S. film equipment leasing company, which keeps my head going, and I enjoy being around the business. I've had a fantastic life. I've been everywhere and done everything, met some amazing people – horrible ones, nice ones. I've worked in deserts, caves, under the sea and in the sky! And I'll show you something that a grip has never ever had, and that's from the British Society of Cinematographers. Last year they made me an Honorary Friend of their Society, and that's unknown for a grip.

John Gutierrez
Boom Operator

Many people probably feel that they have a pretty good idea of what a boom operator does. But until I talked with John I had no idea of the intricacies and demands of the job. In particular, he describes the necessity for memorizing dialogue and for balletic agility, in an account so vivid, that you can visualize him in action.

Moreover, unlike most of the people interviewed who got into the industry by knowing someone, John went to film school and made his own way. Starting out working on low-budget independent movies, his frank account of the union system is also fascinating.

SELECTED CREDITS

Hurricane Streets (Morgan J. Freeman, 1998)
Election (Alexander Payne, 1999)
Black and White (James Toback, 1999)
The Royal Tenenbaums (Wes Anderson, 2001)
Angels in America (HBO TV mini series, 2003)

The sound department on a film basically consists of a three-man team: the sound mixer, who mixes on the board; the boom operator, who holds the microphone on the end of a pole; and a cable person or utility man, who makes things easier for the others.

The pole that the boom operator holds is usually made of a light material, like carbon fiber, that telescopes so you can make it really long or quite short. At the end of the pole is a microphone which, if they are shooting outside, is covered in a synthetic furry fabric which cuts out wind noise. The boom operator's job is to place the microphone above the actors, just above the frame line of the camera, so that it can pick up all the dialogue. He has to memorize all the lines and remember the cues. So, for example, if there are three actors sitting at a table, he must remember when a line is going to be delivered and which of the actors will be speaking, so that he can position the microphone accordingly to get the best sound.

Rehearsals are very important, but also you have to have a certain intuition. You are there with the actors, interacting with them and ready to react if they change something or improvise. You also have to hold the mike very steady, so that it doesn't dip into the frame. The most common things which can go wrong are that the mike dips and is visible in the shot or that a shadow is visible. People are often not aware of this, but as a boom operator, you have to know a little bit about lighting. Imagine that there are lights everywhere to light the scene and then the boom is an added huge pole crossing the lights which could spoil the shot if it creates shadows. So you need to rehearse with the cameraman and the director of photography so that you neither cause a shadow across an actor's face nor see a shadow that looks like a microphone somewhere in the background.

You have to know the best place to position yourself, where you are not blocking any light and where you will create the least shadow. Or you might

John (left, holding boom) working on *Wrestling with Alligators*. (Courtesy of John Gutierrez)

have to climb a ladder and shoot the extended pole above the light and angle the mike. When it is impossible to get a boom to an actor, even by extending the boom to its full length of about 12 feet, a body mike is used. This is usually if it is a very wide-angle shot, or if there is a lot of fast action. A lot of sound mixers will put a body mike on an actor all the time and also have the boom in and they will split the tracks, having each mike on a different track so that the body mike acts as a backup in case they can't get a good result from the boom. But really good mixers tend not to use body mikes unless it is absolutely necessary, because the sound is much more natural from the boom.

One of the hardest jobs I had was when none of the movie was scripted. It was an independent film called *Black and White* [1999], directed by James Toback. He is a very weird director who wrote the script with no dialogue in it, just descriptions, and he just threw his actors into the mix and gave them an idea what the scene was, and then let them improvise the whole thing. He would put on a 1000-foot magazine [the film they put on the camera], which is equivalent to about ten minutes, and would yell "Action" and let the camera roll for ten minutes. You can imagine holding that mike! It's not actually heavy, but you have to hold it with your arms stretched up in the air. And you would do an average of maybe eight takes at ten minutes each and you would be holding up the boom, not knowing who would be talking, but almost performing with the actors. After we did it a couple of times the actors got into a rhythm, and you had to be in that rhythm as well.

Sometimes it is fun if actors change things a little bit – like Al Pacino. He doesn't always go with what is written in the script but changes things around a bit. Some boom operators and sound mixers would find that annoying, but I like to be challenged. When you do the same thing over and over it can get a bit stale and boring, but when an actor brings some kind of energy to the scene it is always fun and it is really nice to be part of a scene that turns out good, and you got the sound. I like shots that are either hand-held or Steadicam shots that are moving around. Then you are moving too and it is almost like a dance. You move with the actors and you move around the camera.

I remember on one movie, *The Simian Line* with Lynn Redgrave and William Hurt [Linda Yellen, 2000], they had two hand-held cameras going at the same time in a small living room. That was the most fun I have ever had on a film. I was climbing on top of furniture to get away from the cameras, and at the same time keeping the mike just above the actors while I was moving around in every direction. One camera would roll out and they would reload it while the second camera was still shooting, and another camera would come in and shoot while the second camera would roll out. Meanwhile I am still up in the air, going on with what the actors are doing. Afterwards we couldn't believe that we got it done. The camera operator was an old-time, experienced guy, and I was just a young kid who was fairly new. I look very young (I'm 31 years old now and I look like I'm 18) so around five years ago I looked like a baby and the camera operator turned to me and said, "That was some amazing stuff, kid; you did a good job." And I just felt like that was *great*.

It was what I wanted to do very early on. I went to NYU Film School and I remember that apart from taking classes in directing and making films, there were other technical classes that you had to take. I took classes in camera and photography and they did not appeal to me, but I remember taking a class in sound and when it came to teaching us about what the boom operator does, the teacher took a kid to help him demonstrate, and I saw the way he was doing it and I thought, "I could do better than that; I could do that." It's like a physical thing and I am a very physical person. I'm also a good dancer, and booming is kind of like a dance. And I just remember looking at that guy and thinking, "Wow, I could do that really good." Anyway I really enjoyed the class and although I took my directing classes, I knew I needed some kind of skill to be able to work in the business, so in my last two years I focused on sound.

I did a lot of sound for student films in my senior year, but after I graduated I didn't know how I was going to get a job and then I got a phone call from a friend from school who had made a short film which I had done the sound for. She was a production assistant on a really low-budget independent movie, and apparently the sound man who was mixing the movie was having a hard time keeping a boom operator, because the job was really disorganized and a bad job and people were quitting on him every two or three days. I would do anything at that time, so the next thing I knew, was the guy called me and told me to show up on the northeast corner of Union Square at 7:00 A.M. I showed up and there was a van there with a bunch of crew members, and I jumped in, and the van drove off to this really bad neighborhood in Brooklyn and I met the sound guy and he started to show me the ropes and teach me what I had to do. That sound mixer was called

Antonio Arroyo, and I went on to do dozens of low-budget independent films with him.

I worked for several years with him around the early '90s when there was an independent film boom, with all the festivals like Sundance and a lot of media attention, because little projects were making a lot of money and competing with bigger projects in Hollywood. Mainstream actors were working on these little projects because the subject matter was more interesting and so there was a *lot* of work. But you were not working with a union or being paid what you should have been and the hours were very long. Independent films shoot six days a week, but I was working in movies and doing something I really loved. From there it just grew and I started working on bigger projects 'til eventually I got into the union and now I am working on really big projects and getting paid very well and getting health benefits.

I've been in the union for over two years now, but it is a completely different world from the independent world. So it was kind of like starting over again because I didn't have any union connections. There are two ways to join the union: One way is to take a technical test and then get voted in. So in my case they would ask questions about sound, like "What frequencies

Boom microphone

are easier to locate?" Then, basically, you also have to know union people and make sure they come to the vote and vouch for you. But that is hard because often people don't go to these votes, so you could be there and they call your name, and they ask if anyone will vouch for you and no one stands up. An old joke in the union is that when you stand up, they say, "What's your name, who is your father, and how is he doing?" It's very incestuous – a long line of close-knit family members – so usually people get in because they are the son of so-and-so.

The other way to get in, which is the way I got in, is that I was working on a project that was eventually orga-

nized by the union. That was happening a lot. There were so many independent films being shot in New York and the union wanted a piece of the
market. So they would come onto the set and try to organize it. They would
ask the workers if they wanted to be in a union one day, and you were either
with the union or against it. Of course, I always thought that the union was
my future, so they organized the job I was working on and I guess I pledged
my loyalty to them and I walked off the job. Then one day they gave me a
form and said "Come down to the office" and I paid them the money that I
needed to, and because I had shown my loyalty to them by walking off the
film, I didn't have to take the test. So now I pay union dues to the union
which covers the grips, electrics, sound, video and props.

Once you are in the union, you cannot take any non-union jobs or you
will get into trouble. So I've had to rebuild my contacts, starting low first. I
am slowly building my reputation again in *this* world. I had a reputation in
the independent world for being really good and people sought me out,
and I am hoping that will happen again. Actually, I have been working
more as a utility man and am getting a reputation as a utility man who can
boom good. At present I am working on a mini-series for HBO called *Angels
in America*, based on the play by Tony Kushner. The sound mixer knew it
would be a heavily dialogue-driven project, with a lot of double booming, or
two booms going at the same time. So he needed a utility man who was good
with the equipment and could also boom, and he heard about me, which is
how I landed this job.

I am the second boom now, so my immediate goal is to become the first
boom on a big project – which could happen on this project because the
first boom on this job is going to move on to something else, so the sound
mixer may find another utility guy and bump me up to first boom. I love
booming and I want to continue doing it. I would like to be the boom operator on really big productions. Maybe down the line, because it is a physical
job, and I guess it will get harder and harder to hold that mike up in the air,
I guess I will have to think about doing something else – maybe sound
mixer. But I'm not really thinking that far ahead. I'm still young and I hope
I can still do this for another ten years, or more.

Larry Prinz
Gaffer

A gaffer is the head of the electrical department. In early English, the word meant "old man" but more appropriately, it has also come to mean "chief."

Larry Prinz is a courteous, soft-spoken American living in England. His eyes twinkle in conversation, as he is by turns frank, funny and informative. What emerges most strongly is the unpredictability of filmmaking, and the importance of a happy crew who work well as a team.

Although eventually Larry would like to be a director of photography, for now he is obviously proud of his title — the name he uses for his email address is lpgaffer@...

SELECTED CREDITS

Caravaggio (Derek Jarman, 1986)
Close My Eyes (Stephen Poliakoff, 1991)
The Snapper (Stephen Frears, 1995)
Kansas City (Robert Altman, 1996)
Sweeney Todd (TV Drama, John Schlesinger, 1998)
The Designated Mourner (David Hare, 1998)
The Lost Son (Chris Menges, 1999)
Gladiator (Ridley Scott, 2000)
Ali G Indahouse (Mark Mylod, 2002)

I grew up in Los Angeles, right behind Columbia Studios and within a mile of Warners, Disney and Universal Studios, and yet at that time I never seriously considered working in films. I went to university and studied marine geology (which still fascinates me) and then went traveling. When I was in Israel I went to Eilat, and in the early 1970s there was a copper mine where they took on people to work, so I lived in a cave with four friends, just outside of town in an area called the wadi. Actually, we were quite lucky to have a cave! There were lots of other itinerant workers, living in shacks and all sorts along the river. We had a pet bat who would fly up and down. One of us would be the alarm clock, and as the rest of us were asleep in the cave he would watch the sun come up over the Jordanian hills. Then he'd wake us up and that would give us time to get dressed, walk into town and catch the bus to the mines. And I did that for about a month.

At the same time, my sister was also in Eilat. She had a job as a chambermaid in one of the best hotels in town, and she got a job babysitting the kids of an American producer called Paul Maslansky, who has since made films like *Police Academy* [1984] and *The Russia House* [1990] and and so on. Anyway, my sister convinced me to go with her one night because she didn't want to walk home in the dark. So, grudgingly, I went along with her, and I met Paul, and when he came back that evening, he offered me a job as second assistant director. I think because he was doing a film with a British crew he missed an American voice! And I guess he took a liking to me. Anyway he was my first guardian angel.

So I said, "Yes, I'd love a job, get me out of the mine, that'd be great!" So then he said, "Give me a call in two days and I'll see if I can arrange it." Well, I thought, "Oh, yeah, he's probably leaving town tomorrow and when I ring him he won't be there." But then three days later I eventually got around to ringing him and his wife answered and said, "Paul's been waiting for your call. He'd like you to start tomorrow!" So I left the mines and started work on the film. I was the runner – the young boy who runs around doing everything and works 18 hours a day, but I was thrilled. The film was called *Big Truck and Poor Clare* and starred Peter Ustinov and Francesca Annis, and it never actually got released. It was directed by Robert Ellis Miller, whose later claim to fame was *The Heart Is a Lonely Hunter* [1968].

On the film I made friends with the gaffer, who was an English guy called Ron Pearce, and we became mates. Ron was in Israel to start a branch of Lee's Lighting, so he was there for several months and he was also doing a couple of low-budget Israeli films. Anyway, I had done some courses in electrics and a film course while I was at university, and I love photography, so I knew a little bit about lighting. So I decided to ask Ron if I could help him out with lighting at all. But he said that unfortunately he had just hired someone so he couldn't take me for his next film. Then three days later he phoned me to say this guy's wife was ill and he had to back out, and would I like to work? So one week later I was on my first film as a lighting electrician. And even though it was low-budget and produced by a scheming shyster

Gaffer tape: heavy-duty adhesive tape, backed with canvas, used by the gaffer and others to secure objects on film sets.

who did everything ultra-cheap, it was fun and I learned a lot.

I worked with Ron on two films in Israel, and then he left to come back to London, but he told me, "If you want a job in London, come and see me." So a year later, having worked on a few more films with an Israeli gaffer, I came back through London really expecting nothing. I was enamored of films, but I really didn't expect Ron would remember me, much less give me a job.

I went to see him just to say hello. Within an hour of meeting him I had probably drunk more beer than I had in my entire life (I was pissed as a rat), and a week later I was working at Lee's in London. Ron was able to claim, which was partly true, that they were training me to run the company back in Israel. So I got a work permit and a visa and worked there for two years, mainly in the stores, learning all their gear and their system and loading trucks most of the time. Occasionally I would go out on a job as extra labor, so I got into the union. I was about 21, and I loved London. I have no real desire to go back to Los Angeles. Knowing that the film industry is a lot stronger out there, I still like a lot about England and there is a lot I don't like about Los Angeles – so I am happy to stay here.

On any film, the first person to be appointed in the lighting department is the director of photography, who in pre-production, along with the director, will hash out the philosophical aspects of the film. Then the DP will say who he wants as his gaffer, and we will talk about locations, about how we see the film. Then it is my job to put it into practical terms – to physically get that done. So I get the equipment, hire the crew, work out logistics and all that. I am also another pair of eyes for the DP, so I will look at how we are lighting a scene, and if I see things which could be improved, depending on the DP, I will go ahead and do it, or discuss it. My assistant is the best boy, who is like the crew foreman and looks after the labor side of it. Then there is a generator operator and however many sparks you need, and off we go.

When I was younger I preferred working on location, feeling that studio work was too restricting. But now I realize that you have a level of control in the studio and you come to appreciate that. I like change, and on a film certainly every week is different. One of my most satisfying jobs was as rigging gaffer – the guy who makes sure that everything is ready for the shooting crew – on *Gladiator* [Ridley Scott, 2000]. It was quite a challenge because of the size of it all – huge amounts of cable. I think I had three miles of mains cable spread out around the set in Malta!

I had a crew of 12 Croatian electricians who were wonderful. If we didn't have something, they would search around the site for bits of scrap metal and make it. They were great. But with a budget that big, the stakes are high, and to keep the shooting crew waiting is a monumental expense. You would just finish getting one set ready and someone would come up and say "They're not going to do that scene now" and you would have to tear everything down and race it over to another set. They might want to do night shooting in the middle of the day, and you would have to set up big black drapes. It was always a race. We had about six huge container-loads of gear and it still wasn't enough.

On a film that large, there is always a lot of pressure – a lot of egos and battles of will to contend with, personality clashes, etc. We kept away from all that, and me and the Croatians had a ball! We worked hard, but we had a good laugh, whereas the shooting crew was under a lot more stress. But when you are dealing with delicate pieces of electronic equipment, there will always be things that don't work when you want them to, like a big light going out, etc. But whereas the camera crew always handle their cameras with care, electricians mainly handle metal and wire and robust stuff, so you don't realize how dust and damp can affect electronics.

You might be on a night shoot and have this wonderful brand-spanking-new remote controlled "cherry picker" – a 150-foot crane with a basket attached – that has all these individually controlled lights, and you spend hours getting it all rigged up. Then you test it all and it works fine, until they all turn up to do the filming, and one light stops working. And then that one starts working and another one stops and it's like musical lights, and I'm on my knees praying every time we switch a light on. I spend a lot of time on jobs praying!

Nothing goes right on films. You turn up at the seaside and the tide is totally opposite of what you thought it would be, so your set is either under water or the sea is 500 yards further away than you wanted. Another time you think it will be okay to get a generator into position on some street, but come the night, there is some idiot who has parked his car there and refuses to move. So you move the generator someplace else and you pray to God that you have enough cable because it's further away, and then someone comes down and says the exhaust of the generator is coming into their house and they want it moved. Or you are shooting in a stately home and you can't even breathe without some sort of restrictions.

One time we were in a house outside of Esher [southwest of London] – a £6,000,000 house owned by an Arab family. I don't know why they let us in, but they did and we were walking on eggshells because everything was precious. We were shooting in the lounge which had these huge curtained windows that went onto a patio, and I very carefully put a couple of lights close to the curtains, but far enough away so that they couldn't burn them. I think it was the director of photography who came along and moved the light a bit so the back of one light touched the curtain. And at the end of the shot I saw this and pulled the lamp away and there was a hole about the size of a 50 pence piece right in the middle of the curtain. Luckily it was in a pleat, so no one saw it, and we just got out of there as quickly as possible.

Once we were in a house where we were told not to touch anything. Then the director came in and sat on an antique table and it collapsed. Other times we have had antique fireplaces, and they have said it was okay to build a fire, but we have built a fire so hot that all the ironwork melted! Crews are pretty good generally about being careful, but we are all human and there are just too many people and too much equipment in too small an area. No film goes by without some disaster, so you have to be relaxed and flexible. You do recces months before shooting, and you've got all your notes and then you get there for the shoot and everything has changed. Or you can't even find the location, or the flight is terribly delayed. In fact, that is one of the fun things about film: You never know what disasters will happen.

I did a film in Jordan five years ago, and I had nine electricians from Egypt, Iraq, Algeria, Jordan, Syria, Lebanon (and I'm Jewish) and only one of them spoke English, and only one was an actual electrician – he was from Egypt and didn't speak a word of English. So you just hope to God that the translation is right and they don't kill themselves hooking onto electricity. Occasionally there is a terrible accident, but there is now much greater health and safety awareness.

Once, up in the Orkneys, I had a crew member who was terrified of heights but too proud to tell me. So I sent him up on a small cherry picker only about 30 feet, and there was a wind blowing and I said, "Frank, can you take it up another five feet," and he said "No, you must be joking. There's no way. It's too dangerous." And when he came down he had a go at me that I was putting my crew at risk and didn't care if they lived or died. I only found out afterwards that he was terrified of heights. I just wish he had told me. Part of our job is to come up with alternatives to get the job done without putting people at risk.

Two lights rigged to "cherry pickers" add to the illumination of an interior second floor apartment.

Years ago, on *Let Him Have It* [Peter Medac, 1991], we had two weeks of nights that were absolutely freezing, and in those days when you had a big crane you had to send someone to sit there for ages, wrapped up as best they could. One guy was a genius at that. He would offer to go up and get himself some polystyrene and build himself a little hut and get a small light to keep warm in there, and have his walkie-talkie beside him and he would fall asleep. Then we would shout and he would do what you wanted and then go back to sleep.

Some jobs are sheer hell to work on, others sheer joy. Ninety-five percent of what makes the difference is the other people who you are working with. You could be in the Caribbean on a job that should be paradise and you can't wait to get home. Or you can be in some awful docklands area of a city in freezing terrible conditions but the crew gels and it's a laugh and great fun. You take your cue from the producer and the director. If they are nice and happy and you respect them and they respect you, then everything goes well. If you have a director or a DP who doesn't know what they're doing, then it can be a nightmare. Or you might get a producer who is just a mean miserable sod who treats the crew like shit.

Nikki Kentish Barnes, one of the producers I worked with most recently, on *High Heels and Low Lifes* [Mel Smith, 2001], was one of the nicest, fairest, most knowledgeable producers I have worked with for ages. She is a filmmaker. She knows what is involved and what's needed – not just an accountant only looking at the balance sheet. Branko Lustig, the producer on *Gladiator*, was a tough cookie. He was a guy who had survived the concentration camps, very lucky to be alive, and he was responsible for a budget of $150,000,000 or so! His head could roll further than anyone's, so he had to be tough, but if you have the money up front, then it's better to spend it rather than possibly spend more on putting things right afterwards.

Generally, money is tighter these days. And I find that filming in general isn't as much fun as it used to be because your schedules and budgets are cut down to the bare minimum. What you would have done in eight weeks five years ago, they want you to do in six weeks now. So you don't have time to laugh, or enjoy yourself as much. It's a bit sad because if you enjoy what you do, you work a lot better – it shows.

Attitude is very important. You need a crew that is positive and cheerful. Lately I have had crews who have made my life a lot easier, but in the past I have worked with crews and wanted to cut my wrists or throat or both just to get away from them! A crew makes a difference to every aspect of the film. In the States it's more common to have female electricians, but it's probably about eight years since I used one. There were some really good ones, but they seem to have disappeared. They had a hard time breaking into the work. There were sexist attitudes and prejudice, and even if they are good at their job, they also have to get along with the boys.

I have a few guys who are quite loyal now and might turn down work to be on a crew with me — five or six really great guys. And in fact attitudes have improved over the years. Thirty years ago, electricians had a reputation for being bolshie, sinking three pints every lunchtime and being the really rough rogues of the crew. But these days nobody can afford to carry people with that attitude. If you can all work together and get on with each other, filming is great.

The mark to me of a good film is if, while I'm watching it, it takes me away or gets me involved so I don't think about the technical aspects. I think the film industry is changing a lot with the increase of digital computer graphics and all the new techniques which are not done on the set but are done post-production. I don't think crews will become redundant, but I think that as computers become more prolific and more advanced, people will say, "Look, it doesn't have to be perfect, we can fix that later." So in a way it can make you a bit more lax and lazy, and there is the danger that some people in some departments may start not to care as much as they should.

On the other hand, computers were responsible for some brilliant effects and scenes in *Gladiator*, like the wide shots of Rome. The basic set in Malta, which we added onto, was a huge Napoleonic fort, which luckily had Roman columns which blended in quite well. We added shiploads of plaster, scaffolding and timber. These guys did magic. When I walked onto the set for the first time, it was the Coliseum — maybe a quarter of the size, but all the statues and temples and everything, all made of plaster with wooden frames and hollow. It was so clever.

But with the addition of a computer, they could make the Coliseum they built, which was 50 feet high, 200 feet high. They could turn 2,000 extras into 80,000 people. You could have a shot where our hero is approaching Rome in a horse-drawn cart and all you might really see is one small building. On the film you see the whole of Rome in the background with birds flying through, and whiffs of smoke — it's all added digitally afterwards. The computer budget on *Gladiator* was probably bigger than the whole budget of most British films, but even so the lighting done on the set was precise, exacting and very demanding. You had the best of both worlds, which combined, made a brilliant-looking film. There's room for both the old and new technologies.

I have always loved photography and I always thought it would be nice to be a DP though I know that at this point, in my fifties, the chances are pretty remote. I have done a small amount of work as a DP and it's a nice thing. The buck stops with you. Your decisions matter and you can make a real visible contribution to the film, and when you get it right it's a great feeling. I mean, it's a great feeling when I get it right as a gaffer, but I don't want to be 60 years old and schlepping lights and cable up the hill in pouring rain. I'd much rather carry the light meter and tell everyone else to carry the other things. But if it doesn't happen, I'll just do the best I can.

Helen Blackshaw
Costume Assistant

I met Helen Blackshaw on a freezing February day on location in King's Cross during the filming of Episode 2 of Murder Rooms, *directed by Paul Marcus. We put a bench in a tiny patch of sun under the railway arches which formed the Victorian backdrop to the BBC drama. Despite the ubiquitous black padded "Michelin man" jacket worn by virtually all crew, Helen still looked slim and pretty.*

She is sometimes treated appallingly by actors, but she adores her job, and was very funny talking about it. What struck me is that women who work on films seem obliged to perform an additional role to their job specification, and it is one which they all seem to do quite willingly — that of confidante or counselor.

SELECTED CREDITS
The Grand I & II (Granada TV, 2000)
Star for a Nite (BBC TV, 2000)
Dream Team III (Sky TV, 2001)
Ruby Wax Dinner Dates (BBC TV, 2001)
Holby City (BBC TV, 2001)
Murder Rooms (BBC TV, 2001)

TV is different from working on feature films: it can be more institutionalized, where people say, "We don't do that at the BBC" and people are more used to working in the studio, and you tend to get different crews.

I got into it by accident. I had trained to act, and discovered that I was an incredibly mediocre actor. Anyway, a friend of mine was working as a makeup artist at the Royal Exchange Theatre in Manchester and she asked me to come and model for her. She said she couldn't get me any money for modeling, but she could get me a job as a dresser. So I did that, but soon afterwards an IRA bomb went off in Manchester, and all the theaters were closed and there was nothing going on. But the BBC were great, and said,

"If there is anyone who wants to work, they can come and work for us."

So I started to do quiz shows and then I lied my way desperately into Granada TV. I phoned a costume designer and she asked if I had ever done any costume drama and I said, "Absolutely loads." And although she knew I hadn't done any at all, she was willing to give me a chance. Costume is more interesting in the long run. If you are doing a contemporary show, you get to shop for the characters, which is interesting to a point, but in a costume drama there is the research and the going out looking for nice fabrics and bits of jewelry. It is a lot more satisfying to know that you personally found something, even a hatpin which no one is going to see. But you know it is real and has history and belonged to someone, and then you see it on screen and think, "Yes, it's just right for that person."

My role here is to prepare the actors' costumes, to do the washing and the ironing for them, and get them dressed at the start of the day, because of course with costume drama it is hard to get into corsets and things. Then I monitor them all day, checking there is no fluff on anything, and being aware of all the continuity – making sure that if we shoot from a different angle, something is in the same place as it was in the first place. On this, Paul [Marcus] is great. Some directors don't like to be approached about costume things – they think it's our job. But just now, I saw Stuart Richman, acting The Respectable Gentleman, without his hat on. But in the period, he wouldn't have taken his hat off, so I was able to go up to Paul and he was happy to change it.

In period things, people get obsessed with hats and lots of producers don't like them because you can't see the character's face. But they're accurate. So it is a compromise between getting it how it would have been and what the audience expects. For example, before I did this I was working on *Holby City* [BBC TV, 2001] and all the surgeons wore masks, but actually in a lot of operating theaters surgeons don't wear masks any more as they are thought not to be really protective. But the audience expects operating theater masks, so you have to go with the audience, or people would write in in droves. You have to get the balance between what's real and what works for TV.

I've done quite a lot of Victoriana, but you still have to keep on top of it. You could think, "Well, I've done this before, so I know what it's like," but it's always good to keep your research going. And it gives you other ideas. So there is that aspect as well as things like the washing. I really do enjoy doing

Helen ironing — a job she claims to enjoy when the shirts are not hers and she can see a perfect result. (Courtesy of Helen Blackshaw)

the laundry — because it's not mine, and at the end of the day you might have ten shirts to do, but you can really see what you've done. I see all those shirts lined up, perfectly ironed, and I'm really pleased!

One of the most satisfying things I've worked on was a soap opera called *Dream Team* [Sky TV, 2001], which is a bit like *Hollyoaks* meets football — a team soap — and they were just the nicest crew I have ever worked with. It was for no money, just scratting about, but you knew at the end of the day that you really had to make it work. We might have 30 quid to go out and buy an outfit for someone who is meant to be a footballer's wife. On contemporary things, the designer is more likely to let me go and do little things myself. Some designers don't want you to do anything because it is their baby, whereas others are more trusting.

Some of the worst experiences are with actors. Certain actors need a lot of attention. I had one actress who was tiny, a size 8 [British], but she was so paranoid about her bottom that she wouldn't go out in front of the camera unless I had stood with her, with our backs to a mirror, comparing bottoms! And I would have to say, "No, it's really tiny, it's a tiny bottom, much smaller than mine." But at the end of it all, I would feel like a great big heffalump.

When I worked in the theater, a very famous actress was wearing a great big frock and she wouldn't go to the bathroom. She would get me to come and hold a sand bucket underneath this big dress while she peed in the bucket! I would never work with her again; she was a nightmare. And then when I left, she gave me a packet of three Marks & Spencer's cheapest knickers as a leaving gift. She was bizarre, and loaded! All the actors know they can't do it without you, because you could let them look a fool, and some of them can't handle that.

Some big names are incredibly "starry" and expect everything done for them; conversely, some very big names do everything for themselves. And you have to judge, too, because some people like to be fussed while others don't. You have to be diplomatic, and sometimes you have to kowtow to people who you know are rubbish and just doing it to wind you up and get some sort of kick out of it. But at the end of the day, my job is to make sure that the actor is okay when he/she gets on stage. Because if an actor has been winding you up and you give as good as you've got, they won't be in the right frame of mind to do their job – and I consider that my responsibility.

Then again, it is good dinner party conversation if you have been working with a big star who is a real bitch. There is one actress who had a minuscule roll of fat over some leather trousers, but she was gagging to wear the trousers. So I said, "Perhaps you could hold your coat closed, so you don't see... (and I didn't say "the roll of fat") because it's nice if we see it closed and it looks really good...," etc.

So we did all that, and then in the middle of the day I went up to her to say, "Maybe you could just close the coat" and she went into this great big outburst of "I know you're just jealous of me" in front of the whole crew. Obviously I'd wound her up by going and faffing with her, but if she had seen herself afterwards with her tummy out she would have been even more gutted. Most of them are okay, though. Once I was working a six-day week, about 15-hour days, and at the end of the week on the Sunday, one of the actresses had booked me a massage!

The thing is that you have seen them in their underwear, first thing in the morning, with no makeup on, with scraggy old knickers, and they have to trust you. I do feel appreciated for what I do by most people and I do have a lot of job satisfaction. You know, it's freezing cold and miserable at half five in the morning, and you are standing outside the wardrobe wagon smoking a fag, and you see all these actors walking past in period costumes and you think, "I'm really privileged to be doing this." It's not like a proper job; that's the best thing about it.

Kenneth Dodd
Best Boy Electric

Whenever I talk to people outside the industry about film crew, the term "best boy" is the one that most often intrigues. Yet Kenneth takes his title for granted and did not know its derivation – which, according to the Internet Movie Database, "is likely borrowed from early sailing and whaling crews, as sailors were often employed to set up and work rigging in theatres. There are no 'best girls' per se; female chief assistants are also called best boys."

In the U.S., Kenneth's title is best boy electric, as opposed to best boy grip, whereas in the U.K. there is just one best boy, who is the chief assistant of the gaffer and second in command of a group of technicians. Either way, the best boy is not a beginner or a very young man, as the name might suggest. Kenneth, in his thirties, is someone who enjoys working with different people in changing situations, although he admits that his job is not glamorous and can even be boring. Talking with him, I became very conscious of the particular lifestyle of many film crew: long hours; closeness with co-workers; constantly changing jobs; and the need to keep on working.

SELECTED CREDITS

100 Center Street (TV Series, 2001)
The Devil and Daniel Webster (Alec Baldwin, 2002)
The Palace Thief (Michael Hoffman, 2002)
Analyze That (Harold Ramis, 2002)

When people ask what I do, I say, "I do lighting for movies." Then they think I work in movie theaters and I say, "No, I do lighting for films," and then immediately they ask, "Who have you met?" When you first start out, it is really cool that you are working with all these stars but now it is no big thing; they are just normal people like everybody else. And film crew are pretty normal people too. On a regular crew, I handle around seven guys,

Kenneth Dodd (Courtesy of Kenneth Dodd)

although it might be as many as 25 on some days. My job is to tell the guys what to do and I also do a lot of paperwork, to take the pressure off the gaffer. He mostly stays on set with the cameraperson and my job is to handle the behind-the-scenes things, like ordering extra equipment, keeping track of the men, time cards, making sure I have the right stuff on set for what we are doing, and getting organized for the next day.

I started out as an electric and naturally progressed from there. I always *knew* eventually that I would work in films, but I only started when I was 23, because I wanted to have a life before that. So I had a regular job – I worked in electrical supply, and in an electrical rental house – I wanted an eight-hour-a-day job because I wanted to do the normal things that young guys do. I wanted to hang out with my friends and things like that which you can't do when you work in movies because you don't get home sometimes until Saturday morning and you are doing 12- and 15-hour days. Now I have been in the business about seven years, and eventually I will move up to gaffer and then maybe I'll try to get to be a director of photography.

I enjoy the different things every day. No one on the crew is an office-type person. That's why you have this job – because you don't want to be in an office seeing the same people and doing the same thing for 20 years. When you are on a long movie, after two months you get tired of the people you are working with, because you are not used to seeing the same people for so long! Also, you are stuck with them for 15 hours a day: you see the people you work with more than the people you love. So you try to hire guys that work hard and that you get along with. You can't have personality conflicts or you'll be killing each other! Normally if you don't like someone you work with, you try to stay away from them, but in this job, you can't.

If you have a nice director and there is a good feeling, it makes you want to work harder and go that extra. I did a movie recently called *The Palace Thief* [Michael Hoffman, 2002] and from everybody down – the director, cameraman, production manager, all the way to the bottom – everybody was great. If you get someone who is really bad, you don't want to do the job. Even though you try to be professional, your emotions always come into it. It's hard when people are nasty or when the set is tense. But the great thing about our job is that you know you can put up with anything for three months. Most people, if they have a job in an office and their boss stinks, end up quitting; I can stick it out and then go on to a new job with totally new people.

At present I am working on a film starring Robert De Niro [*Analyze That*, Harold Ramis, 2002]. There are certain people you always want to work with and De Niro is one because I think he is amazing. Actually, he is a lot funnier than I thought he would be, because of his ad-libs. Then also, the bigger the stars, the more people see the movie, and the bigger the budget, and that's all good for your résumé.

So I make sure everything runs smoothly and I save the film money: by knocking guys off early if I can, and not getting them meal penalties. Because that is how you *do* get the next job. If you spend a fortune, the production manager is going to notice, and next time she has a job she'll think,

Lighting cable

"I don't want this guy." The production manager's job is to keep the money as low as possible, so you try to make other people look good and then they want you to be on their next movie. I get my satisfaction making them happy and getting more work.

Of course, sometimes things go wrong – naturally I've walked into shots – and then we all play practical jokes on each other because you *are* working long hours so you try to keep it funny and stop it getting too tense or too boring. For instance, you might set up and then sit around for three hours. So you might tie someone to a sand bag and give them 50 feet of cord and then they can't walk any more. Or you tie soda cans to the end of a long piece of string and spring-clip it to someone's shirt or pants and they walk a hundred feet while the film is shooting and then all of a sudden the cans start rolling and the person keeps walking because they don't know it is them because the noise is so far away. You send location guys to the VIP section of restaurants saying the whole crew is going to go there and then you never show up. Little things like that lighten up the mood. Actually, no one has ever done much to me, because they know I will get them back because *I'm* usually the practical joker.

People who have regular jobs, think working in movies is very glamorous, but it's not. They don't realize that you go into condemned buildings that are dirty, that have asbestos and rats. You might be working in Harlem down an alley at three A.M., and I mean the building is abandoned for a reason and you are filming in it. And people disregard things they shouldn't, sometimes, so you hear of crew falling through roofs when it is not secure enough, and there are stuff like nails and glass. In California if you film in an alley, they go in and clean the whole alley out and then bring in their own garbage! But in New York, they don't do that. You are filming in real garbage sometimes. On the other hand, going away for short spells on a movie is great: You stay in a hotel; you don't have to worry about cleaning or food; it can be much easier. And because people *think* it's glamorous, you do get treated as someone special.

Peter Hutchinson
Special Effects Supervisor

Special effects are illusions created on a film set, as opposed to visual effects, which are created by the camera, and digital effects which are added in post-production.

Peter Hutchinson has 35 years' experience in special effects, and while he may not get fired up over pyrotechnics, or heated over explosions, his easygoing manner does not conceal some strongly held views. He is adamant about safety; annoyed by lack of recognition of his craft in the credits; and angered by penny-pinching. Along with many crew members, Peter reiterated how important it is for the director to know what he or she wants and to be able to communicate it, but Peter's job satisfaction is also determined by budget, and in this respect, his account of his experiences is surprising.

SELECTED CREDITS

Yanks (John Schlesinger, 1979)
The Long Good Friday (John Mackenzie, 1980)
Local Hero (Bill Forsyth, 1983)
The Mission (Roland Joffe, 1986)
The Crying Game (Neil Jordan, 1992)
Smilla's Sense of Snow (Bille August, 1997)
Star Wars Episode I: The Phantom Menace (George Lucas, 1999)
Hidalgo (Joe Johnston, 2004)

First of all, a special effects supervisor who has been successful in getting the job reads the script and compiles a special effects budget and breakdown. He also chooses a crew made up of senior technicians, technicians and probably some trainees, depending upon what type of effects are required. For instance, if it is a drama set at sea where there is lots of rain, wind, water, and maybe putting part of a ship on a hydraulic rocker, then you would have guys who you know are good at working on the floor making the rain and wind work and talking to the director to insure everything runs smoothly, but who also have some engineering skills to make the ship rock back and forth.

A different type of film might involve car chases with stunt men where you might need to make rigs to help them make cars turn over, or put cars on wires to crash into specially built houses made to collapse, or even fire cars out of a cannon in order to hit something with a lot of impact. There are also explosions and pyrotechnics, and although most people in the industry are multi-skilled, there are always people who really shine in one area rather than another.

Once you have chosen your crew and the budget has been accepted, you then set up a workshop and start putting everything together. This can take several weeks and you could go anywhere in the world from the poles to the equator. If the film was set, say, in a rain forest in Africa, or in a desert, everything would be loaded from the home base into containers and shipped out and a workshop would be made at the location. In Europe, we would use road vehicles and keep one as a mobile workshop and the others as store vehicles – it can become quite a big circus.

On the other hand, there could be just me and one other person on a job, if it is a fire in a grate, which believe it or not, comes under our jurisdiction, because of the health and safety element. It sounds simple, but the fire is always driven by propane gas which makes the flame, and we normally have inert logs and coals so that continuity remains the same. If you use wood, of course, it changes all the time, and you might be in a room for three days shooting, and yet script time might only be ten minutes. Propane gas is very heavy, and lays on the floor, and if someone inadvertently turned it on and then someone else struck a match, there would be a tremendous explosion which would blow the house apart. So special effects look after small things like that, as well as blowing the house apart, if that is what was wanted.

If it is a big war film, there might be a special effects crew of 30 or 40 people. On a Bond film, the supervisor has between 50 and 100 people at his disposal. I haven't worked on one of those, but I did work on *Star Wars* [George Lucas, 1999], which actually was a big disappointment to me. It is a high-profile production where you would expect that they would have enough money to spend to do things properly. But no, they didn't. They wanted to do everything as cheaply as possible, and then when it didn't

Peter at home

come up to standard on the set there was moaning and groaning that it wasn't working properly.

On *Star Wars Episode I: The Phantom Menace* we had quite a bit of trouble with [the robot] R2-D2, and it was purely because we didn't have enough manpower or enough money to spend on him. If I had been allowed to get the crew that was required, we wouldn't have had problems. There were all sorts of political reasons for it as well. The director didn't want some of the people who had worked on earlier *Star Wars*, which was absolutely ridiculous. Presumably there had been a clash of personalities in the past, but they were denying me the choice of the full range of crew. There was one guy in particular, who had worked on all the previous films with R2-D2, so he would have been a magnificent choice, as he already knew a lot of the problems we were going to face.

Star Wars, for me, was quite an unhappy picture. I thought, "Wow, I should be able to do a really nice job on this, and come out of it very well," but it didn't work out like that. We were out in the desert in Tunisia, ahead of the shooting unit, testing R2-D2 and one or two other things. It was vital that R2-D2 could run properly on the sand, because they had experienced problems with him on the previous three films, where he just used to sink into the sand and stop, and they had to put boards down for him to run on. But they didn't want to do that this time; they wanted him to run properly. We spent an awful lot of time working this out. We drove him with an extra motor because he really has three "feet," each with a wheel and we had him with all wheels driving, which hadn't been done before (they had only driven two). We also made the motors bigger and went as large as we could with the wheels, without disfiguring the shape of R2-D2. We achieved this extremely well, I think, because he never got stuck in the sand in Tunisia.

But there were certain unpleasant things which used to happen, like I got a phone call from the producer complaining that we were only working half a day. We were getting up at about four and leaving the hotel at about 4:30, because the hotel, being Tunisian, didn't do much of a breakfast, and we were always in the desert before sun-up. We worked the same as everyone else (like the construction crew), through 'til about half past twelve and then drove for an hour back to the hotel. We were doing a full day's work in temperatures of over 100 degrees. You couldn't touch metal because it literally burnt you, but we were instructed that the next day we were to work through lunch, from 4:30 A.M. until 5:30 P.M.

One of the art department fainted in the air-conditioned hotel, and the Tunisian doctor said, "You're mad. Not even the Bedouin travel at midday. And you are contemplating *working* out here. Well, I'm going at noon and if you are silly enough to stay here, then it is up to you!" So we tried it, and I had some really seasoned men, who had traveled the world on productions, but at two o'clock we all had to give up. It was just ridiculous. It is about the only production that I feel a bit upset about, because of the way we were treated – even our credits were wrong! We were credited as second unit, but we did main unit and second unit, and were main unit stand-by, all the way through it.

We also learnt that ILM [Industrial Light and Magic], who do all the computer-generated images, built an R2-D2, and he cost nearly as much as our entire special effects budget – probably 20 times more than we spent on our R2-D2, and it all seemed a bit of a thing to try and drive us down but bolster ILM. *Star Wars*, to me, is beginning to look a bit like an arcade computer game. The first three had soul. The guns fired blanks and you had the spent shells ejecting and the flash from the muzzles; but there is none of that any more. To me it doesn't cut it any more and I think a lot of the audience feel the same way.

Everything else I've enjoyed. I did the special effects on *The Mission* [Roland Joffe, 1986], which was extremely hard work but everyone was appreciated. Roland Joffe was certainly one of the best directors I have ever worked for and he was also easy to work with. By that, I mean someone you can talk to, and who can give you the information that you need to do the effect that he wants. With some directors it is quite difficult to actually get out of them what they want, perhaps because they don't know what they want until they see it. Roland Joffe always knew what he wanted and he tested not only special effects, but every department, to the limit by his demands. And they were artistic demands for excellence. His camera is always tracking and moving in some direction; it is never static.

He really tested us one day with a rain job where he wanted to rotate the camera through 360 degrees. I have never known anyone do that before. Normally, to produce rain we have rain stands which are like tubes that point in the air about 20 feet high – they are on a big tripod. But all of a sudden he decided he wanted a shot where the camera pans all the way round and goes back to where it started from in a circle, so we had nowhere to hide. So we hauled the rain stands up palms and lashed them to the tops of the trees. The one in the middle really had nowhere to go, so we had to walk it, and a hose to feed it, around, as the camera rotated.

There weren't an awful lot of effects but we were kept busy all the time: there were explosions, the big fire at the mission at the end, and there was a shot of canoes going over waterfalls which were all mechanical dummies and – even if I say it myself – I think they looked very good. Actually, *The Mission* was nominated for a BAFTA for special effects, and though it didn't win, it was fantastic to be nominated. It was one of the most demanding, but also one of the most satisfying films I've worked on.

Unlike visual effects, which are now mainly done in conjunction with computers, everything we do is done "in camera" – they shoot on it there and then, and they can see it the next day in "rushes." Sometimes we are needed to enhance the visual effects. For example, on *Dinotopia* [TV series, 2002] you would get a dinosaur crashing through the woods, but we would have to make branches whip out of the way and snap off and puffs of dust fly from the dinosaur's feet, or grass flatten, or splashes of water go up for each foot, in time to the beast crashing through. Everything had to be carefully choreographed with the visual effects department and then when they put their monster in, it all interacts properly with the surrounding landscape. Although visual effects could do the whole thing, it would take them far longer to try to do the effects that we did. So they can generate work for us, and vice versa.

Recently I also worked on a film called *The Rocket Post* [Stephen Whittaker, 2002], a true story about a man who invented rockets to deliver the post in the western isles of Scotland. They assumed that we probably wouldn't be able to produce a rocket the same as this guy built, and be able to fire it, so they had the visual effects guys standing by. If we could have made the rocket go ten feet and then fall to the ground, they could have digitally carried it on as far as possible, but we actually achieved the full flight. It took off and sailed up into the sky, leaving a nice wide plume of smoke behind it and carried on for about a mile in the air. The director and the producer both came up to me afterwards and said, "That's fantastic. You've saved us thousands of pounds," because doing it for real saved a lot of money.

Visual effects were still used, because the rocket then crashes into a lawn of a stately home very near people, and we couldn't be sure that it wouldn't break up and hit someone. So our part there, was to fire a fountain of earth in the air and just do the rocket coming the last few feet while the visual effects boys brought the rocket right in, marrying up with our real one hitting the ground. We work very closely together on many occasions. But generally we work most closely with the director, the lighting camera-man and camera operator. In fact, we rely on the camera operator's input quite heavily because he is the one looking through the camera and he will often say, "Well, if you move that over to the right six inches, it will look a lot better."

Actually, I started out as a photographer. I didn't really know what I wanted to do when I left school and, I think in desperation, my father put me on a course of photography at Berkshire College of Art and so I did a two-year course and came out as a stills photographer. But you didn't become a photographer straight away, you had to work in a darkroom first. So I started doing that and then I progressed to working for the BBC in their darkrooms, but I found it a bit like being a mushroom, and didn't enjoy it too much, so I was looking around to see what else I could do.

My father was a production designer, so in the school holidays I would go to the film studios. I hadn't left school with the intention of going into the industry, but I knew I had to earn money to survive, and I started looking into the film industry and realized it was a very interesting business. I looked at all the departments and I knew a guy whose father was a special effects supervisor and that seemed to me to be the job that was the *most* interesting.

In those days you had to be a member of the union to work on a film, but I was lucky because I was working for the BBC so I could get into the union, which was the ACTT then [now BECTU]. I started out as a stills man and runner and general dogs-body on a few commercials and that got me thinking more about the industry and I decided it was definitely what I wanted to do. Then, luckily for me, my father got a job as production designer on *The Dirty Dozen* [Robert Aldrich, 1967] and I asked him what the chance was of getting on the special effects team, and he said, "I'll put a word in for you and we'll see." I actually started on *The Dirty Dozen* in 1966, in the art department, and then moved across to special effects when it got closer to shooting.

That was my first film where I worked in a special effects department, and I've stayed in it ever since. There have been highs and lows in the industry; times when work has been extremely scarce, when the industry in this country has almost gone under, but not quite. MGM [where *The Dirty Dozen* was made], which was an exact replica of MGM in Los Angeles, closed down and it was probably the best studio we had in this country, but others survived, although always on a knife-edge. I would like to carry on doing special effects – I think I've got quite a few years left in me still. One does start to slow down, and it is a very demanding job and a very serious department because there is the potential of causing damage to people and property. Things don't go wrong very often, but I remember one occasion when they did.

I was working on a film about the Royal Navy for the BBC and we had to make harpoon missiles which the Navy uses. They are actually American and they are big, about 12 feet in length and 18 inches in diameter and they cost about three-quarters of a million pounds each. So there was no way that the Navy was going to be able to get hold of them to fire them, so it fell to us to make something that would look like the real thing. In this case there was enough information available about what they looked like and how they worked for the art department to draw one for us, but then we had to decide the best way of making it work and what materials to make it out of.

The brief here was to go full size and we made a Fiberglas shell and managed to purchase the propellant. We needed about 700 pounds of thrust to get this thing in the air, so we built a launching ramp for it which wasn't going to be seen. The Navy actually fires them out of sort of long square tubes, but they didn't want us to use theirs, or use ours alongside theirs, so we had to fire ours from mid-ship. We fired one on land first to make sure it worked okay and it did. Then on the day we fired a pair on the frigate; they took off, one after the other, and went the required distance, and then crashed into the sea and everything worked fine.

Then the director wanted a single one, so we fired one which went out, and then, I don't know why, because the motors on those things burn for

about three seconds, enough to get it a good way out, about a mile away from the ship, this one's motor cut out. It suddenly turned on the wind back towards the frigate, which I never would have expected. And although it was only Fiberglas it probably weighed about 50 pounds, so it was a fair chunk of weight if it had landed on the radar equipment or something. Luckily it crashed into the sea, well short of us, but it did give the captain rather a hard time for a few minutes and he said, "Right, we won't be doing *that* again!" In fact, we had another two, but as we had got the shot we didn't need them.

I look upon that as a fairly light-hearted incident, and on that film, the director, Graham Moore, was actually very good to work with, but again there was a problem with the budget. We could have made it so the missile destructed when it got to the end of its flight, so that the motor burnt out and it just blew itself up and fell as a lot of confetti; or we could even have had a parachute system where that would have stopped it at the end of its flight and it would have floated gracefully down into the sea. But there wasn't the money to do that. There is sometimes a balance between health and safety and getting the effect. Sometimes things do go wrong, but normally if it does, it is designed to fail-safe.

That is why we very rarely use remote control for firing charges. It is always line-of-sight and it is hard-wired on a switch. It can happen that a scene is rehearsed, and the stunt man runs across the set, with a particular path to go, and he may have some quite big explosions either side of him. And in rehearsal he will go down his chosen path and then we are going to do it, so we make all our stuff live, and it is "turnover" and he starts to run and for some reason he goes the wrong way and he is going to go right over the explosion, so you just don't fire. There are some people in our industry who like to use beams that you break through which then fire the explosions, but it is dangerous because you can't stop anything like that happening. It might sound old-fashioned, but a switch and a piece of wire to the explosion is certainly the safest and best way to do it.

What keeps me going is the knowledge that something is safe and will look good on screen and will entertain people. The other thing I think of is that, rather like writing a book, your work will always be there. You can

Opposite: A film crew including stunt divers, electricians, grip, gaffer, assistant director and camera crew watched by an owl on the Thames in London.

always go back and see what you've done, and hopefully in the future, some of the films will be shown again on television. So although you are getting older, your work is still being viewed by people.

I really enjoy my work, but I do have one more complaint – the credits! I don't understand why we are so low down. Often special effects are down with the caterers, while people like the costume designer are way up at the top. Yet it might be, say, a war film, where the costumes have already been designed and are just being reproduced or even borrowed from a costumier. Occasionally the special effects supervisor is credited a bit higher (and he can ask for the positioning to be written into his contract) but the crew are always really low down – it is all up to the producer. Sometimes I feel we are thought of as a necessary evil. We are quite an expensive department because safety is so important and often quite a lot of the budget is used before anything else happens – but then, no film is worth risking a life for.

Chris Lyons
Special Effects Dental Technician

Chris Lyons is a partner in a company delighting in the name of Fangs FX, a business run from a regular dental practice where various certificates adorn the walls, and white-coated personnel wander in and out. Chris himself is a casually dressed, large, confident, jovial man who is proud of his work and enthusiastic about it. He is willing to do anything and go anywhere for his job because "it is pure escapism."

SELECTED CREDITS

Legend (Ridley Scott, 1985)

Richard III (Richard Loncraine, 1995)

Evita (Alan Parker, 1996)

Entrapment (Jon Amiel, 1999)

The Mummy (Stephen Sommers, 1999) and The Mummy Returns (2001)

Harry Potter and the Philosopher's Stone (Harry Potter and the Sorcerer's Stone)
  (Chris Columbus, 2001)

Harry Potter and the Prisoner of Azkaban (Alfonso Cuarón, 2004)

We find vampires boring. But we can make sexy vampires, or horrible ones; it depends on the actor or actress. When we did a recent vampire series for TV, it had a male, vicious vampire, and a female played by an American actress who was a very attractive lady so we gave her sexy "vampires." You do little tricks to the teeth to make them look more sexy – they might be slightly curved, and a bit more subtle. Actually we also did *Shadow of the Vampire* [E. Elias Merhige, 2000], which got an Oscar nomination for the makeup [headed by Willem Dafoe].

Sometimes you don't even see the teeth on screen. On *Star Wars*, you didn't see any of our teeth. The best ones we did had fluorescent red gums, bright blue teeth, and each tooth had a black triangle in it, but you didn't see them – it was just cut. When we do normal teeth, that's the beauty, the art of what we do. We want you not to know. We did William Hurt in *Lost in Space* [Stephen Hopkins, 1998] and you would never know he was wearing teeth, but he just wanted to change his character very subtly. So then the art of the craft is for people not to notice. Or sometimes you want people to look at a character and think, "Hang on, there is something not quite right there." So their eye is drawn in. That's what we specialize in really.

I got into this by pure fluke. An optician working on *Superman III* was having problems making metal-colored lenses. He went out to dinner with a friend, and relayed this story. That friend went out with another friend who happened to be a dentist, who said he knew some guys who might be able to help out. So we got a phone call from the optician, and we cast some chrome cobalt, which was stuck onto the surface of the lens and used on the film. He then went onto *Legend* [Ridley Scott, 1985], where they had problems with the teeth, and he got in touch again, and we did all the teeth for the film.

At the time we were just normal dental technicians. We still do normal dental work, but now I much prefer the film side: you never know what you are going to do, where you are going to go, or who you are going to work with. My phone could ring and it's tickets at the airport and you're off! We have two aluminum cases with us which are packed and with me all the time. One case is fully equipped to take impressions and cast models. The other case is for fitting, adjustment and repair. So if I get a call, I can literally pick one of those cases up and go. Some of the work is repairable, some isn't, but some of our work is down to less than half a millimeter thick, the majority, in plastic. At present, there are other people in the U.K. who do small stuff, but as far as the big features and big TV go, there is only us. Our nearest competitor is one guy in the States, and actually we work together quite often.

In our company there is myself and two partners who do the film work. I am the one who normally does all the negotiating and appointments and I get dispatched out to sort out any problems. My father is another partner. He started the business. And the third one I've known since I was about nine – we're almost like brothers. We're all dental technicians, and we'll do anything from lumps of jawbone and a tooth floating around in space, to teeth with diamonds in. It used to be mainly horror and sci-fi, but now it is close to 50-50 nice and horrible.

We've had several actors and actresses whose teeth aren't the best in the world, so we'll give them "the Hollywood smile." Or if they've got gaps between their teeth and the character they are playing doesn't have gaps, if it is a true-to-life film, then we'll make a little piece to close the gap for them, as we did for Madonna on *Evita* [Alan Parker, 1996] and *The Next Best Thing* [John Schlesinger, 2000]. We did teeth for Jonathan Pryce on *Evita*, too. General Peron was apparently known as "Colonel Tooth" because his teeth were very white, almost artificial-looking, so we got actual pictures of Peron so we could copy his teeth. We did that with Bob Hoskins too, in *Enemy at the Gates* [Jean-Jacques Annaud, 2001]. And we did a facial distortion from the inside for Ian McKellen on *Richard III* [Richard Loncraine, 1995].

It is normally the makeup department who will phone and sometimes

Chris working on a plate in his lab. (Courtesy of Chris Lyons)

we are given a totally free run where they ask what we think should go with the makeup. Other times they will ask for something specific, and we will be given verbal or drawn guidelines and we interpret those into what will work in a human mouth. The teeth we make have to be 100 percent comfortable: The actors have to be able to speak, sometimes sing, drink. Sometimes we will be on set all day, other times we will be in when the actor turns up, fit them and then go away and either someone from makeup or the actor themselves will take them out – it depends entirely on who it is and what they want and how difficult the makeup is. Makeup is getting so good now and the cameras are getting so close, that if they give the teeth to other professionals it is one less thing to worry about.

When we did Gary Oldman in *Lost in Space* he had full prosthetics, contact lenses and teeth. Then they computer-generated it and the only thing that remained original was our teeth. Everything else was enhanced. So Makeup and everyone phoned up and said, "Have you seen it? You lucky bastard, its only your teeth which stayed original." That's quite rewarding, that they liked the teeth that much! On that film we did have quite a lot of influence because Makeup had several ideas that the director didn't like and I said, "I can see what the director wants. Just give me the budget and let me go away and make the teeth." So I did and the director loved them. You get to learn how the directors' minds are working.

Computers haven't affected me yet – in fact, I've helped them. On *The Mummy* [Stephen Sommers, 1999], there was a shot where they wanted to go right down inside the mummy's mouth, and they wanted a grid on the teeth to match up on the computer, so we made some white templates, which they could use. We've made rigs to go in the mouth so you can have a 12-foot remote-control tongue coming out of the mouth. Nothing is odd, we have got so used to it.

I've got all the teeth mothballed. I've got *Star Wars Episode I* [George Lucas, 1999] teeth all in storage, in case they needed them for *Episode II*, although actually that was done in Australia. I wouldn't be allowed to use those teeth for anything else though. But we did teeth for *Harry Potter and the Philosopher's Stone* [Chris Columbus, 2001] which we mothballed and are now using for *Harry Potter II*. For the first *Harry Potter* we did all the goblins, Filch the caretaker, Marcus Flint, the Slytherin Quidditch Captain, and we also looked after all the kids, because they were all at the age when they were losing teeth! If one of them lost a tooth, we would have to go in and make them a little plate to fill the gap. I also did some buck teeth for Hermione Granger [Emma Watson] but they ended up not using them. We hand-make each individual tooth and it's built up in layers. To make a standard set of monster teeth for, say, the goblins in *Harry Potter* – each goblin would be just over a week's work. They fit over the actor's own teeth but look all spiky, interlocking like a mantrap.

They said the goblins had to look fairly mean and I thought of the jagged look and did a design and showed them and they said, "Yes, that's fantastic." Sometimes you have a lot of creative input, other times you don't. You can also match the skin colors to the gum colors, like for *The Mummy*. We never say no, basically. Whatever ideas, however wild and wacky, we'll try and fulfill them. We do hair lips, fake orthodontic braces, metal finger extensions, all sorts. It is a trade secret how we put the teeth in, but they just click in and out in seconds. We've got a patented design. A lot of the actors and actresses who have worn our teeth will only come back to us.

Actors don't get edgy with *me* but they might get touchy over other things and you might walk in at the wrong time in the wrong place and get the brunt of it. I don't put any airs and graces on and that's the way I deal with them. They all come in here [the practice] – only the big names won't – and we take all the impressions and make prototypes and fit them here, or go out to location and fit them. If they have a problem, we will travel wherever. Sometimes you'll turn up, and they're filming in like, an hour, and you've turned up to put the teeth in, and as you put them in they break, or they don't fit. So you say calmly, "I'll be back in one moment," and you go outside and get on the phones and ask if anyone has any bright ideas, and we get round it.

I've got one female actress who phones me up on quite a regular basis because we do her all the time, and she can phone me when I'm having lunch with the in-laws, and you feel like saying, "Look, I'm having lunch," but you can't and the in-laws don't believe who is on the other end of the phone and that she is just phoning me up because she is sitting in New York and is a bit bored and wants to know how her teeth are doing. I've had phone calls where they say, "I need to see you," so I might drive all the way down to the other end of Wales or something and you get there and ask what the problem is and they say they just wanted a chat! There are some awkward people who I won't name, and there are some worse than others, but the majority are just normal people doing a job.

I've had a couple of directors, too, who won't make their minds up or keep changing their minds. They might say to you, "Can you just move that *one* tooth?" and they don't realize that that's like a whole week's work thrown away, moving one tooth one millimeter which you are not going to see anyway. So you might take it away and work two days and two nights on it, and take it back, and he'll say, "Actually, I think I might have preferred the first one." And you feel like smacking him, but it is the director's prerogative. They're paying the bills so I don't care, although sometimes it can be very demoralizing. And because we go through Makeup, sometimes the directors won't even know us. We'll just appear. We've been threatened with being thrown off films for industrial espionage because the director and producer don't know us!

Sometimes you get directors, like on *Harry Potter*, Chris Columbus, he's fantastic. He'll give loads of feedback, lots of praise when praise is due, and he tells you it's rubbish if it's rubbish, which is great. And some actors and actresses are really good to work with, like Helena Bonham-Carter. We gave her buck teeth in *The Revengers' Comedies* [Malcolm Mowbray, 1997] and we also did her in *The Theory of Flight* [Paul Greengrass, 1998]. She plays someone with motor-neuron disease with muscle wasting so we made her lips plump forward as though the muscles had gone in her mouth, which affected her speech, but helped her get the voice that she needed for the part. Helena is great. She's our favorite. She's just a nice lady. The majority of them are, although a few are bastards. You get to know which ones you have to play carefully, and other ones you can say what you want to. I've got some actors who, if they swear at me, I swear back at them, and we get on like a house on fire. Others it's like, fine, he's in a rough mood, so I'll just leave him alone.

I am amazed how some of them remember me. Like four years after working with Jimmy Nail, he remembered my name, out of all the people he must meet daily. Another nice guy is Roy Hudd. He's really funny. He dragged me outside the makeup bus once to ask me if I had any new jokes because he was running out! So we stood outside for about three quarters of an hour having a smoke and chatting and telling each other jokes and having a laugh 'til the makeup woman came out and said, "Are you bloody coming back in here or what?"

It's almost surreal. You see these actors on TV, and you think, "Hang on a minute. I'm just a little bloke who works in Harrow and I've knocked on their front door and sat in their lounge and had a cup of tea, and some have offered to make me breakfast." Lots of friends of mine just do not believe me. They think I'm winding them up! I don't brag about it, but if people ask me, then I tell them. Why not be proud of what you've done? I love what I do, and want to carry on as long as I can. We've created a niche market, and obviously we want to keep it to ourselves, so we don't really advertise, but we love it. You see, it's pure escapism.

One of the most challenging jobs I have had was on *Event Horizon* [Paul Anderson, 1997]. They wanted a guy to basically get an ice pick in the back of the neck and in real time (not just a cut shot) they wanted to show the pick going in and coming straight out, smashing teeth as it went. That was a tall order, but we achieved it! Actually, a friend of ours had a car accident and lost a load of premaxilla, which is bone in the upper jaw, and he played the part in the film – it was just a small part. So we had a big space to put a crossbow bolt in, and with a flick of his tongue, the bolt came out three inches and the tooth comes flying out with the root as well, and all the gum splits. It's pretty sick, but it was quite challenging! Most of them are a challenge because they're all one-offs. So we'll go in and say, "Yes, we can do that," and then we will walk away and think, "Christ, how the bloody hell *are* we going to make it?"

On *Event Horizon* we also did teeth in the cheek and lip in a self-mutilation and torture sequence. And there was a woman who has a halo screwed round her skull with bars coming out and screws which go onto the teeth. The bottom teeth were hers, and the top ones ours, and each screw was handmade in plastic. Unfortunately, we do get involved with some quite sick and horrible stuff. Sam Neill's character in *Event Horizon* had tribal scarring and was supposed to be reborn. I came up with the idea that if he has tribal scarring on the outside of his body, why not have it on the inside of his body as well? So he's got three scars running through his lips, which carry on through the gum and through the teeth. It all matches up and gives the appearance that not only is he scarred on the outside but all the inside of his body is scarred as well.

I used to go to the cinema in my late teens with my girlfriend at the time, at least once a week. Now I generally watch films on video or Sky, but only because I don't have the time, and I have two young children as well. Horror and sci-fi is what we mostly get involved with, so if I want to see those at home I have to wait 'til the wife goes to bed because she likes the

"Kleenex jobs." She wouldn't come to see half the films I've done! I took her to see *Alien 3* [David Fincher, 1992] and I got grief for about the next three months.

The youngest person I have done is a five-year-old, and that was my son. The BBC called me and said they wanted some cat's teeth for a five-year-old, but the child wouldn't let me do it because he was getting frightened, so I asked how important it was to have that child, and they said "Not really. Why?" I said, "My son would do it because he knows what I do." So I gave them some pictures and he got the part, which was good. Now my son asks, "Have you met Harry Potter?" and I say "Yeah" and he says to his friends, "*My* dad's met Harry Potter!" He's only five and they don't believe him, so when I see him it's like, "Have you *really* met Harry Potter?" and I say "*Yes.*" The other day he had a Harry Potter activity day at school and accidentally I had my *Harry Potter* crew jacket on and I walked into the school, and he said to everyone, "I *told* you my dad worked on *Harry Potter*!" and he turned to me and said, "You've been to Harry Potter's house, haven't you, Dad?" And I answered "Yes" in front of all his friends.

Jemma Scott
Contact Lens Technician

Most people could be forgiven for not knowing what a contact lens technician does on a film. Indeed, at a hurried reading of the credits one might think it was something to do with camera lenses or perhaps with actors who normally wear glasses. Nor at first, would one be much the wiser when visiting Jemma Scott, the young director of the Reel Eye Company in Radlett, Hertfordshire.

I entered a perfectly regular-looking shop called Grant & Glass Opticians with rows of display glasses lining the walls, almost like a front for some covert operation – or was my imagination getting the better of me? I descended some stairs and met Jemma in a rather dark basement, sitting at a scruffy desk where there was still no evidence of her unusual occupation: She designs, provides and fits colored contact lenses for actors on numerous films.

SELECTED CREDITS
Braveheart (Mel Gibson, 1995)
The English Patient (Anthony Mingella, 1996)
Star Wars Episode I: The Phantom Menace (George Lucas, 1997)
Sleepy Hollow (Tim Burton, 2000)
The Beach (Danny Boyle, 2000)
Lord of the Rings: The Fellowship of the Ring (Peter Jackson, 2001)
Harry Potter and the Philosopher's Stone (*Harry Potter and the Sorcerer's Stone*)
  (Chris Columbus, 2001)

Originally I came to work for Richard Glass, who has actually been in special-effect contact lenses for films for 20-odd years [*Return of the Jedi*, Richard Marquand, 1983, was one of his first big films]. But I came to work in the shop above, as his manager, and I didn't realize at that time that he did lenses for films! I am trained as an optical assistant, which is similar to a dispensing optician except that they don't do the fitting [when the health

Jemma (Courtesy of Jemma Scott)

and curvature of the eye is checked].

So I was managing the practice and then Richard had an awful lot of film work and he asked if I would like to go on a "stand-by day" on a film set which is to go and actually put the contact lenses in for people. So effectively I worked for Richard and then I got much more involved in it and people would start ringing me about the design of lenses and eventually I couldn't handle doing the two things. So Richard stayed in the shop and we split into two companies and that is how the Reel Eye Company was born, in 1996. Now we tend to do most of the big films in Europe – we've pretty much cornered the market.

For example, although I didn't go to New Zealand, and although most of the lenses for *Lord of the Rings* [Peter Jackson, 2001] were made there, some, which had to be unique, were done by us. In Australia and New Zealand, lenses cannot be hand-made, so they can't make up a design. They have to choose out of catalogue, which does have quite unusual lenses like yellow ones, but we made all the specialist lenses. People might think we gave Elijah Wood [Frodo Baggins] blue lenses, but actually those are his natural eyes, which are just an amazing blue color. But there is a part in the film when he is being chased through a wood by characters on horses and Liv Tyler is trying to get him to safety. Anyway, he is ill and his eyes look thick and bloodshot and cloudy, and we did those lenses. We also did some lenses for Liv Tyler and her fairy people, who wore a very pale kind of pinky-blue.

There was an optician in New Zealand who did lenses for the background people and he did all the lens fittings for us [for Elijah Wood, Liv Tyler and Orlando Bloom, who played Legolas Greenleaf]. He e-mailed me all of their details, so we did everything pretty much by e-mail and then he was there on set to put the lenses in and take them out and look after them. We did the designs through Peter Owen, who was the makeup designer.

Normally makeup artists or someone from production phone and say

Dining bus. According to the Internet Movie Database, on *Lord of the Rings: The Fellowship of the Ring*, 1,460 eggs were served to the cast and crew for breakfast every day of shooting!

they want to change a character's eye color, or make someone look like they have bloodshot eyes, or to look dead, or whatever, and then I arrange a contact lens fitting and then correlate those details to a design of lens. Next I order the lenses, which are made by a company called Cantor and Nissel, who have a very good hand painting department. They make therapeutic lenses as well, for instance for someone who has got a damaged eye and wants to make their eye look good. The two industries have actually helped each other. We will push it in a film to try to get a certain design because that's what the concept designer has thought of, and Cantor and Nissel will try different things out, which have helped their therapeutic lenses because they have been able to find new colors or designs.

On a film, you try to have the actor see through the lens as much as possible, so they can walk about comfortably, but it may not be the most important thing. On a blind lens for instance, the whole lens is made opaque and the actor won't be able to see through it – which can end up as being quite a good prop for them. On a hand-painted lens we make the pupil three mils in diameter, so that when a bright light is on the actor we can't see their own eye color behind the lens. So their peripheral vision is slightly restricted.

I love my job because I have an office where I have a regular nine-to-five day, on my own, but when I do the films it is completely varied – they can choose any hours of the day they like. And you get to meet loads and loads of different people. One of the nicest films I worked on was just a small film for Hallmark called *Leprechauns* [John Henderson, 1999] which was a fantasy, and the whole crew was just so nice that we had a really lovely time. We were filming outside quite a lot, in the summer, in the country and I would just really look forward to going to work every morning. I usually look after everybody's lenses for them while they are filming. I put them in, take them out and take care of them so the actors don't have to worry about it. I had hundreds and hundreds of lenses on that film. There were fairies who had jewel-blue eyes, leprechauns who had Irish-green eyes, and hairy, acrobatic creatures with bright red eyes. It was a magical little film.

I worked on the first *Harry Potter* [Chris Columbus, 2001] and I am presuming I will be on the next one. Zoë Wanamaker [Madame Hooch] had yellow eyes, because she is meant to look a bit like an eagle; the goblins had black eyes all over; and Alan Rickman [Professor Snape] had really dark brown lenses. I'd worked with Zoë before so she always asks for us now anyway – she's lovely, a really nice lady. She was brilliant with her lenses and just got really excited about it all. Alan Rickman was very quiet and I thought at first that he didn't like me, but it was not that at all; I think he is just one of those people who takes a long time to get to know somebody. Actually at the end he was really kind and bought me a bottle of champagne and I hadn't really spent *that* much time with him, and he said that he wanted me to do the next *Harry Potter*, and not disappear (I had to go off before the end and do *Blade II* because *Harry Potter* overran quite a lot). He was really sweet.

Some actors have a tolerance problem, which is another reason why I am there. I make sure they don't overwear the lenses and get a couple of breaks during the day so that psychologically they don't feel like they are wearing bricks all day. After a week or so you get very used to them, but the actors often don't get that time. They will wear them one day, and then again maybe a couple of weeks later, and some actors find it easier than others.

One disastrous shoot I remember was a big Levis advert many years ago, where there was a very beautiful girl from outer space who wore a silver-mirrored bra, and had big purple eyes. Unfortunately she was allergic to the solution, so I would put her lenses in and she would be fine, and then about 20 minutes later, her eyes would start suddenly streaming all over the place. And she had all this iridescent makeup which was a nightmare with water, because it just slid off her face! So she was meant to look absolutely beautiful and her eyes were getting puffier and redder, and I was just thinking, "This is awful, I don't understand." Eventually I rang Richard and we changed the solution and everything was fine.

Then the next day, the pod or spaceship that she was meant to come out of was made out of a glowing substance which smelled of menthol. Well, menthol makes your sinuses run, but wearing contact lenses exaggerates that effect, so there she was, for her close-up, with her eyes streaming again. She was obviously really sensitive to anything like that and it was just awful. We got through it in the end, giving her loads of breaks, and patching her face up until the last minute when they were absolutely ready to shoot, and then dragging her away again!

Actors don't get cross with me because I hold all the cards – I can make it hurt! Basically, we are all there to do a job, so you get on with it. I have just spent four months in Prague on *Blade II* [Guillermo Del Toro, 2002], where I was Wesley Snipes' Personal Contact Lens Technician. I think that's a ridiculous title, personally! I was terrified going out there because I didn't know what he would be like, and a lot of these stars have their own really close, personal people who work with them on all their films and they all know each other really well. So I thought, "This is going to be horrible. I'm going to walk in and be the new girl." But they were very easy to get on with and really looked after me, and welcomed me into the clan.

To be honest, I didn't spend that much time with Wesley Snipes. I would literally walk into his trailer, put his lenses in, and he would chat a bit, but I never spent long with him, and he didn't wear the lenses all the time. His lenses were actually made in America. I was simply there to stick them in and pull them out again – they were a kind of hazeley-orangey-color, because he is a vampire and all the vampires had lenses. They were quite unusual, but I don't think one will notice them all that much, to be honest, on the film. So I was totally amazed that they paid for me to be out there for the whole film. Really, I didn't work that much. Sometimes I get a bit bored, but I am a world-class chatterer now! And I ended up helping the makeup department, begging them to give me a job to do.

I did lenses for *The Beach* [Danny Boyle, 2000], too, but I wasn't there with Leonardo DiCaprio. We found a Thai optician to put the lenses in because it cost too much to bring me out there. Leonardo DiCaprio had been beaten up in the film at the end, and the makeup artist wanted to give him a subconjunctival hemorrhage, which is a burst blood vessel. So I designed a large diameter schleral soft contact lens for him which was 22 mil across, and had the bloodshot effect painted on. I either draw it, or write down exactly what I want for the person who paints it.

I designed the lenses for Darth Maul in *Star Wars* [George Lucas, 1997], with the makeup artist, Paul Engelen. That character wasn't meant to wear contact lenses originally. The makeup department got drawings from the concept designers and designed makeup to fit the character. So Paul Engelen had drawn the red and black of Darth Maul's face and put the horns on and suddenly realized that his eyes just stood out because they looked really white and one was suddenly aware that the character was human and not a creature.

I was having a meeting with Nick Dudman, the makeup artist who was the head for all the creatures, and he showed me a Polaroid of what they had done so far and said he felt the character needed contact lenses. He said, "What do you think?" I had a really crude pair as part of my sample kit that I'd taken along – a red and yellow blend – and I said, "I think yellow, because that is the most unnatural color I can think of for an eye to be, and we'll make the red stand out, so it looks like it is all part of it, because half his head is red." He said, "Yes, I kinda like that idea," so we made a pair up to see what they looked like, and camera tested them and George Lucas obviously liked them because they stayed. Some directors are particularly nice to me. Danny Boyle is. I've just done *28 Days Later* [2002] for him, and he needed lots of lenses for that film and he loved them all and was always coming up and chatting to me and was really sweet. Normally I'm known as "lens girl" and people shout, "Hey, lens girl!" but he was really nice.

It's a really bizarre job. Even other people on a film ask, "What do you do?" and I say, "Contact lenses," and they can't believe it. But there is a demand there. It's unbelievable the amount of films that have lenses in them. Like in *The English Patient* [Anthony Mingella, 1996], Ralph Fiennes, when he is burnt, has got our contact lenses in. With all that burnt makeup, his eyes would really stand out unless they were deadened, to take the color out. If we have done our job right, unless it is a character like Darth Maul, the audience shouldn't realize the actor has lenses in. It's a fine line between going completely outrageous, to very realistic. I'm not sure what I'll be doing in five or ten years time – but I don't think I could go back to being an optical assistant. I don't think they'd let me loose on the customers!

James Moore
Mouth/Beak Replacement Coordinator

James Moore came from New Zealand to England expressly to work on the animated feature film Chicken Run, *released in 2000. It was the first feature-length film made by Peter Lord, Nick Park and the Oscar-winning team behind such popular shorts as the Wallace & Gromit films and* Creature Comforts. *It tells the story of the daring escape of chickens, helped by Rocky (Mel Gibson), "the lone free ranger," from Tweedy's Egg Farm. The film was created with Aardman's distinctive brand of clay animation, and James Moore's part in the process was unique.*

It was therefore with high expectations that I traveled to Aardman Features in Bristol to interview James. But as I exited Parkway station in pouring rain and drove past uniform brown pebbledash houses to an industrial park, my spirits started to sink. Nor did they revive when on entering the Aardman studio I was asked to wait, sign a confidentiality form and was told not to ask anything about the forth-coming feature Tortoise v's Hare. *Next I was ushered into a meeting room by Adam Barriball, the Publicity Unit Assistant who informed me that he would be present throughout the interview.*

James was rather shy and nervous and very serious. In contrast to the Aardman puppets (which "we like to call characters"), James did not smile and I never saw his teeth! Yet his explanation of his job was amazing. I thought a mouth/beak replacement coordinator meant a dialogue synchronizer: replacing a human mouth with a puppet beak. Actually, it means someone who literally coordinates the changing of tiny plasticine mouths or beaks in a puppet's head. On Chicken Run *there were over 60 interchangeable beaks, each one corresponding to a different phonetic sound, and each had to be exactly the right color blend, achieved by using a converted chewing gum machine in the Aardman studio.*

SELECTED CREDITS

Oscar and Friends (TV Series, Gnome Productions, New Zealand, 1996)

King Kong (Feature Film Remake, Peter Jackson, 1996)

McDonalds Happy Meals (Commercial, New Zealand, 1997)

Chicken Run (Peter Lord and Nick Park, 2000)

Tortoise v's Hare (Peter Lord, 2003)

I worked on *Chicken Run* for nearly two years, and most of that was actual shooting time. Each second of film that we view is broken down into 24 frames! You make a tiny movement of the character on the set, then you take a shot (a frame), and then there is another little movement which is shot, again and again and again. So depending on how much activity there was in a sequence, the animators would be shooting an average of two or three seconds of film a day, which would be about 50 or 75 movements, so it is an incredibly time-consuming process! And the mouth movements are just a part of all that. Each puppet has an internal skeleton, so virtually every part of them is able to move. I think Rocky had 159 moving parts to his skeleton. Then the plasticine on top has different press molds, and each part, e.g., the teeth, tongue, etc., has a different mold measured to the precise thickness. It is keeping these all consistent that makes the character believable.

All the characters have cowls (scarves, or necklaces, or *some*thing round their necks) which hide the seam where the head comes off and a different head on a stick, with a slightly different expression can replace it. But within that head there are also removable mouthpieces which can be changed.

I got my title because I wasn't strictly model making or supervising (because I wasn't that senior at that stage), so I became a coordinator. Then they had to think up something that fitted more particularly, and they came up with probably the longest job title in existence!

I only did mouth/beak replacement for *Chicken Run*. It basically came about because in the model making department they really needed some-one to oversee that part of it: to make sure all the mouths and beaks were done the same way and that someone knew how and why they had been done in a certain way, instead of it all being split between different people.

All the sound recording is done first. So Mel Gibson and the rest [the "voice talent," as they are referred to at Aardman, for of course the real actors are the chickens] would rehearse and do all the recording very early on. Our job is to get the dialogue (on a Walkman at this stage) in synch with

the character's mouth movements. Each phonetic sound and the corresponding shape the mouth makes, like "ooo" or "eee," is broken down by someone
else onto what is called a "dope sheet" which is given to the animator. So he
might for example have four mouth shapes for Rocky saying the one word
"Ginger." I don't have to actually get involved in all that.

There is also of course an overall mouth design typical of Aardman,
with the teeth and the overbite, which will be worked out at the beginning
with the key animators and the director. The mouth movements are the
most important part of the animation of the face. It is up to the individual
animator to decide on other facial movements, like the eyes.

Originally, in the early days of model making at Aardman, part of the
animator's job would be to sculpt the mouth shape each time for each phonetic sound. They didn't have replacement mouths, just a whole pressed-
out solid head. Often it would end up that they would keep having to repeat
the same mouth shapes over again, which was a bit daft and time-consuming.
It also meant there was not such good continuity in the characters.

So the idea of replacement animation is that you replace the mouth
each time with another mouth shape already made. So you might have a
box of Ginger's heads, and another box of her mouths which each fit into

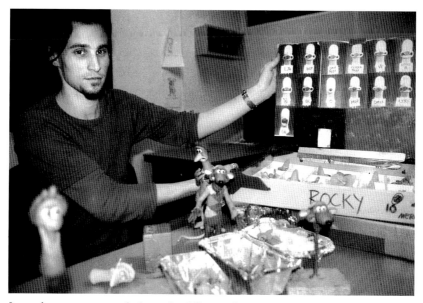

James demonstrates mouth shapes for different phonetic sounds. Foil boxes (foreground)
contain plasticine puppet heads.

the heads separately. Of course, there is a problem with plasticine, because it is so delicate, in getting them to all be the same, and for them not to get damaged, but really the idea is to save time, and therefore money.

The plasticine is mixed to a certain consistency so that it is as firm as they can get it, "the Aardman Mix" which is made in-house, but it is still very labor intensive, in a way shifting the work from the animator to the model maker. Instead of using a sculpted head in its entirety, the model maker divides it into separate parts. A chicken is complicated because the beak and cheek areas are different colors. So you generate a master, generic cheek and a master beak plate, which is like a blank, and make a press mold of it which always stays the same. Then you press out 15 or 20 beaks, say, which the animator will insert into the head and sculpt into a different position. Then he/she'll test them on the computer to see what it will look like on film. Then you'd get a box back of all the different sculpted mouth and beak shapes — about 16 different vowel or consonant sounds for one character.

A lot of the creative part of the look of the characters is down to the original sculptor and the animators. The model maker's job is to replicate things and produce them *en masse*. By the end of the film there were 32 units in different stages (e.g., building sets, rehearsing, shooting). There were about 15 sets where shooting was going on simultaneously, so you might need 15 puppets of, say, Ginger, and one set of mouths isn't going to last very long. So I would need to make molds of everything so we could produce as many as we needed.

Originally there was me and one other guy making all the molds for all the chickens and then there was just me, and so I became the coordinator, because I knew how they all worked and how to test them out and everything. So my job was to replicate the original sculpt without changing it or damaging it and work out a way of producing sets of them as quickly as possible. I had to keep things consistent and accurate, because in animation you do want some things to be constant. Like, the beak can't shift around within the face, so we had to put a solid piece of resin inside the plasticine.

At the beginning it was quite hard to make sure the beaks didn't shift around. How tightly they were fitted into the head made a big difference. And even getting exact consistency of color was difficult. If there were any tiny differences of any kind it would ruin the look of the film. So it was a minefield of difficulties. You might have just pressed out a whole load of beaks, which because of a problem with the "core," which attaches them into the head, would pop in and out of the faces and move around. Or you'd finally get the beaks right but they'd get damaged being taken in and out all the time.

I had never done anything exactly like this before. I started off doing commercials in New Zealand, mainly live action stuff. I did a little model making and special effects. Ever since I was about 17 I used to hang around a model making company in Auckland in New Zealand. In my school holidays I would just go on shoots and assist. I always wanted to work in film – more live action than animation at that stage. Then I worked on a children's TV series and in fact it was the director of the current Aardman film "Feature 2" who came over to New Zealand and helped set up the series around six years ago. So I had about two years work on that series, which was really my biggest training because there was some model work and a bit of mouth replacement on that. So when I knew that *Chicken Run* had started, I contacted him, Richard Goleszowski, and he helped me get a work permit and I came over here because I wanted to work on a feature film.

There isn't that much animation work in the world or that many experienced people. The other advantage of animation is it generally involves you in quite a good block of work. We are on project-based contracts so although you're not staff, it's more regular work compared to other films. Some model makers come from college, but here we've got a doctor and all sorts. Bristol is quite a pool of talent because of Aardman (which grew from the two directors working here off their kitchen table with camcorders) but also people come from all over, like Belgium, the U.S., etc. Now I'm working on prototypes, which is when you make the very first puppet of a character and there is a lot more problem-solving work instead of just factory stuff. You might be just one of three people working on that character and a lot more is expected of you to really produce.

With the crediting in model making, they try to credit you with the thing you did mostly or the highest profile thing you could be recognized for. So someone might get credited as a sculptor and have worked on a film for two years, but just have sculpted for six months. You can't get more than one credit, so a guy I knew got to pick his credit because he worked in layout and sound and as a runner. I think my title was quite funny because it sounds like such a madeup sort of fabricated thing. I think it was either someone in production or at the top in model making who thought it up, as a kind of one-off. On my passport I just put "model maker."

James Cosper
Location Scout

James Cosper was working on The Sopranos *in New York, and since they would not allow me on set, I met him in a café near Silvercup Studios. I gave a cab driver the name of a street that I had misheard over the phone. He had never heard of it and for a while we were lost – which seemed a bit ironic as I was meeting a location scout.*

James is confident and bubbly. But his marriage didn't survive his work. As he explained, it didn't help when he used to keep phoning saying, "I don't know when I'll be home." However, he sees his five-year-old daughter regularly and when he lent me the photo of himself working, he said that his ex-wife was extremely anxious to get the photograph back.

Selected Credits
Night Falls on Manhattan (Sydney Lumet, 1997)
Sex and the City (HBO TV Series, first aired 1998)
The Insider (Michael Mann, 1999)
Flawless (Joel Schumacher, 1999)
The Sopranos (HBO TV Series, first aired 1999)

I got into being a location scout because I needed to get a real job. But that's not how I started out. I grew up in a very small town in the state of Washington and when I was 18 and graduated from high school I moved to Hollywood to be a movie star. I went to the American Film Institute for a while and also the Sherwood Oaks Experimental Film School, which was run by a crazy guy and it was a really, really great experience. But then about four years into it, I woke up and decided I didn't want to be in the film industry any more; it was too confining, there wasn't enough creativity. This was the early '80s when independent film hadn't really taken off yet and the big boys really controlled the shots.

James scouting in his car. (Courtesy of James Cosper)

So I became a modern dancer. I used to go to the punk rock clubs and I thought, "Well, the film industry sucks and I'm going to be a dancer!" I moved back to where I'm from – Portland, Oregon – and got a degree in Dance and did my own performances and videotaped my shows, which is the closest I got to film at that time. Then I moved to New York and worked with a modern dance company and I got married. I met a girl and I fell in love and I got married and I had a baby. As soon as I had a baby, I had to get a real job because there is no money in dance. I had one connection, and I called this girl and she said she would make a phone call and maybe she could get me some work on an independent film.

That's how I started. I scouted on a Peter Falk independent film that went straight to video. But by going to the one-hour photo-lab where all the scouts put all their pictures together, I met other scouts and I started to get jobs. It was word of mouth. When they need someone, they need someone *now* – you've got to go to work today – and I was available. So I did a few little independents and then I hooked up with *The Sopranos* [HBO TV Series about a mob boss and his family in New York, first aired 1999] and then I got a six-month job with them and I really fell in love with it at that point. It was something I was good at, and this is my fourth season on *The Sopranos*.

A location scout is not the same as a U.K. location manager [who arranges with authorities for permission to shoot in specific places and finds and manages all the locations]. Sometimes, particularly on features, I will scout the show and then work on the set, but on *The Sopranos* I just scout: I read the script and I go out and I find the locations. When I worked on *Sex and the City* [HBO TV Series first aired 1998], I would scout the locations and then work on them, making sure that all the neighbors were happy and that everyone on the location was okay. On *Sex and the City* we were working in restaurants which had million-dollar pieces of art on the walls, and you had to make sure that [costume designer] Patricia Fields didn't smoke her cigarettes next to them! You have to make sure that nothing gets ruined and that the crew are clean and courteous – it's a whole different job. I prefer just to scout.

As a scout, you go out and take pictures, but in a certain way. You turn the camera so you take vertical shots to get maximum depth between the ground and the ceiling and you stand in one spot and take photos next to each other so you get the whole panoramic view and then you put those photos together. Any old camera will do, a high quality Olympus "point and shoot" will do for this. It's not about artistic photography, it's about covering the location so that when the director looks at the pictures, they get a good idea of what that area would be like to film in. At the one-hour lab we use, they have the double-sided tape and the cutters and the manila envelope. Michael Mann, who directed *The Insider* [1999], wouldn't even look at a folder of photos unless it was put together in a certain way.

When I shoot a place, I always look to see where the trucks could park and make sure they would be out of the scene. I'm always two weeks ahead of the show. You need to get permits, and get police officers involved, but I don't do the paperwork. The most important thing is to get the pictures in focus and get the contact of the person who says, "Yes, you can shoot here." You want the people to be into the fact that you are coming to their place to shoot. That's important – you don't want to be going to a place where the people aren't into it. Basically, they want to let you use a location because they love the TV show, or because they want the money. It doesn't matter which one they want, so long as they want one of those – then there's no problem. Sometimes you need a gorgeous, beautiful house and the owner just lets you in and you wonder why.

It takes about 11 or 12 days to shoot a 50-minute episode of *The Sopranos*. Of that, usually about six days would be done in the studio and about five on locations. Today I'm photographing baseball fields in New Jersey that are close to a school. At first we were just looking for Little League fields for a half-day shoot which we wanted to be close to where they would already be shooting. Then as concept meetings progressed, new ideas came up, and last night they told me that they needed the ball field to be near a school. But schools are hard to clear, so I will be looking for a ball field which is not actually part of the school. That would be the ultimate find: we could shoot in the ball field and have the school in the background.

Every day is a new experience for a location scout. You go out and meet new and interesting people. Anything is possible. On *Sex and the City*, I remember once they were looking for a log cabin which was not too far away. After two weeks I finally found one in Jersey and it was a Girl Scout camp, which had nine old log cabins, and we shot there for three days in the woods. It was a great experience, but I had to deal with the crazy Girl Scouts. The lady who ran the camp there was bombarded with local Girl Scout people saying "How dare you let a show like *Sex and the City* shoot in our Girl Scout cabins?" But I was like, "Who cares? We are giving you a lot of money to fix up your cabins!"

Recently, for *The Sopranos*, I had to go out and find four crack houses in a row. That sent me to East Orange, which is probably the worst area I have ever been in my life – worse than Harlem, worse than Patterson, New Jersey. East Orange is probably the most drug-infested town I have ever been. I had to find three burnt-out, boarded-up houses, next to one house that people were living in. The concept was that we were going to go in and film the crack-heads sleeping and smoking crack in the house and then we had to go in and kick them out for the episode.

So basically I was out scouting in a very bad neighborhood. I got pulled over by three undercover agents who put me up against my car and one of them just didn't believe that I was a scout with *The Sopranos*, no matter how much I told him, and he gave me a really hard time. But what were they going to do? Bust me for being in a bad neighborhood? Anyway, finally they let me go. It was a very tough thing to go through, but I found the location, and it's in the new episode of *The Sopranos* and I actually worked on the set for that episode because I got to know the neighbors. In fact, the neighbors were phenomenal. They were very accommodating, partly because we were giving them money, but also Jim Gandolfini, the star of *The Sopranos*, is brilliant with people. He will talk to anyone on the set and is very giving that way. A lot of the people had never seen the show because they don't have cable TV, but they'd heard of it, and they came up and talked, and actually everyone had a really good time.

That was a very interesting location to find, although in this business no one really thanks or praises you. But I kinda like it that way. It keeps it even – there's no competition within the scouts to find stuff. You could go weeks without finding anything or you could find something every episode. Of course I would like to have one of my locations in each episode, but it is not demanded of me because you never know the luck of the cards. There are three location scouts on *The Sopranos*; on *Sex and the City* there were four, but two were on set all the time and two looked for locations; on a feature there will be five or six at the beginning but once the locations are found they are not kept on.

I enjoy meeting new people each day and I enjoy taking pictures of all the different stuff that I see all day long and immediately taking the film to the photo-lab and looking at the pictures that night. But different scouts work differently. Some pick up a phone book. I go out and I get lost, but I am constantly looking for something new; I don't want to go to a location that has already been used. A lot of scouts use the same places because it is easy and they know about it, but my challenge is to go out every day and find something new and different. I just did two weeks looking at cemeteries, which I enjoyed! Or they might want a middle-class house that could belong to an ex-cop, on the ocean, where you can park a car. So you drive to the Hamptons and Queens and Asbury Park and Jersey – all over.

I've been on *The Sopranos* four years now so I really have an idea of what they are looking for and I know the Italian mob world. You get a few

James looking for a beach house location on *The Sopranos*. (Courtesy of James Cosper)

hardcore Italians who think the show is a disgrace to them, but they tell you up front. Then you just walk away. You have to keep your wits about you, be as friendly as possible and convince people that they want to have a film company come into their house. Jersey is a lot like where I came from – suburban small townships, where the people are generally happy for you to shoot. Manhattan, on the other hand, is a monster to work in; it's just a bitch. Parking the trucks is a problem; blocking the traffic; and the neighbors don't want lights at their windows late at night. So something like *Sex and the City* is a really tough shoot.

Everybody wants to become a location scout. Everyone I tell, thinks I have the greatest job in the world. But you have your 12- and 16-hour days where you are out looking for something you can't find and you need to find it before you come home. You also have to be a pretty good driver, unless you are in Manhattan. A few scouts in Manhattan just ride the subways. Most people get into the business by knowing somebody, and then "shadowing" them – training by watching them work. Learning how to do it only takes a day or two and then it is up to you to hustle and get the jobs. Sometimes there is a high demand for scouts but then when the job is over you have to figure a way to survive.

When *The Sopranos* finishes, I have no idea where I will work. I am fishing at the moment; like a trawler out at the ocean throwing out a fishing line looking for that next job. I like the steady work of TV, and I like being able to schedule in seeing my child, so I hope to get on a new TV show I have a good time. And I still dance. I go out honky-tonking once in a while.

Will Scheck
Greensperson

I was keen to interview Will Scheck because I liked his job title and was not completely sure what it meant. At 7:30 in the morning I got a call in my New York hotel to meet him on the corner of the street in his pick-up truck, which he could not leave nor park easily. The truck was filled with barrels to be used with plants as set dressing. But to find out exactly what a greensperson does – from providing flowers, to altering the seasons, to estimating the price of leaves – read on!

SELECTED CREDITS

Marvin's Room (Jerry Zaks, 1996)
The Ice Storm (Ang Lee, 1997)
K-Pax (Iain Softley, 2001)
Kate & Leopold (James Mangold, 2001)
Far from Heaven (Todd Haynes, 2002)
The Royal Tenenbaums (Wes Anderson, 2002)

I am the person on a film who is in charge of all of the plants, flowers, trees, soil and grass. I work under the production designer, who hires me if they are interested in that kind of decorating. The designers I work with give me some leeway so that I can pitch ideas and be quite creative in my work. First I would look at the location, and if a garden is required there we would design it from the ground up. We also do indoor plants and provide pretty much all of the organic material on a film.

It is also a Hollywood tradition that the greensman provides all the dirt roads. So on a job I did recently in Brooklyn for a period film, *Kate & Leopold* [James Mangold, 2001], set at around the time the Brooklyn Bridge was being built, the designer installed all these makeshift construction buildings and my job was to get rid of all the paved roads and make them into dirt roads. We brought in about 30 truckloads of different kinds of gravel and dirt material and covered all the roads with it – a long way from flower arranging, although that was actually my other job on that film. I often do the research myself to find what flowers are appropriate on a period film. Mostly I use the library of the Horticultural Society at the Bronx Botanic Gardens. So for *Kate & Leopold* I looked at formal Victorian table arrangements, like three-tiered platters using flowers such as tulips.

Another film I enjoyed was *Far from Heaven* [Todd Haynes, 2002] with the designer Mark Friedberg, who is probably my best client. The film actually has a gardener as a main character. A woman falls in love with her gardener, so on a film like that you are going to have a greensperson because the flowers are a part of character development. Also that film takes place in the 1950s and we were trying to recreate the Technicolor, washed-out look of films at that time. We used many silk and plastic flowers because it was meant to look like a movie not like reality, so we flaunted their look. In the '50s and '60s, scenery was less sophisticated than it is now, so we used flowers which were unnaturally gaudy and too big. It was set in the fall, and we painted leaves in garish colors and pasted them individually on the ground to create this artificial look. I did all the house plants, too, lots of exotic-looking tropicals.

There was also a flower arrangement on *Far from Heaven* that had to be made specially. It had to have a flower with an interesting name, which the characters find growing outside and cut and bring home and it had to be large enough to photograph well. So in the end we invented it, which was really fun. We decided with the director that it would be a witch hazel, which blooms in the fall. But real witch hazel is a bit small and on camera it wouldn't captivate the audience. So we made a larger, exaggerated version. Another Hollywood tradition is that you can make up the names of plants for films, so I found an artificial leaf and an artificial stem and an artificial flower and put the three together and we called it winter hazel – which is actually a plant but not what we made. We made a 20-foot shrub of this, and then an indoor arrangement.

But in most of my jobs we are looking for realism and on most films I use real plants. About three weeks ago I got a call to do a rooftop garden for a commercial. We went up there and looked at the location and the art director had a drawing of decking and so forth. Then I had two days, and a budget of about $10,000 to go out and buy all the plants. I have a little tour of about five wholesale and five retail nurseries that I do. I start at

Will's pick-up truck.

about seven in the morning and by about three in the afternoon I will have seen about 30,000 plants and taken digital photos, made choices and tagged things along the way. By about four o'clock I go home, download all the images and decide what I am going to take the next day. Then I get all the checks cut, get everything in order, and make another round and hand-select everything I have decided on and then another truck comes and picks it all up.

Everything goes to location, where I have a crew waiting to bring it all to the roof and I place everything. We actually built that garden out of plywood, so instead of hauling huge amounts of dirt up to a roof, we cut holes in the quarter-inch ply and dropped the plant containers in the holes and just used some mulch on top of the wood. It looked like there was six yards of deep soil on the rooftop, but in fact it was just a sprinkling on top. Similarly, on a film I did about Jackson Pollock, we made a vegetable garden out of a combination of artificial vegetables and fruits and vegetables that we bought from the grocery store and plopped in the ground – full heads of lettuce and cauliflower. Making a realistic-looking vegetable garden in one day is a tall order.

As a greensperson, I don't get paid as much as a union construction worker – which is ridiculous, but I also don't work all the long hours. I don't stand-by on set. I get there before, during the prep time, and then leave and take it down. There is usually someone else who stands-by for 14 to 16 hours a day, but I function more as the designer or coordinator, working eight to ten hours.

At the end of the day, I normally take a step back when everyone is clamoring for plants. Mostly the actors don't get involved, but the producers often want the plants, and the "higher ups" in the art department, and my crew. Many fights break out. I let them take what they want, and what is left I'll take home. Generally what I have at home are the runts of the litter — the plants that couldn't make it and nobody wanted, but I try to nurse them back to health. Some have made it and some haven't. The film business in New York used to be very corrupt. At least, corrupt on a kind of low level, but film crew used to do better about 20 years ago. Some of the old-timers remember the way it was. For instance, in the prop department, basically, if you bought a prop, it was yours! But now things have changed. Now money is really scrutinized.

I started as a prop man and I did that for 15 years. But I am an avid home gardener and my mother is also a big gardener, so about ten years ago I decided to see if I could make a go of specializing and it has worked well. When I started, there was no one in New York specializing in this, and I kind of made it up as I went along. In the past ten years, my job has got slightly more competitive. Now there are three or four other people doing this work here, and because the film industry has its ups and downs, there are times when everyone is looking for the same jobs and negotiations have gone in favor of the studios. There is one guy who specializes more in the heavy equipment side; he has moved rivers! There are several people who just do flowers; I do a kind of mixture.

The movie business is famous for doing work that is never seen. We dress the whole of Park Avenue, and they decide to shoot on Madison. On the other hand, cost-cutting is sometimes a mistake. I worked on a film called *Joe's Apartment* [John Payson, 1996], which was about cockroaches building a garden! My kids loved the movie, though it got very mixed reviews. We took a square city block which was leveled; there was nothing there and we built a garden in three weeks, including 30-foot trees and a pond. Actually, the cockroaches built it overnight, to make amends with the character because they burnt down his apartment! Anyway, we had about 20 pounds of sod [grass] delivered, which has to be laid the same day or it starts to rot. The producers got cold feet and decided they didn't want to pay the overtime, so all the sod rotted over the weekend and when we put it down it was all

Will makes notes about tulips.

brown and it all had to be painted, which did *not* look good. There were some aerial photos of the garden taken, but my set of photos, to put in my portfolio, I had to have retouched!

So although we use many real plants, there are also advantages of artificial ones. We use a lot of silk flowers because they last. I have 40 or 50 huge boxes of silk flowers that I take with me on all my jobs. On a film, you often have to see a location many times, but it is not all shot at once, so it is a problem if flowers deteriorate. There is also a problem with visibility. Silk flowers actually photograph better than the real ones.

Another thing which the greensperson is often called upon to do is change the season. For example, a company may need to shoot a Christmas

Will counting leaves.

scene outside of the Waldorf Astoria Hotel or Bloomingdale's, in August. So I would set up Christmas trees, bring trees in with their leaves taken off, and with lights wrapped around them. Once I was working on a movie called *Autumn in New York* [Joan Chen, 2000] where, although it was shot in autumn, we had to create a lot too. So we were out in the street with giant lifts to bring us up to the top of 50 foot trees. The trees had all lost their leaves, so we were putting artificial painted fall-colored leaves on. Someone came up to me and asked what I was doing and I said, "We're putting the leaves back in the trees." He asked, "Why?" and I replied, "You want fall here, don't you? This is how it's done!"

We generally buy all the leaves, and in fact all artificial plants, from about ten huge factories in China which sell them to about 50 companies who sell them for different prices with different names. So one of my jobs is doing pricing. An interesting part of my job is when I am brought to a tree, and the producer or location scout says, "How much will it cost to take all the leaves off that tree and make it into a fall tree? How much material, labor and equipment rental?" So I go to the tree with a grid and pluck some leaves and count them and then multiply it to determine how many leaves are in that tree. Then I'll know approximately how long it will take to remove all the green leaves.

Next I go to the catalogue and find leaves. They are sold in branches, and I will order samples and count the leaves on the sample and multiply that to know how many branches I'll need. Then I start looking for the best price for that branch, because I would need about 2,500. Sometimes you are looking for fall leaves at the end of December and they are all gone because the factories don't make more than they can sell in that season. They are really made to be used in arrangements, and styles change in the floral industry. So you have to be quick and know what you want, and then figure out how many people you need to put the leaves on. It might be that there is a whole alley of trees and I know that in each lift I can have three people and they can do about 40 square feet an hour, so what will it take to do it all?

Meredith Tucker
Casting Associate

On any film, there are often three people involved specifically with casting. These are the casting director (usually credited before the film starts), a casting associate and extras casting. Ultimately it is almost always the director who will choose his/her cast with the producer also having a say in major roles. But directors and producers rely on the casting director to assist them with assembling the perfect cast for their production. It is the job of the casting director to suggest people to the director who he/she may not have thought of, and to liaise between the director, actor and their agents, while casting directors also negotiate the deals with agents and are responsible for the contract once an actor is cast.

Casting directors often work with an associate (or assistant). Both need to have a vast knowledge of different actors, for together they audition and help select all the actors with speaking roles in a film, TV show or play. To some extent, as Meredith explained, the job is made difficult because they are unusually reliant on the performance of an actor at an audition on a given day. The person who does extras or background casting selects all of the non-speaking roles and chooses them more for their appropriate look than their talent.

Casting is an example of a vital role in film that is not generally recognized. Far from the elegant "casting couch" kind of office one might expect, Meredith works on Broadway, but in a dingy building where one is quite relieved to find her large airy room at the end of a dark and slightly ominous corridor.

SELECTED CREDITS
Stealing Beauty (Bernardo Bertolucci, 1995)
That Thing You Do (Tom Hanks, 1996)
The Truman Show (Peter Weir, 1998)
The Ninth Gate (Roman Polanski, 1999)
The Sopranos (HBO TV Series, first aired 1999)
What Women Want (Nancy Meyers, 2000)
Ciao America (Frank Ciota, 2002)

Meredith in her office.

In a sense, casting people essentially perform a weeding-out process. What happens here at Walken/Jaffe Casting where I work, is that we get a breakdown of the characters we are going to be looking for, either for a TV show or a film. Next the breakdown is sent to the agents, who send us pictures of their clients who they think would be right for the part. We pick out whom we want to see along with names of people whom we are always considering and then we narrow down through auditions and availability. We take the "finalists" to the director or producer who will make the ultimate decision.

At present I work mainly on *The Sopranos* [HBO TV Series, first aired 1999], which when it is up and running is kind of all-consuming. But before I joined this company, I worked mainly on feature films, usually larger-budgeted ones. I did some acting in college – I was terrible – and I was taking a semester off in 1990 and there was an alliance of off-Broadway theater companies that had an internship program and they set me up with some interviews and I ended up interning with New York Theater Workshop, doing stage management. But they also had a weekly reading series for new plays, which needed to be cast each week, so I ended up helping the woman who was in charge of that and just fell in love with doing it.

If it is just a reading, you can have your pick of a lot of actors because it only takes one afternoon out of their lives. And I thought, "This would actually be a good job for me." I had worked in a video store during vacation at college and people would come in and ask if something was a good movie and I would always say, "Yes, so-and-so is in it." I had a good memory for stuff like that, which is really important in this job. It's always useful if, say, you have seen an actor who stands out in a play in a certain part, and you remember, and can suggest them for a similar part in a film.

Then in the summer between my junior and senior year at college, I interned for a film casting director in New York and after college I worked as a casting assistant for various casting directors until I worked for Howard Feuer for about six and a half years, going back and forth between New York and Los Angeles with him. I worked on films like *To Die For* [Gus Van Sant, 1995] and *Beloved* [Jonathan Demme, 1998] and *The Truman Show* [Peter Weir, 1998]. *To Die For* was a phenomenal experience because it was a great script and I actually got to read with many of the actors, which I never did again. It was really, really fun. And my boss was involved with choosing Nicole Kidman for that. I didn't really meet her, but you are normally only disappointed when you meet the big stars.

On *The Truman Show*, Jim Carrey was already set up to play the part from the start, as is often the case with a big movie; it gets the go-ahead with a star as part of the package before starting casting. Then we did the rest of the casting for it in New York and Los Angeles long before shooting, which was mostly in Florida. But the prep time with Peter Weir was fascinating. He was very inclusive. And you really felt that he was using the whole casting process to figure out how he wanted to do the movie, in a much more apparent way to me than it had ever been before. Usually you would think a director had an idea in mind and was looking for that, but on *The Truman Show* ideas evolved. We had an actress who we tried to cast as the wife but it didn't work out, so we moved on to a couple of other actresses and then the original actress became available. But Peter Weir's whole process had changed, so she was no longer right for the part and we ended up casting Laura Linney, who was fantastic in that part.

We also cast a guy named Paul Giamatti, who had a very small part in the movie [Control Room Director], but he became central to how Peter saw the control room. The piece of casting expanded to the whole concept, and we could see the process. It seemed things were in flux and Peter was more open to everything and that casting was really helping him develop how he would handle a lot of things, which was really neat, and he was so appreciative. Most directors are nice, although there are a few horrible ones who can be mean, especially in LA – people are full of egos, particularly in the film industry.

Tom Hanks was really wonderful to the actors who came to audition for him on *That Thing You Do* [1996]. I didn't get to sit in on a lot of his auditions, but the walls were very thin in that office, and I could hear him! One of the things he did, that no other director has done who I have worked with, is that he would actually tell the actor in the room that they got the part. That must have been thrilling for the actors, to have Tom Hanks tell you point blank, "That was great; I'd love you to take the part." Usually the agent will tell actors if they have or haven't been successful.

Around that time I would sit in on a lot of auditions, and help set up everything, going through the photos, but now I actually get to audition on my own. On a film you will have about three months to cast 20 parts, whereas on *The Sopranos* we'll have six days to cast 15 parts – some of them one-liners – and when we are really crazed we will see 80 people in one day. For even one person to sit in the room the whole time is torturous but to have two would be masochistic! So we often split the day and video everything and I might see 40 people. Then the final auditions are done at Silvercup Studios when the actors will read for the producer and director.

Meredith looks through artists' photos.

We take into account the actor's appearance and their résumé – if they have only done soaps or musical theater, we might be less welcoming. One young girl fresh out of some new acting studio auditioned for me once and she did this crazy method acting and she read a line about how she was beaten as a child and all of a sudden there was this truly blood-curdling scream, and I had to leave the room and compose myself, it was so awful!

The Sopranos is so specific that sometimes it is better for us to get some guy who has never acted before, from Arthur Avenue on the Bronx, which is the big Italian section. But the *real* types do not want to come near us. In Little Italy there was a bar that I was in and there was an older man – I don't know if he was a mobster – but he really looked right for the show and I went up to him and introduced myself and said he would be great for a part we were casting, but he wanted nothing to do with us. The real people don't, it is the people who think or pretend that they are real, and there are enough of those guys to go around that we don't need actual mobsters!

When I first started working here, we had an open call in New Jersey and we had 14,000 people come! It was insane. We caused a traffic jam. We saw about 5,000 and then they had to shut it down because people were just pushing and getting crazy. So we got their photos and then we saw about 150 people and hired about ten people. Two people had fairly big parts, one of whom had never acted before. She was a legal secretary but was a heavy-set Italian-American woman who just looked perfect.

When you find the right person, it is very exciting. I remember I was working on the movie *What Women Want* [Nancy Meyers, 2000] and the director was primarily a comedy writer, so if someone wasn't making her laugh, her energy would lull. But there was this one guy, Mark Feuerstein, who ended up getting cast in the movie as Mel Gibson's best friend, who just came in, and he had done a pretty good job when he came in to see my boss originally, but this time he just turned on the charm like you wouldn't believe and the director was just giggling. He charmed *everyone* so much and it was a really good audition and we were *so* excited and it was great. Sometimes, even if the person doesn't get the part, but they do a really good audition, there can be something really wonderful about it.

I would like to cast something entirely on my own, but I am also interested in producing, partly because we are not unionized, so we get no benefits. There have been talks, since I have been doing it, over the last ten years, to get unionized, but it hasn't happened. I think, and many people say this, that we have remained non-unionized because casting is primarily done by gay men and women – maybe because many are frustrated actors. Being a freelance crew person here is problematic and it is very badly paid – the same with costume departments, which are also primarily gay men.

Another thing about casting is that it is not really appreciated. There is an Emmy for casting, but there is no Oscar, and when an actor wins an Oscar they will very rarely thank the casting director. And it is weird that you are so dependent on other people spontaneously being able to do well. Your livelihood is actually resting on a lot of other people, which makes it very pressure-filled and a bit problematic. You might have a director's session the next day and there is really nothing you can do but hope the actor does a good job, which means a kind of lack of control. You can prepare them as much as possible, like even if someone is well-known, my boss will always offer for them to come run it with her. So we try to give them little clues as to how to do it in front of the director. Then if they do a better job than you anticipated, it is all the better. We work insane hours, and it is very intense, but when someone comes in and does a great audition, the hair on the back of your neck raises up and the excitement and energy is palpable.

Dianne Greaves
Foley Artist

Foley artists (formerly known as footsteps artists in the U.K.) are named after Jack Foley 1891-1967, born in Yorkville, New York, and credited with creating the techniques for adding post-production sound effects to films. Many of his methods, despite developments of modern technology, are still used today — with the practitioners using props such as boots, a stalk of celery, coconut shells, to create the sounds of footsteps, breaking bones, horses' hooves, etc. These sounds then embellish or replace the original soundtrack. Sounds such as explosions, car engines, gunshots, roaring tigers, etc., are generally taken from pre-recorded sound effects libraries. But only a Foley artist can match the unique sound and timing of the footsteps of a particular character in a certain mood.

I met Dianne at the studio where she works. Behind a curtain she showed me different doors for opening, shutting and locking: a car door set into the wall, a wrought iron gate, a stable door and a house door. There was also a working sink with various jugs and bottles and a watering can. Then she pulled away a portion of carpet to reveal different surfaces for walking: sand, wood, linoleum, etc. Finally she opened a huge walk-in cupboard that looked something like a cross between a junk shop and Aladdin's cave. It was crammed with swords, bicycles, guns, broken glass, chains, china, old furniture, saddles, bells, bridles, fabric, boots, bags...

Dianne was disarmingly nervous about her interview, saying, "I am a dancer, not a talker." And indeed she looked like she had been a dancer — petite and trim-figured, with platinum blonde hair. She also had an ageless, almost child-like quality which seemed to fit with her joy in dressing up, using props from her store and creating "magic."

SELECTED CREDITS

The Cook, the Thief, His Wife & Her Lover (Peter Greenaway, 1989)
Orlando (Sally Potter, 1992)
Little Buddha (Bernardo Bertolucci, 1993)
Four Weddings and a Funeral (Mike Newell, 1994)
Secrets and Lies (Mike Leigh, 1995)
Chicken Run (Peter Lord and Nick Park, 2000)
Last Orders (Fred Schepisi, 2001)
Bridget Jones: the Edge of Reason (Beeban Kidron, 2004)

You have to be a bit weird to be a Foley artist – but it is a lovely job. In the past, Foley artists only did feet, but in the last 15 years it has grown to more and more special effects. We do Foley because when a film is being shot, and the mixer is concerned with the actors' voices, a lot of sound is lost; some never happens, like maybe fighting with swords which are not real; and some is not wanted like the sounds of aircraft going across. If dialogue is lost then, it is replaced. Everything else needs replacing too, like clothing movements, so you have a clean soundtrack, which is what people expect. We also do a whole soundtrack of a film without the dialogue which is sold all over the world and then they put their own dialogue in with, say, Russian actors doing the voices.

We have an editor and sound mixer working with us. A Foley editor transfers the film onto video and charts out the whole movie into cue sheets for the Foley sound mixer [recording engineer] and Foley artists to follow. These consist of time codes for an action to start and stop and a description of the action, such as "car crash at 300 feet." The Foley sound mixer records the sounds from microphones onto separate tracks (smashing glass, two car doors slamming together, etc.). He also puts what we do into perspective – he might bring our footsteps from a distance to closer up while we are actually just walking on the spot. He makes us sound real. Then the tapes are combined and manipulated and fitted by the sound editor for precise synchronization.

All these people, who work in post-production, are different from the sound department who worked while the film was shooting. Sometimes the director will come in and see what we are doing, but not very often. Usually, in England the post-production sound is all done in a week – two if we are lucky, but in America I think they get a month because they often have more money to spend.

I have been doing Foley work for 20 years. I was a dancer since I was three, and performed on television with people like Lionel Blair, and then one day an agent said, "Will you do some Foley?" I had no idea really what it was, but the money was very good at the time and I said, "Yes, I'll do it, *whatever.*" Normally, now, it would be the sound editor who would ring me to give me my work. At first I was no good at it at all – it took me a good year to learn how to create sounds, how to improvise and how to get my timing right. For example, sometimes you can't see the actor's feet and you have to watch their shoulders or hips to synchronize the timing of their steps.

Because you have to have good timing, a lot of the people who work as Foley artists, even the men, are dancers or have had drama school training where they have learnt to dance. Or one of my colleagues, Jason Swanscott, is a footballer – a very big guy, but very quick and nimble on his feet, so he is very good at synchronization. If you are doing children, however big you are, you have got to be nimble – but most of us are ex-dancers. It's where the dancers go when they are too old to dance! Actually, I sometimes still get to dance. I did a tap routine on *Plots With a View* [Nick Hurran, 2002] and I did the tap on *Billy Elliot* [Stephen Daldry, 2000]. I didn't do the Foley for that but the Foley artist couldn't tap and tap is what I am good at, so I was brought in to do Jamie Bell's tap. He did the dancing, but you couldn't hear it clearly while they were shooting.

There are only about a dozen of us in the whole of London and we help each other out, but when I started there were five Foley artists. In the U.S. there are many more because they make more films. Here if there were lots of Foley artists, we wouldn't all make a living. But the older people teach the new people. I was taught by the sound mixer in this studio – Ted Swanscott. He had been doing all the *Alien* films with Beryl Mortimer, a footsteps artist of that time, and he taught me how to walk and scuff my feet properly – everything. You have to learn the tricks of the trade from someone. And now I can teach people.

We did a film last year, *Kevin of the North* [Bob Spiers, 2001], and it is all set in Alaska in snow. A new person would come in and say, "Where is the snow?", but I would show them what we do for snow. If it is thick, crunchy snow, we use a big pillowcase full of cornflower and you get that lovely crunchy noise. If it is ice, you use silica gel with some sea salt scattered in, and when you walk on that it gives a gorgeous icy noise. I learnt all these sounds from older footstep artists and editors.

There is a charming old editor called Peter Holt and we did a film called *Mary Riley* [Stephen Frears, 1996], which wasn't a brilliant film, but it was big, and the characters all walked on old cobbled streets and we wanted their steps to sound gritty. But if you walk in the old leather shoes that they wore in those days, on grit, it sounds horrible and scratchy. So Peter Holt brought in tins of mixed herbs and by walking on them it created a lovely dirty but soft sound. The whole job is just tricks, really.

We still use coconut shells for horses' hooves, and carriage noises are made with a battered old suitcase on a chair. A creaking door sound is made using

Coconut shells are still used for the sound of horses' hooves.

old film tape. If you put the tape round metal or wood, it will make a brilliant creak and you can do that to the exact timing that you want, whereas an actual door might creak one day and not the next. On *Chicken Run* [Peter Lord and Nick Park, 2000] we used wire round an old aircraft wing, which we pulled to create creaks in the doors. Quite a common effect is the sound of squelching feet in mud – we use soggy wet newspaper to walk on.

All the big studios, like Pinewood and Shepperton, have enormous prop cupboards. We have our own little squeaks and cracks which we keep in our bags, and a Foley artist never throws anything away, but most things are provided. Actually, the first feature film I worked on was *A Room with a View* [James Ivory, 1985] and although we had turf in the studio, we brought in extra foliage to sound as though the characters were walking through long grass. Every film is a challenge and every film is different. It's a fun job; it's lovely.

Yesterday we were doing a new film called *The Kelly Gang* [Gregor Jordan, 2003] and we had to do the sound of slicing a horse's throat. It was quite revolting, but we had good fun doing it – slicing a cabbage and doing gushing blood with our mouths. That's a Foley artist's fun. I told you, you have to be a bit weird to be a Foley artist! It's often good when a man and a woman work together because a man is good at the heavy work and the woman can add the lighter feet – anyway, there was me and a man working on a track yesterday where they were shooting bottles off a shelf in a bar. So if one of you does the smashing glass [hitting broken glass in a bucket with a baseball bat], the other can do the liquid [smashing a glass with water in it] and the two combined makes a much bigger, better sound.

In contrast, another film I enjoyed working on was *The Borrowers* [Peter Hewitt, 1997] about four-inch high "little people" who live under the floorboards. There was a scene when the little boy lands on a light bulb and you can hear his little hands and feet landing, which was my fingernails on glass – those little things that you add make a movie magical, I think. A Foley artist really does add magic to a film. If you listen to *Gone With the Wind* [Victor Fleming (and uncredited, George Cukor and Sam Wood), 1939], there is no Foley. In the first scene they are all on the boardwalk and there are no feet sounds or crinoline dresses and although it is a beautiful film it is very flat without those sounds.

We would do everything now and it would sound much livelier. We would walk holding a big silk crinoline dress, which we would swing, and add all the men's steps in their boots. We recently did a film called

Diane creates the sound of shattering glass by pounding pieces of glass in a plastic bucket with a baseball bat.

Napoleon [Yves Simoneau, 2000] for television, with Isabella Rossellini in it, which is a lovely production and all the ladies wore crinoline dresses in that. We also had to create the sounds of armor and bayonets and all the noises of 50,000 people marching in an army and we did that with two of us but building up many tracks.

Sometimes you have to improvise. For instance, we have just done a film about thieves who were all on skateboards. You can't skateboard in a studio, so you have to do it with rollerblades and rollerskates on your hands. We had to do it on different surfaces, which was quite hard work on the hands. Rollerblades on their own don't make a noise so you have to work at creating a sound which makes the film sound exciting. Sounds have got to be believable, even though they are not the real sounds – that is the difficulty of the job.

The more you do it, the better you become. People do it 'til they really want to retire, into their sixties and seventies. We have a man, Stan Fivepence, who probably wouldn't like me to tell his age, but he is still doing a great job. You learn to invent more. And because we are not in front of the camera, it doesn't matter what we look like – which is just as well really, because we get filthy! We get muddy and dirty; it's not a glamorous job at all. It is a hard tough job and sometimes you get hurt and cut the top of your finger off or something. Of course we get to giggle about things too, like when we do sounds like farts, which you usually do with your hand over your mouth, vocally. We do a lot of vocal sounds, like gushing blood or sauce bottles, eating, drinking, kissing – you just kiss your hand.

There is so much sound! If a person went to a movie, and the sound was awful, they would complain. So we work to a very high quality. I walk up and down escalators following people, listening to their shoes! I love movies, but I always watch for every single sound. And when I go and see a movie, even if they use a little bit of my feet, I have put something into it, and I think, "I did that!" The first star I ever did was Goldie Hawn's feet and I was really proud. I thought I'd reached "the big time." Well, it beats working at the till in Tesco's, doesn't it! I wouldn't want to do anything else. It is like when you are little, you play, and when you are grown up you can play and get paid for it!

Richard Bradshaw
Stunt Performer

When Richard Bradshaw told me he would pick me up from the tube in a black Porsche, I suspected I might be meeting rather a flash guy. So I was surprised to find the remains of chewed bones left by his pet Alsatian in the well of the car's passenger seat, and that he lived in an unpretentious suburban house. Richard was down-to-earth and modest, and contrary to some preconceptions, this stunt performer was also intelligent and sensitive.

Richard enjoys stunt work because he is always learning, and because it combines acting with his favorite sports, in particular scuba diving, which enabled him to work on films such as Titanic. *While totally dismissive of the "knocks" that it is the job of a stunt performer to take, his concerns are with professionalism and safety. In fact, the stunt register has a remarkable safety record. All other activities involving sports to which an element of danger is attached have a higher number of fatalities. The key to stunt work is not necessarily involvement with danger, but getting something right, and doing it first time.*

SELECTED CREDITS

White Squall (Ridley Scott, 1996)
Tomorrow Never Dies (Roger Spottiswoode, 1997)
Titanic (James Cameron, 1997)
Sleepy Hollow (Tim Burton, 1999)
Billy Elliot (Stephen Daldry, 2000)
Star Wars Episode II: Attack of the Clones (George Lucas, 2002)
Sahara (Breck Eisner, 2005)

Originally I trained as an actor. I went to college, studied drama, did all that, and worked a bit (mainly on stage) but not very successfully or satisfactorily. So I got a bit frustrated with it and got completely out of the entertainment industry for a while. Then I moved back to London and decided to have another go at it, and I met someone at an audition who was training to become a stunt man, and got chatting to him. Suddenly it all seemed to make sense – this was the performing that I wanted to do professionally, plus most of the stuff that I did for fun. I always enjoyed scuba diving and rock climbing; I've owned motorbikes for years; I do horse riding when I can; martial arts – I was a junior international fencer – that's the stuff that I do. And the idea of being able to make a living with a combination of acting and sport seemed fantastic.

There are two levels of training you can do. The first is about different sports, like the ones I just mentioned, that relate to stunt work, and you can go away and get a reasonably high qualification from the governing body of that sport. For example, you have got to be brown belt (which is one below black belt) in martial arts. You have to get qualifications in six sports (spread quite broadly, you couldn't just specialize in different martial arts) from a fairly extensive list which includes gymnastics, water sports, fight skills, riding, driving skills, etc. You also have to get a full Equity card, which can be quite a big deal if you are not already an actor. Then you can get onto the stunt register and are in effect an apprentice – learning to relate these sports that you've done to the actual job. And for the first few years you keep a record of everything you do, which gets signed by the stunt coordinator.

The stunt coordinator is usually the person who employs the stunt performer on a film, although occasionally if there isn't a stunt coordinator it might be the producer or the production manager or the director. They phone me up and tell me what is needed and in virtually all cases I'd want to accept it – because they wouldn't offer something I couldn't do, like in my case skydiving. Stunt work is about creating the right shot, so that the effect is as spectacular as you want while still being within the boundaries of acceptable safety. And the only answer to what constitutes "acceptable safety" is that I always intend to be able to work the following day!

The first time you do anything completely new, there is a certain amount of concern about what it will feel like and what you actually have to do to get it exactly right. But a lot of what makes a good stunt man is being able to harness the inevitable adrenalin, whether it is a big stunt or not, and focus it, so that you can deal with the element of pressure to get it right the first time round.

A lot of the work isn't about massive peril. Doing a hand-brake turn in a car, you are not in a particularly dangerous situation, but they might

Richard flies through the air after an explosion on a space ship in *The Fifth Element*. A small trampoline enables him to throw himself against the wall, which has had two of the vertical pieces of wood cut away to make it safer. (Courtesy of Richard Bradshaw)

want you to stop quite close to the camera, so you would need to make sure that all the camera crew were completely safe. You would want to be doing it exactly as planned and arrive exactly on the mark so that they get the shot. The director is going to be much happier with that, than with someone who does the same thing ten times bigger but it's completely off-camera so you don't see it. So a lot of it is about the reliability and professionalism of the person.

In my early career I would get an immense amount of satisfaction after a film if I could say "now I understand this," or "now I can do this." Initially my biggest influences were other stunt people – the stunt coordinator or a more established performer on the job. As I went on, I became more interested in cameras and editing and what makes my bit of it look good on screen. That's something I am very interested in now. I just recently bought a computer with editing facilities and I am in the process of learning all that. Not that I necessarily want to be an editor, but I think the more I understand editing, I will be able to make suggestions as to how cameras are positioned, how we string a sequence together, that sort of thing. One of the most challenging things about my work is that I am always learning and there is always something to think about.

Terry Forrestal is a stunt man who taught me a huge amount. Recently there was a program on BASE Jumping,* which looked at a number of different groups of people who did it, and why they did it, and Terry Forrestal was on it. He was a guy in his mid-fifties or so who had worked as a stunt man for years and had a reputation as an exceptionally gutsy performer to the extent that some people thought he was a bit too reckless.

He would do some extraordinary things, and hurt himself pretty spectacularly along the way, but as a coordinator he was incredibly conscientious and aware of safety and aware of the need to look after his performers. He had a very different attitude to looking after others to what he did himself. He was also a second unit director and was really the first person who gave me a sense of the importance of, and appreciation of, the cameras and the way they are set up. Anyway, during the program Terry and a group were BASE Jumping on holiday with a documentary crew filming them. It wasn't actually for a stunt, but tragically Terry got killed. A BASE Jump went wrong. And I think it hit all of us on the register very hard.

Since the stunt register came into existence in 1977, we've only had one person killed doing a stunt, which if you look at any other sport which has got any sort of element of danger in it, is actually an extremely good record. Yes, people have broken bones and had knocks and that sort of thing, but actually the safety record is extremely high. So when something like that happens, it affects us all deeply.

I have been doing stunt work for about seven years. I have also done some doubling — for Ted Danson and Pierce Brosnan, for instance. In *Tomorrow Never Dies* [Roger Spottiswoode, 1997], I just did the underwater scenes for Brosnan — in a picture that size, the lead actor will have several

---

* An acronym for Building Antenna Span Earth, BASE Jumping is parachuting from fixed objects, such as a mountain, instead of out of an aircraft.

stunt doubles, particularly as there would be several units working at once. I did a couple of months' work, in a sequence where Bond dives down to a boat which has been sunk and something has been stolen from it, and there is a fight down there and they get trapped and then they escape. Working underwater takes a long time, so I got to know Pierce a bit. He's a lovely guy. Really, really nice. Very professional and good at working with a team.

He did quite a lot himself if it was safe, like a lot of the driving of that boat. But when you're getting the boat jumping over another boat and do-ing a 360-degree barrel roll, you've got to ask yourself, "Is it really going to be him?" My father-in-law told me that he watched *Tomorrow Never Dies* on a transatlantic flight in the middle of the night. Suddenly he shouted out to the amazed other passengers, "That's Richard!" The fact that people might think Pierce Brosnan did the stunt doesn't actually affect me. Other profes-sionals in the business know the work that I've done and know what I can do and the respect of my peers is what counts. It is always nice going to the cinema and hearing someone go "oooh" at something that was in fact me. That's nice, but it's not so important.

From quite early on in my career, I got a reputation for being someone particularly capable in, under, around water. There are probably about three others with a similar reputation. So I got quite a lot of work and met lots of people who I really enjoyed working with. It's lovely going out to a nice location like, say Malta and having a day off and being able to go off and dive for pleasure.

On *Titanic* [James Cameron, 1997], I died horribly, nightly, for about three months. It was a very, very busy time – from January through 'til April. It was the whole sequence of the boat sinking: people jumping overboard, people getting washed away, sliding down the deck – I was lots of different people. There were about 120 stunt people altogether during that time and it was nice because it was a very international stunt crew with an English stunt coordinator, and it was all done in Mexico. Just the mod-ern-day bits were shot around Halifax. So it wasn't too cold although, as it was winter, the nights could have been warmer and we were working six nights a week. But it was quite an experience working on something that scale!

Jim Cameron had a very unusual way of shooting. A lot of the stuff was shot from quite a long way away, often on long lenses, so shooting fairly tight, and then coming in and out. But it meant that because of where he physically was while he was shooting, we really had no sense of what was in shot when. So there were massive long sequences (much longer than normal "takes") that were happening with all sorts of mayhem up and down the boat. And seeing it cut together in the finished film, there are little snippets here and there, and it is pretty much the only film I have ever been involved with when I know I'm in there somewhere, but I'm really hard pushed to spot me! He managed to get the sense of frenzy and chaos, even from the people involved, which is unique.

The boat that was built was I think 90 percent scale — enormous — and running alongside it he had a huge crane and off the jib of the crane in a basket was him and a number of cameras. And this crane would be running up and down the side of the boat, sort of swinging out across the boat, shooting at different angles as they went. So a lot of it was up above us, or around, and we didn't know where he was going to be. But that didn't stop what we had to do. Even so, there were a fair number of "takes" and because it was such a big scale it took a massive amount of time to set up again. Often we'd get maybe three shots done in a night.

Cameron is extremely demanding and as a result not an easy person to work for, but at the time you also got a sense that he was someone with an extraordinary sense of vision. I always find films that are based on fact exciting, and working on them you do get a special sense of what the actual people went through at the time. Jim Cameron was quite a fanatic about the *Titanic* and had been a member of some international *Titanic* society for about 20-odd years. It's his passion, and being involved with that was very interesting.

We actually sank the *Titanic* one night by mistake. There was a big hydraulic winch which lifted the thing up and down so you could see the water rushing on the deck, and that broke. It went down and wouldn't come up, so we had two or three nights off, which was fine by us! No one got hurt with that, although there were some people on the film who got banged around a bit, but they were doing some pretty big stunts. There was one shot where someone falls off the back of the ship and falls about 200 feet, hits the propeller, bounces off and, spinning through the air, falls another hundred feet into the sea. I have had numerous people say to me with great authority "a stuntman died on *Titanic*" referring to that scene, and of course you would die if you really did that. However, the stuntman who did it was alive and well and having a cup of coffee an hour later because the coordinator had created a very clever shot to produce an amazing effect.

There can be a vast difference between what the public sees in the final cut and what physically occurs and is captured in a particular way on film. Although on *Titanic*, because it was such a multi-national crew, there were occasionally some language problems. We had a group of extremely good and capable Czech stunt men, but not all of them spoke much English. And there was a particular shot which Cameron wanted with this one guy trying to climb up the railings of the ship and I was meant to hit him in the stomach so that he would fall back. I had to decide, in the kind of criss-cross diamond pattern of the railing, a particular one of these that I was going to go through.

So we rehearsed it with the guy climbing up, and I saw where his stomach was, and it was fine. Cameron was shooting it from the side, so you couldn't cheat it. But obviously the Czech guy hadn't quite understood how committed I was to that particular square to go through to hit him, and he climbed up six or eight inches higher than he had in rehearsal, so when I whacked him, he went down not a happy man! But in the end, we are there to take the knocks. That's why we get employed and why we get paid the money, and professionally our job is to reduce the likelihood and the severity of injury.

If you are going to get knocked down by a car on film, the chances are that you will come away with some bruises. But hopefully they will not be so bad or severe that if they say, "You need to do that again," well, fine, you do it again. So people do get hurt, and occasionally bones get broken, but that's why they pay us. We have our own insurance which covers loss of earnings, which is part of the professional package that we offer. For that, they usually pay us a good amount of money and we hope we won't actually have to make a claim and we can make a good living.

As a professional I have a price for my work, and some companies want the world for twopence halfpenny, which means they simply don't get me. So a job where they're not prepared to pay for the skill, potential hazard and likely discomfort incurred is something I wouldn't do. I would want to work 30-40 weeks of the year, not necessarily all week; a lot of TV stuff you just work a single day. Certainly if I was working less than 30 weeks, it would have to be either that those weeks were very intensive or it wasn't a particularly good year.

I enjoy my work, so if it is properly priced, why turn it down if it is

offered to me? But there will come a time when I don't want to throw myself around and take the knocks any more and then it's a very natural progression into stunt coordinating. Probably within the next five to ten years I would like to be getting a regular mixture of coordinating and performing so that as I get older I am already established as a coordinator rather than having to make a shift. But for now, I am happy as I am, and also, as well as performing and doubling, I sometimes do safety underwater for other stunt people on films.

If you're going over a waterfall or some rapids, you want to be able to give as much as you can but have someone come in and be right there when you need them. Similarly, if someone does a fire job it will be a stunt man who will be the first person to put them out, because you want someone who knows what you are going through and can feel when you are in trouble. However capable a professional fireman may be, if they see someone on fire they want to go in and put them out, whereas I might want it to run for a little bit more and give a little bit more performance.

It's obviously better if the actor can do their own action shots and you can actually see their face while it's all going on. But they have to be put in a position where they can't get hurt – not because they couldn't take a knock but because if they've got a black eye they would have to stop filming. In *Mission: Impossible 2* [John Woo, 2000], there is some great action very cleverly shot so that it looks like Tom Cruise is doing the most spectacular and outrageous bits of action, and yes it is him doing it, but they found a way of making it absolutely safe. Tom is the sort of person who I think would spend a lot of time and effort in finding a way to do the action rather than use a stunt double. He's really into that sort of thing. He loves cars and bikes and going off rock climbing – that's him.

Generally, most actors that I have worked with have been very good, wanting to get the best performance they can, and therefore listening to different people who can help them. There are inevitably going to be some that don't want to learn in that way, and that's down to them. Possibly coming from an acting background myself helps. I think stunt men have earned the reputation over the years of being slightly dim thugs, which I would like

Opposite: Richard Bradshaw (left) and Tom Aitken (right) are blown up on *Soldier, Soldier* (TV series, 1991). Both stunt doubles work closely with the special effects supervisor as grenades are activated – but Richard still got a singed eyebrow! (Photo copyright Carlton Television, courtesy of Richard Bradshaw)

to think certainly isn't the case these days, and I think breaking down those barriers can be something that is very important.

In *Titanic*, there wasn't really a huge amount of major action that the main cast was involved in. So yes, they were in the water getting wet and cold, but at least Leo was able to wear a wet suit under his costume; Kate wasn't. She got very cold. But she was fabulous to work with. She's great, lovely, so cheerful and positive and lively the whole time. I worked with her again on *Quills* [Philip Kaufman, 2000], about the Marquis de Sade. I was doing some tests for different torture chamber things! There were various unpleasant things which people had to go through, so we went through them first to check they were safe. In fact, you can easily do a couple of months' work on a film and be nowhere near the camera.

I did another historic job in Plymouth, a while back, on a film called *Dead End*, for the Fuji Film competition. I had to do a hanging sequence, which is not a big deal – you get harnessed up, and it can look really good. But this was one of only two still functional old gallows that had been used over the years, and there was this low-ceilinged old room that had been locked up and shut away for goodness knows how long. It had one massive old oak beam across the center with the place where the rope marks had worn it, and the trap door underneath. At the time, with a sackcloth over my head and my hands tied behind my back, standing there, with an actor playing a priest, reading the last rites, I could feel some ghosts there. It's more often the historical things that get to you.

Normally the preparation and rehearsal you are likely to have gone through before doing anything puts it on a different level from the nightmare, for me anyway. But my partner, Sonia, is probably happier to see the final product than the shooting. On one film I had to jump from Tower Bridge into the Thames. She and some friends came along to watch and one friend, who stood beside Sonia, took a video of it. When he played it back, you could hear Sonia's intake of breath as I jumped into the river. Then there was a pause as you see the splash and a little while later you see me resurface in the water, and you hear Sonia's sigh of relief.

Karen Fayerty
Unit Nurse

The nurse on a film set is an unusual member of the crew who is not constantly rushing around but knows everything that goes on. It is her job to watch, and be available, often treating nothing more serious than a hangover.

Karen admits that she does her work partly for the money and that she misses the buzz of hospitals. But she also tells of the friendships she forges, and the fact that as she has no children or conflicting interests at present, she finds her work strangely addictive.

SELECTED CREDITS

The Winslow Boy (David Mamet, 1999)
Honest (David A Stewart, 2000)
Snatch (Guy Ritchie, 2000)
Bridget Jones's Diary (Sharon Maguire, 2001)
The Importance of Being Earnest (Oliver Parker, 2002)
Harry Potter and the Chamber of Secrets (Chris Columbus, 2002)

As a nurse out of uniform, it is a bit odd asking a director to drop his trousers – to get a jab. He might be going away to work and need immunization, a tetanus injection or something, but it doesn't feel right somehow for me. In a hospital, you feel you are in your working mode partly because of your uniform. But here I am in my jeans and boots, and part of my work is to be friendly and chatty and I can feel a bit strange trying to get an antiseptic trolley into the back of a truck or somewhere.

I am a registered general nurse and a registered sick children's nurse and used to work in the casualty department of a hospital called Ashford, which is near Shepperton Studios. One day we were just talking about earning extra money and a friend of mine said she was going on a flight retrieval thing, off to some foreign country to bring back someone who was sick.

PLEASE BE AWARE
**REAL GLASS USED
IN ALL EXISTING
WINDOWS AND
FLATTAGE**

FIRST AID

Health and safety on set — the main
concerns of the unit nurse.

Then a paramedic said he had been working for an agency which got him work on film sets, and he suggested that I join them and earn a bit more money that way.

So a friend and I joined an agency within Shepperton Studios, and started doing it like that, on our days off, weekends, holidays. I never even knew the job existed before and it showed me a whole different world that goes on. I did it for about six months, in Shepperton and on location, and then I decided that I wanted to do it full time. It was in 1995 and the National Health Service was starting to fall to bits and I couldn't really do my job properly as a nurse. I noticed a lot of people around me getting quite burned out, and I was starting to get less and less job satisfaction, so I left.

I took the bull by the horns and am completely self-employed now. Normally the production manager or the production coordinator will hire me when he hires the crew. When I first started out, it was mainly word-of-mouth. We all know each other and keep in touch and if we get asked to do a job and can't do it I would say, "I know someone who could do it." So that is how I started to get work, with people recommending me. Then I started to build up my own contacts and now I have production managers that I know who will just phone me up.

Health and safety is the main concern. Some film companies will just have a qualified first-aider on the job; some will always have a unit nurse. Basically I am there to look after the health and well-being of the crew and everyone involved in the film. Everyone has their own way of doing the job. Some people don't like to stay on set as much as I do. Some nurses will always have their walkie-talkie and so they can wander around more. The main thing is that you have to be available, because if someone has a headache and they don't see you, then they are quite likely to think, "Oh, I can't be bothered, she's not here."

There are some days when we don't do anything all day, but a lot of people will just talk to you about things. It's important that you are friendly and chatty, because lots of people just come to tell you their problems. They might say they are having a bad day, or a relative is ill. And because the nurse is sort of neutral (I don't belong to any department), if someone is fed up with a particular department, they can come and tell me about it and know that it won't go any further.

When you do your nursing training, confidentiality is really drummed into you and I still keep to that. Here, if someone is ill, everyone will come up to me and say, "What's wrong with so-and-so?" and I have to say, "I can't really tell you. If they want you to know, then they will tell you." Touch wood, I have been quite lucky and never had any really serious illness on set. I have had people sprain their ankles and one man dislocated his shoulder. He was pulled over by a cow! He was a cow handler on a period film, with slippery costume shoes on. Anyway the cow moved, and pulled him over and he said he was okay, but he was brought over to me with his hand down by his knee, and I knew what he had done and sent him to the hospital. But the first assistant director still said, "Can we just get this shot done first?" I had to say, "No, I think he might faint if he doesn't go to hospital right away."

Everyone just focuses on their own job, which is why it is good to have a nurse to determine the level of how important something is. But the main things I deal with are hangovers, headaches, upset stomachs. It's worse on location when people go back to a hotel at night. I always stay sober, because if I have a hangover I can't bear people coming up to me whining about theirs. There are also quite a few twisted ankles because people are always

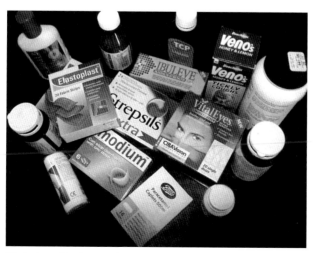

Typical medication used on set.

tripping over cables. Also bad backs, because they are always doing lots of lifting. Occasionally people get electric shocks from the lights, or get nasty cuts on their fingers, but one of the hardest things is exhaustion. People often really need to go home and rest but don't want to lose money, or can't go off for continuity reasons. Most shoots are happier in summer. People always seem to feel better running around in T-shirts.

On almost all jobs, I'll pick up one or two friends. You meet strangers, and by the second day of shooting you often feel that you've known them for ages. Because you work 12 hours a day, six days a week, you see colleagues more than you see your family. So there are often people that I will keep in touch with after the filming has finished. But other than that, I don't really get much job satisfaction. When you work in casualty, someone will come in with a broken leg, and you'll treat them and fix the leg, and get an immediate sense of satisfaction, but here it is mainly minor things.

I miss the chaos of going into a really busy casualty department and doing an eight-hour shift. The advantage of filming is that we get paid well. It is also much less stressful. I can switch off at the end of the day. I might moan about the hours, but actually, for the moment, I wouldn't want to do anything else. It's an odd way of life, but it's quite addictive in some ways.

The first time you go and see a film you've worked on you don't really concentrate on the story because you are so excited seeing it all put together and thinking back to what you were doing at each stage. So sometimes you have to see it a few times. But sometimes, when you know the story, it spoils it a bit. Then if it is, say, a TV series, you get friends badgering you to tell you what's going to happen and you can say, "No, I'm not telling you the end. You wait and see!"

Jim Clubb
Animal Supplier and Trainer

Stalked by a pair of crested cranes, I walked towards a pre-fabricated office, passing some South American penguins, a giant tortoise and a tiger! I was in Britain's largest privately owned collection of wild animals that is not open to the public, having come to see Jim Clubb, managing director of "Amazing Animals," based at Heythorp Zoological Gardens in rural Oxfordshire.

Housing animals in cages or enclosures is never ideal, although I got the impression that Jim and his staff did genuinely care for their animals' welfare. They are constantly seeking to improve their facilities, and as well as providing animals for film, TV, stills photography and special occasions, they are also glad to provide them for educational purposes and for charity events. Jim himself has always loved animals and is an interesting, proud, jovial man with plenty of stories to tell.

SELECTED CREDITS
Octopussy (John Glen, 1983)
Blott on the Landscape (TV Series, Roger Bamford, 1985)
The Secret Garden (Agnieszka Holland, 1993)
Twelve Monkeys (Terry Gilliam, 1995)
101 Dalmatians (Stephen Herek, 1996)
Fierce Creatures (Robert Young, Fred Schepisi, 1997)
Lost in Space (Stephen Hopkins, 1998)
Harry Potter and the Chamber of Secrets (Chris Columbus, 2003) in association
   with "Birds and Animals"

I got into this business by running away and joining a circus! It's true. I went to an English public school and was expected to go into my father's sand and gravel business. They were probably one of the largest sand and gravel readymix concrete companies in the southeast. I was the eldest son and supposed to go into the business but I didn't want to be involved. So I joined a circus and became a lion tamer! And the people I worked for happened to be heavily involved in the film industry. In those days the only way to get zoo-type animals for films was to get circus animals that were trained and used to noise and bustle. For example, they took 12 of their circus elephants to Rome for the filming of *Cleopatra* [Joseph L. Mankiewicz and others, 1963].

But my interest in animals started way before then. As a boy, I kept unusual animals as pets. From the age of eight until I left home when I was 16, I kept monkeys, fox cubs, fruit bats, snakes, alligators, crocodiles, in a little private collection. At that time, people weren't keeping animals like that. The rich and famous were, and the big estate owners like the Rothschilds had private zoos, but there weren't many amateurs. People kept fancy birds and fish but they didn't keep mammals and reptiles as a hobby.

I became a keen herpetologist, keeping reptiles, and joined the British Herpetological Society and got my knowledge from that. I was also very lucky in meeting up with a local chap, older than me, who was a photographer who also kept reptiles and a few other animals. We used to go and visit zoos and he taught me about keeping reptiles and amphibians. Then on holidays I used to work in the local pet shop, and I could also ride. My family was very into show jumping and racehorses and my grandfather bred and kept greyhounds very successfully – so animals were in my blood. I was also, and am to this day, a keen zoo and circus historian. I am interested in anything to do with the keeping of animals in captivity and it has helped me all along.

I left the circus in 1977 and started my own company. I had done quite a lot of filming with the circus then, but they didn't want to do it any more and the film business was taking a dip just then, but I persevered and we did whatever came along. We always had lions and bears and a camel and a zebra and reptiles and it grew very fast. None of those animals is difficult to breed in captivity; there are more tigers in captivity than there are in the wild. We have been in the business 32 years and 99 percent of our animals have been bred over many generations. Originally the animals came from zoos and other establishments – 20 years ago you could buy them from animal dealers – but our stock has gradually built up over the years from breeding. Occasionally animals may become aggressive or do not adapt to

Opposite: Jim and Cleo the Camel (Courtesy of Amazing Animals)

the work. Often those animals are kept as breeding stock, or they might be swapped at a safari park or zoo.

We are careful not to have too many animals and only breed when we want to. At present we have about 140 species and up to about 350 animals. The most popular, after the big cats, are the smaller monkeys, camels and zebras. But not all our animals are big. That 350 includes about 60 to 70 reptiles: small lizards, tarantulas, scorpions. I also have another business in Reading which specializes in domestic animals – cats, dogs and farm animals. We couldn't survive without domestic animals, reptiles and fish – we also have about 200 to 300 varieties of fish. We do some big events and high society parties where they want a big aquarium set up for just one *night*. We did a party last year that cost £10,000,000 – Elton John was the cabaret! That is a very specialist field because the fish get upset and stressed very easily if you don't have the water quality exactly right. So we take all the salt water with us from here. But that is just one part of the business.

We are unique worldwide because we employ the trainers 52 weeks a year. Normally, both here and in the U.S., all the trainers are brought in for one particular film. We employ 18 people year-round and are able to find just enough work for them. The facility here is also unique. The animals are kept in 100 percent modern mainstream zoo conditions, but the animals are kept here for the sole purpose of filming. We work a bit with the American Humane Society who came here for an "open day" and they were so pleased with our facility and said they had never seen anything like it in the world. Other people might have a group of big cats or wolves in the U.S. but we are so diverse and do everything. Zoos can't do our sort of work because they don't have trained animals, and other companies supply animals – there are 105 suppliers of animals for the film industry in the U.K., but we are now exclusively the only ones legally licensed to supply zoo animals for films. Everyone else will tell you they can, but all they do is sub-contract them from us.

In America they call animal-trainers "wranglers." It used to always refer to horse people and then it spread to apply to all animals. On a film you might also have an animal coordinator who could be someone like myself or our head trainer and then there would be maybe six other trainers. I am not as actively involved in training as I used to be. I employ trainers who I normally teach. Every animal is different – you can't have favorites, although I do still work with the big lion. I would never try to hand him over to anyone else because he is too late in life now. But we have three young lions coming along now, being trained. Big cats are actually often easier to train than smaller animals.

Animals are trained first through feeding. We hand feed them, getting a bit closer each time. To start with we carry a board in front of us, from the waist down, or a little riding crop, for protection. Gradually we will approach nearer and nearer 'til there is a trust built up between the animal and trainer. And they go on being trained here all the time. We rehearse with them and put them in different situations and play with them. There are different schools of thought about training. Some people like to handle the animals a lot, but actually I prefer to keep my distance. If you have strict boundaries, it is much easier to keep safe, and both you and the animal know where you stand.

Of course, accidents are still bound to happen and trainers definitely get hurt. Wild animals are never going to be domesticated, and even if they

Jim hugged by a Canadian black bear. (Photo by David Jamieson)

try and play with you, they play like they do with other lions and tigers, so you always have the risk of being injured. Only the slightest claw can result in horrific wounds. We are, all of us, always frightened. You have to respect the animal, and that involves caution. We know the job, and animals don't suddenly attack you, it is a build-up over weeks and you have got to spot those times. You've got to think to yourself, "Okay, he's not too good today. Let's call it a day. Let's not continue working with him." You have got to have the experience to be able to do that.

I was bitten very badly by a puma on a TV commercial once, but that was the director's fault and mine, because I should have just said, "No," but the director just wanted us to do more and more. Nowadays I would just say, "No, that is it." But when you are younger, you are not so confident. Now, when it is the wild animals, I rule the day. I run the show on that day and I have to have full control or I don't want the job, because accidents will happen. I know how many times the lion will come out and do what they want before it is dangerous.

I never believe in telling a director that we can do something we can't. It is much easier when a director is willing to take advice as to what an animal can't do but what it might be able to do instead. Sometimes a director will spend hours repeating something over and over again until an actor gets it right, but they expect an animal to come in and do it right straight away! Stills photography is usually easier when you just have to get the animals in position, maybe with their mouth wide open or whatever.

Our main business really comes from commercials. There are not that many films, made in England, that suit us. And if you leave England, the animals have to do six months' quarantine. There are plenty of films that feature the odd dog or cat, but the biggest film I have done in recent years, which used a lot of big animals, was *Fierce Creatures* [Robert Young, Fred Schepisi, 1997] with John Cleese, Jamie Lee Curtis and Michael Palin, which was a delight to work on. We had a three-month training and preparation period for that film and then shot for 16 weeks, so we were involved for a *long* time. I was jointly involved with another coordinator, but all the stock and training and staff was done by us.

First they send you the script, which is confidential, and you do an animal budget for it. That can take you two or three weeks if you are doing it very thoroughly. At the same time, we would write our opinion as to the ways the animals should be used and presented. In this day and age, when people are very sensitive about animals, animal welfare plays a major role. For instance, wherever possible we always have our veterinary surgeon present on the film and we have him written into the payroll. On *Fierce Creatures*, the whole film takes place in a zoo and it featured tigers, lions, sea lions, camels, llamas, snakes – a lot of animals.

We also had five "hero" animals that were featured all the way through, and they were a baby wallaby, a baby ostrich, a ring-tailed lemur, a coatimundi [a white-nosed, raccoon-like mammal] and a little deer. We set up a kind of zoo, or holding facility at Pinewood Studios where we trained all the hero animals and their doubles. Like if John Cleese was doing a scene with the ring-tailed lemur, and getting it to sit still by feeding it raisins, and then it had had enough raisins and was getting fidgety, we would substitute the lemur's brother, and he would sit and get fed raisins and look just the same!

There were three trainers with those animals there full-time. The bigger animals, which only featured in backgrounds or simple roles, we kept here and rehearsed here, and brought them down to Pinewood three or four days before shooting. We have a kind of studio here with a green and a blue screen so animals can get used to color and their moves and everything. Sometimes scenes are shot here too, and then used as split-screen in a film, or sometimes our trainers will take on a doubling part in a film involving animals. But on *Fierce Creatures* we worked with the actors constantly. You either can work with animals or you can't, and we were very lucky with that cast and really didn't have a problem. John Cleese used to correspond with me for a long time after the film. He was always buying me presents and inviting me up to his house.

Another thing I enjoyed working on very much, was back in the '80s when I did a TV series called *One by One* [BBC drama, 1984]. It was a lovely series about a zoo vet that was based on *our* vet, David Taylor, who is still around, although he is semi-retired now. The series lasted three years, 36 episodes, showing him becoming one of the world's leading vets. We used lots of animals and lots of the stories were about us so it was quite funny. Jimmy Ellis, who had been in *Z Cars* [TV series, 1962-1978], was in it and he became a great friend of mine. And Rob Heyland, who played the vet, was great fun to work with.

I did quite a few acting parts in it as well, which I have often done since. Peter Gilmore gave me enormous help with acting and it was a good time. But now we do so much, I forget. We do a job of some description every day of the week, and some days, two jobs with two different teams. A lot of them might just be a dog at a bus stop, but it is all work that needs to be done and that we want to do because this place takes a lot of running.

Jamie, my son, works alongside me, and Sally, my wife, though we've parted now, has stayed a director in the business and we have always remained great friends. She was the mainstay of the business right from the beginning. She is a very experienced, knowledgeable animal person – it was her family I went to work for in the circus! She has always run the office side and the general day-to-day caring of the animals and their staff. She used to go filming in the early days, but as we got bigger she stopped going and now even I can't go because I have to run the office. We have 18 full-time people here. Michael, our general manager, had a grandfather and father and auntie who were all animal-trainers. His father was killed by a lion!

In general, we use the big cats the most. We have lions, tigers, leopards and black panthers, which are really black leopards. I had a job once, many years ago, where they asked us for a black panther and we were too expensive. In those days, there were other people who could supply them and so we didn't get the job. Another chap arrived with a black panther, which was a tame, hand-reared zoo animal, but it wasn't trained, so it wasn't used to the environment. It is one thing having a tame animal, but a trained one is completely different; a trained animal is able to accept the situation and the environment.

Anyway, during the shoot, they had let the panther out into the studio, with no security caging, because in those days you didn't have to have it. First the panther attacked the camera operator, then the director, then the supplier, and then it disappeared up into the gantry! This was at Bray Studios. Well, I got a phone call towards the end of the day: "We've decided we think we might want to go with *you* with the black panther." So I said, "Oh, really?", and they replied, "Yes, the one we *were* going to use is not really suitable and the director doesn't like it. Do you think you could come down?" So I agreed and they confirmed a booking for a black panther at eight the next morning.

But when we went down there, the stage was all closed and locked. Then the first assistant came along and said, "We've got *one* problem." And I asked, "And what's that?" and he said, "The panther we were going to use is still loose in the studio!" It had been there overnight and they couldn't get near it or it would have killed somebody. So we went in with our team and our vet dart-tranquilized the panther before we could do the shoot. So that was an unusual one.

But we had another interesting experience with a black panther! We were filming down in south London, in a studio in Woolwich – a strange place for a studio – and we were doing a commercial. We had three or four panthers and had set it all up, but we did notice that there was something a bit strange about the studio manager and all the people who worked there. All of a sudden, there was pounding at the door and the whole studio, apart from the photographer and his assistant and me and our trainers and the vet, they all disappeared.

There was more pounding on the door, and by *that* time they were breaking the door down and it was the police! Fifty armed police with dogs came into this little studio and saw the black panthers. The dogs turned and were gone and so were all the police! So I got the panthers back in their traveling cages and then the police told me that the studio was suspected for a drugs smuggling racket. They said they were going to arrest everyone there except for us, and seal the studio. So they arrested all the studio staff

John Cleese discusses his BBC TV series *The Human Face* with Jim Clubb. (Photo by David Jamieson)

and within a few hours they had found £2,500,000 worth of drugs hidden in cat litter which was stored in the studio!

Smaller funny incidents happen, too. I remember having a lion cub on *Blue Peter* [Children's TV Series, 1958] and it messed all over Valerie Singleton [Presenter 1962-1972] on the Monday at the BBC in London and then we went down to BBC Bristol to do *Animal Magic* [Children's TV Series, 1962] in the same week with the same lion cub and it messed all over [Presenter] Johnny Morris! They didn't really mind, actually. Johnny Morris was *great*, really good to work with.

There is also a more serious side to our work when we provide animals for documentary films. For instance, John Cleese did a BBC series called *The Human Face* [four-part BBC documentary, 2001] and used one of our baby lemurs to show how human skulls and faces have developed from those of monkeys and lemurs. We have also used our studio here to film wolves and vultures scavenging a model of a mammoth carcass, and once we even disguised an elephant to resemble its prehistoric ancestor for a TV natural history program.

We have helped people visualize the past and the future. On *Walking with Dinosaurs* [Animated documentary TV Series, 1999], the animated characters performed realistic-looking movements because they were based on films of our animals. And the movements of the little alien in *Lost in Space* [Stephen Hopkins, 1998] were achieved with the help of our Rhesus monkey, Kate. Our animals are used in so many different ways, the company's name is really appropriate – Amazing Animals.

Beccy Tiller
Location Caterer

Beccy runs "Bad Catering" from a van proudly displaying that name. She is mobile, adaptable, smiley and very hard-working. I sat with her on a double-decker bus marked "extras" (as opposed to "crew"), where her meals are eaten. These old buses, typically found parked at the edge of film sets, provide a brief respite for their occupants, who can sit down out of the cold and eat and chat.

The meals are substantial, and always include several choices, with hot dishes, a salad buffet, cheeses and puddings. A full English breakfast is always served, and tea and coffee are available throughout the day from large urns. Beccy never knows exactly how many people will be eating her meals, what special requirements there might be, or what stories of woe she will be told.

Selected Credits

The Scarlet Tunic (Stuart St Paul, 1998)
Love Is the Devil (John Maybury, 1998)
Play (The Beckett Film Project, Anthony Minghella, 2001)
Time Team (TV Series, 2001)
Los Dos Bros (TV Series, John Henderson, 2001)

My company is called "Bad Catering." I used to have a business partner called David so it used to be "Beccy and David" and one evening a friend of mine was thinking about names, and she had had a few glasses of wine and came up with "Bad Catering." We thought it was amusing but no more than that, and then I took it up because I liked it. It's catchy and people don't forget it. There are loads of people who call themselves things like "The Good Catering Company" but nobody else has the gall to call themselves "Bad Catering." Also it means that you can't live up to that name, or at least you try not to.

Beccy's Bus

I come from a restaurant background. I managed restaurants and troubleshot for large corporations, Grand Metropolitan, people like that, and I worked for Langan's Brasserie as Manager. But I became disillusioned with catering after a while and a friend of mine was working for the Rock and Roll Stage Set Company and they needed an administrative bookkeeper and I dropped out and did that for a while and loved the people.

That company sadly went bust about four years later, but I didn't want to go back into mainstream restaurant work. I felt I could deal with the egos and personalities this side of the industry, and I ended up working for a rock and roll catering company that did rock and roll tours. They had the odd video and bit of TV work and I took that department and marched on with it and built that side of the business up until there came a time when I wanted to do it for myself.

When I was in college I didn't even know that location catering existed. I think most people fall into it by accident, as I did. The main difference between this and a restaurant, from a catering point of view, is that I appear every morning and build my kitchen before I start! One of the most extraordinary places was Sanday up in the Orkneys in Scotland. I was working for a Channel 4 archaeological program called *Time Team* [TV series, 2001] and we got to see some great places all over the country. The day they phoned up to see if we could get to Orkney was marvelous. It took us three days to get there with all the equipment. In fact, we didn't take the truck up, we worked from a school domestic science lab, which was hysterical.

We were cooking for about 70 people out of about six small domestic ovens set up in four kitchens, like you have in school, and we were literally legging it backwards and forwards all the time. There were two of us and a local helper and we had to take everything with us because the facilities on the island were so limited. The people there would have to go to the mainland or live on what the boat brought once a week. So our helper took everything that was left over home with her at the end of the day, especially things like fresh vegetables. By the time she got home, there would be about 30 people, mainly family, sitting on her doorstep waiting to be fed!

They were fantastically friendly people there and looked after us so well and were lovely. And they also had this strange tradition. On Sundays the whole island, about 500 people, would have an outing, and descend on different people for tea, but if there was something particularly interesting going on they would all turn up there instead. Anyway, one Sunday afternoon everyone on the island came to the film shoot just to have a look at our menu board, because there were things they would never get! Things that you and I would take for granted, like Stilton and Brie and standard ingredients that we just pop to the corner shop for, they just don't have. That was really my favorite spot – it was so beautiful up there, even if there was a strange set of requirements and you could never think "Oh, damn, I've forgotten the cream today."

Today I started work at 5:15 A.M. I was up at 3:45 – that's fairly average on a film shoot. We will finish on site at about 4:30 P.M., but then of course there is the shopping and organization for tomorrow. We need to keep buying things fresh, especially because of the limited storage space. Sometimes we will literally decide the day before, what we are going to cook the following day, and sometimes we will organize all the menus for a five-week shoot in advance. But the numbers always change, and we won't find out how many people we will be catering for tomorrow until 4:00 P.M. today.

That's part of the challenge of location catering; that along with changes in times. Yesterday they said we would have lunch at 1:30, and then at 12:15 I hear that the director has shouted that they'll stop and have lunch now, and obviously it isn't cooked. Then they want to know how quickly you can do it, so you give them a time and then in fact they don't turn up 'til an hour after that anyway. Sometimes you have to put your foot down because legally you are only allowed to keep food hot for so long. Occasionally crews will start disappearing off and then appear three hours later expecting lunch and so you have to be fairly stern and say, "You get back here and have your lunch or it's going in the bin!"

I get special requests for food all the time. It is very much the "in thing" at the moment to be intolerant or allergic to just about everything. Wheat is the fad at the moment. I have quite a lot of sympathy because I am a vegetarian and have an intolerance to cows' milk. But what I get upset about is if someone appears at breakfast time and announces they are a vegan, and they expect you to create something specially for them for lunch, and then they come back for crumble and custard. At that point I would tell them that I might not be putting myself out quite so much the following day. But if someone genuinely doesn't eat something, of course that is not a problem and we will provide for them.

We have tea and coffee going all day, and usually do three meals a day – on a pop promo we'll have four or five meals. There will be a full cooked English breakfast, a full lunch with four to five choices (red meat, poultry, fish and vegetarian every day), a choice of dessert and a cheese board. The crew and cast all eat exactly the same food. Occasionally, if extras are only working limited hours, they might only get two of the meals.

I enjoy it because you get a group of people who you are with for around six weeks and you almost eat, dream and sleep with each other. You are working a 12- to 14-hour day together and then you go home and go to bed. There is no social life outside of the film set. The girls might ask if you want to go out for a glass of wine at night and you have to point out that you have to be up at 3:30 A.M. I don't even know how you could fit a family in! I have two cats who eat at strange hours and have just got used to it. I say, "Oh, hello, it's breakfast at four this morning; oh, no, it's a day off, we'll have breakfast at nine." All those veterinary books tell you you have to give them a routine, but no, they do all right.

Typical crew tea break

You would have to have a very understanding partner to put up with it. But it suits those of us who do it. We tend to work like mad things, and then maybe have a couple of weeks off. I have regular contracts, and employ four or five people. You have to be organized, and be able to work in very confined spaces. Chefs out of restaurants just don't understand it, and are not prepared to do the cleaning and washing up and general tidying up that is needed – and crews do tend to be very messy, and they do eat a lot!

If you are up at four, you get hungry. And when you're tired, your blood sugars are all over the place, and if you are out in the cold, it's nice to go and sit on the bus. Stodge in the winter is very important. Bacon butties and spotted dick and custard are top of the bill. But every crew is different. Some are very plain eaters, wanting things like steak pies and what from our point of view is boring food, and other crews are mainly vegetarian and very adventurous, which is nice.

There are a few people you would rather not see again, it has to be said. I am mentioning no names. Some actors will have you running around wanting bizarre things at bizarre times of day, almost trying to false-foot you. Like they might ask for the same thing four days running and then on the fifth day ask for something completely different. So you might be in the middle of nowhere and have to think, "Okay, how do we do this?" At other times they are absolute sweeties.

Sometimes they will come into the kitchen and have a chat, and that is also part of the job. Certainly, with the crew, you know what all their children look like because you've seen photographs of them all. You know who is having teething problems, who is having marital problems, if someone's house plant is dying, if the cat's not well, and who's got a hangover! So you are handing out hangover cures one minute, tea and sympathy the next, and then having a right old giggle about their exploits down the pub the night before, and that is very much part of the job – something you wouldn't get in a restaurant.

Also, if someone is having a bad day, the first person they come and kick is a caterer. It works both ways. But the idea of going to the same place to work day-in day-out seems awful now. We get to see some very pretty places. Last year I was driving up to Northumberland, and driving across the causeway to Holy Island, with the sun just coming up, was truly beautiful. Sitting out on the step of the van that morning, peeling potatoes in the sunshine, was lovely. However, when it is lashing it down with hail like it was this morning, and you are in some goods yard in north London, it's not quite so great.

I shall carry on doing it until I think of something else. It is physically very hard, and does take its toll. You have to love it or you couldn't possibly do it, but I think that's the same with everyone on the crew.

"I was definitely told 1:15 lunch break *after* the Etruscan battle ... no one said anything about you lot being killed in early skirmishes..."